Wisdom or Knowledge?

ISSUES IN
SCIENCE AND THEOLOGY

This series is published under the auspices of the
European Society for the Study of Science and Theology (ESSSAT)

Editors

Willem B. Drees
Professor of Philosophy of Religion and Ethics
Leiden University, the Netherlands

Hubert Meisinger
Campus Minister and Associate Lecturer in Systematic Theology
Technische Universität Darmstadt
Protestant Church in Hessen and Nassau

Advisory Board

Wisdom or Knowledge?

Science, Theology and Cultural Dynamics

Editors

Hubert Meisinger
Willem B. Drees
Zbigniew Liana

T&T CLARK INTERNATIONAL
A Continuum imprint
LONDON • NEW YORK

Published by T&T Clark
A Continuum imprint
The Tower Building, 11 York Road, London SE1 7NX
80 Maiden Lane, Suite 704, New York, NY 10038

www.tandtclark.com

British Library Cataloguing-in-Publication Data
A catalogue record for this book is available from the British Library

Typeset by YHT Ltd, London
Printed on acid-free paper in Great Britain by
Antony Rowe Ltd., Chippenham, Wiltshire

ISBN 0 567 03099 7 (hardback)
     0 567 03100 4 (paperback)

Contents

List of Contributors   vii

Preface and Acknowledgements   xi

Abbreviations   xiii

Introduction: Mapping the Issues   1
Hubert Meisinger

Progress in Science and Theology   10
Dirk Evers

The Reliability of Science and its Cultural Impact   25
Mariano Artigas

'Don't Drink from that Dirty Stream!' The Decline of Science
and Theology as Sources of Wisdom in Europe   38
Chris Wiltsher

Disjoining Wisdom and Knowledge: Science, Theology and the
Making of Western Modernity   51
Peter Harrison

Wisdom through Communion and Personhood: From Patristic
Theology to Contemporary Science   73
Alexei V. Nesteruk

Walking on Hermeneutic Territory: The Horizons of Sense for
a Pilgrim   91
Lucio Florio

Where Streams Meet? Ecology, Wisdom and Beauty in Bulgakov,
von Balthasar and Aquinas   108
Celia Deane-Drummond

Biotechnology and Ethics: A Locus for the Reintegration of
Science and Wisdom? 127
Michael Fuller

Food Safety and Food Justice: Impacts of Scientific and
Religious Cultures 135
Antje Jackelén

To Know is to Make: Knowledge, Ignorance and Belief in a
Technological Society 145
Walther Ch. Zimmerli

Index 153

List of Contributors

Mariano Artigas holds a Ph.D. both in physics and in philosophy. He is professor of philosophy of science in the University of Navarra (Pamplona, Spain), where he has served for ten years as Dean of the Ecclesiastical Faculty of Philosophy. He is ordinary member of the Académie Internationale de Philosophie des Sciences (Brussels), and of the Pontifical Academy of Saint Thomas (Vatican). He has published fifteen books, among them *The Mind of the Universe* (Templeton Foundation Press, 2000), and *Galileo in Rome* (Oxford University Press, 2003), and many articles. He also is head of the group Science, Reason and Faith (www.unav.es/cryf).

Celia Deane-Drummond has a personal chair in theology and the biological sciences at the University of Chester (UK), where she directs the Centre for Religion and the Biosciences. As a plant scientist (Cambridge, Reading) she published over thirty articles in international scientific journals. She also has a doctorate in theology from Manchester University. Among her books are *Theology and Biotechnology: Implications for a New Science* (Geoffrey Chapman, 1997), *Creation Through Wisdom: Theology and the New Biology* (T&T Clark, 2000), *Biology and Theology Today: Exploring the Boundaries* (SCM Press, 2001), *The Ethics of Nature* (Blackwells, 2004), *Genetics and Christian Ethics* (Cambridge University Press, 2006) and *Wonder and Wisdom: Conversations in Science, Spirituality and Theology* (Darton, Longman & Todd, 2006). She is co-editor, with B. Szerszynski, of *Reordering Nature: Theology, Society and the New Genetics* (Continuum/T&T Clark, 2003) and editor of *Brave New World: Theology, Ethics and the Human Genome* (Continuum, 2003), *Teilhard de Chardin on People and Planet* (Equinox, 2006), *Future Perfect? God, Medicine and Human Identity* (Continuum, 2006) and editor of the journal *Ecotheology: Journal of Religion, Nature and Environment*. She is currently chairperson of the Science and Religion Forum (UK).

Dirk Evers, PD, Ph.D., studied Protestant theology at Münster and Tübingen Universities and at Tamilnadu Theological Seminary, Madurai (South India) from 1983 to 1989. He is an ordained minister of the Lutheran Church of Württemberg. Since 1994 he has been working as assistant lecturer in systematic theology at Tübingen University (chair of Eberhard Jüngel). In 1999 he received his doctorate in theology with a thesis on 'Space – Matter – Time: Christian Theology of Creation in Dialogue with Scientific Cosmology', which won the ESSSAT prize in 2002. He completed his postdoctoral project (*Habilitation*) in 2005 with a work on 'God and Possible Worlds: Studies in the Logic of Theological Discourse on Possibility'. He has published numerous articles in systematic theology and science and religion and lectured widely in that field.

Lucio Florio, D.Theol., is priest of the Roman Catholic Church and a systematic theologian from La Plata Archdiocese, Argentina. He studied in La Plata, Rome and Buenos Aires. He teaches in the High Seminary of La Plata, at the Catholic University of Argentina and the Santo Tomás de Aquino University, both of them in Buenos Aires. He is the director of the Argentinian edition of the *Communio* review. Florio has written many articles and has published a book, *Mapa trinitario del mundo: Actualización del tema de la percepción del Dios trinitario en la experiencia histórica del creyente* (Trinitarian map of the world: updating the perception of the trinitarian God in the believer's historic experience) (Secretariado Trinitario, 2000). He was a lecturer at several science and religion workshops. Florio also was the President of the Organizing Commitee of the International Meeting 'Sciences, Philosophy and Theology: At the Search of a Worldview' held in La Plata in 2003 and belongs to several academic institutions.

Michael Fuller is an Anglican priest. He studied chemistry at the University of Oxford and theology at the University of Cambridge. He is Pantonian Professor at the Theological Institute of the Scottish Episcopal Church, and an honorary fellow of New College, University of Edinburgh. His publications include *Atoms and Icons* (Mowbray, 1995) and some twenty articles, exploring the interactions of theology with the natural sciences, and discussing theological themes in Russian literature and in music.

Peter Harrison is professor of history and philosophy at Bond University, Australia. His chief research interest is early modern intellectual history with a particular focus on relations between science and religion. He is author of *'Religion' and the Religions in the English Enlightenment* (Cambridge University Press, 1990) and *The Bible, Protestantism and the Rise of Natural Science* (Cambridge University Press, 1998). His next book, *Adam's Encyclopaedia: Theology and the Foundations of Scientific Knowledge, 1500–1700*, will be published by Princeton University Press in 2006.

Antje Jackelén is associate professor of systematic theology/religion and science at the Lutheran School of Theology at Chicago and Director of the Zygon

Center for Religion and Science. She studied theology in Bielefeld-Bethel and Tübingen (Germany) and in Uppsala (Sweden). She earned her Ph.D. (D.Theol.) from Lund University in 1999. From 1999 to 2001 she was Regional Director for Europe of the CTNS science and religion course programme. Her publications include *Zeit und Ewigkeit* (Neukirchener, 2002), ET *Time and Eternity: The Question of Time in Church, Science and Theology* (Templeton Foundation Press, 2005), *The Dialogue between Religion and Science: Challenges and Future Directions* (Pandora Press, 2004), as well as numerous articles in theology and in religion-and-science.

Hubert Meisinger, Ph.D. (D.Theol.), studied theology at the University of Heidelberg and at the Zygon Center for Religion and Science in Chicago (USA). He is an ordained minister of the Protestant Church of Hesse and Nassau and works as campus minister and associate lecturer for systematic theology at Darmstadt University of Technology. In 1996 he received the first ESSSAT prize for his dissertation on 'Liebesgebot und Altruismusforschung. Ein exegetischer Beitrag zum Dialog zwischen Theologie und Naturwissenschaft' (Love command and investigations on altruism: an exegetical approach towards the dialogue between theology and science) (Fribourg University Press; and Vandenhoeck & Ruprecht, 1996). From 1996 to 2004 he was ESSSAT scientific programme officer, since 2004 he is vice-president of ESSSAT for publications. He has written numerous articles in theology and religion-and-science and co-published several books in that field, including *Physik, Kosmologie und Spiritualität. Dimensionen des Dialogs Zwischen Naturwissenschaft und Religion* (Physics, cosmology and spirituality: dimensions of the dialogue between science and religion) (Lang, 2005).

Alexei V. Nesteruk, Dr, is a lecturer in mathematics, philosophy of science, science and theology at the University of Portsmouth, and a visiting lecturer at the Institute of Orthodox Christian Studies in Cambridge. His main research projects are 'Towards a Neo-Patristic Synthesis of Theology and Science' and 'Phenomenology of Cosmology'. He is the author of 85 papers and a monograph, *Light from the East: Theology, Science and the Eastern Orthodox Tradition* (Fortress Press, 2003).

Chris Wiltsher is an associate lecturer for the Open University, teaching courses in the mathematics of computer software, education and the history of religion. He worked for many years in adult education and theological education, teaching systematic theology, philosophy and ethics. His publications include books and papers on topics in science and theology and in systematic theology, ethics, education and computer systems management.

Walther Ch. Zimmerli, Prof. Dr, D.Phil., h.c., is the founding president of the Volkswagen AutoUni, Wolfsburg, member of the executive board, Volkswagen Coaching GmbH, and also of the Topmanagement, Volkswagen.

He studied at Yale College (Connecticut) and at the universities of Göttingen (Germany) and Zurich (Switzerland), where he completed his Ph.D. in 1971. From 1971 to 1978 he was an assistant professor in philosophy. From 1978 he held chairs at the universities of Braunschweig (Germany), Bamberg, Erlangen/ Nürnberg and Marburg. From 1999 to 2002 he was the president of the private university of Witten/Herdecke GmbH. He also was visiting professor in the USA, Australia, Japan and South Africa. In 2002 he was awarded an honorary doctorate by the University of Stellenbosch. His further awards include the 1996 International Humboldt Research Award. Among other things he serves as corresponding editor of the *European Journal of Ethics*. He has published and co-edited several books, including *Einmischungen. Die sanfte Macht der Philosophie* (Darmstadt, 1993) and *Wissenstechnologie. Die Rolle von Bildung und Information in Lebenswissenschaften und Gesellschaft* (Cologne, 2001).

Preface and Acknowledgements

This volume will consider science and theology and the nature of knowledge and wisdom. Is scientific knowledge wisdom, or is it more limited – effective, useful, applicable, but not what we mean by wisdom? And is the wisdom of ages past, embodied in the great religious traditions, still wisdom for our time, as we have to face new challenges and responsibilities? To what extent are science and theology determined by their cultural setting? To what extent do they influence the development of culture? Which new opportunities have shown up in our days, both for science, theology and culture, and for their interaction?

From 1 to 6 April 2004 the European Society for the Study of Science and Theology (ESSSAT – www.ESSSAT.org) organized its Tenth European Conference around the theme 'Streams of Wisdom? Science, Theology and Cultural Dynamics' in the wonderful city of Barcelona, Spain. It attracted more than two hundred participants mainly from Europe but also from the rest of the world, who attended the five plenary lectures and more than 100 paper sessions in which participants presented and discussed their own papers which had been reviewed in advance. Since Barcelona also hosted the Forum of Cultures in 2004 the organizing committee decided to take up the notion of culture for the conference's programme and discuss the interconnectedness of science, theology and culture, questioning whether science and theology can be described as streams of wisdom and/or knowledge.

This volume contains extended versions of the five plenary Templeton Lectures given by Manuel Artigas, Celia Deane-Drummond, Lucio Florio, Peter Harrison and Walther Ch. Zimmerli as well as five outstanding contributions from the paper presentations at the conference given by Dirk Evers, Michael Fuller, Antje Jackelén, Alexei Nesteruk and Chris Wiltsher. Together, all of them offer insights into the wealth of contributions presented at the conference and its wide-ranging discussion of the conference theme from the viewpoints of philosophy, ethics, ecology, hermeneutics, history and Eastern Orthodoxy and with respect to a few selected practical issues. The variety of perspectives presented in this volume, from different cultural backgrounds themselves, reflects the role of culture on the meta-level of writing and reading. And the reader herself or himself will be encouraged to 'drink' from the streams of wisdom and knowledge which will be investigated in the book in order to think anew about the rather simple separation between the two cultures which has prevailed for a rather long time in scientific, theological and cultural thinking. Those who want to dive even deeper into that topic will also be referred to 23 other papers published in *Studies in Science and Theology*, vol. 10 (2005–2006), the yearbook of ESSSAT, which appears every second year. These papers are also outcomes of the presentations and discussions which had taken place at the heart of every ESSSAT conference.

We express our gratitude to the Facultat de Teologia de Catalunya, which hosted the opening session, the University Ramon Llull and especially its Institut Químic de Sarriá (IQS), where all further meetings took place, and its *Enginyeria La Salle*, which took care of the transmission of selected presentations to thirty other groups and institutes in Spain and the Spanish-speaking world to plant a few more seeds for that worldwide dialogue. Especially we thank the local organizers Manuel Doncel and Llorence Puig, assisted by a group of people dealing with science-and-religion questions, for all the work done on site. For financial support we are most grateful to the Fundación IQS and to Epson Ibérica & Fundación Epson. The John Templeton Foundation not only sponsored the plenary lectures and our publicity programme but also made it possible to give grants to younger participants, of whom there were visibly more than in former conferences. The Radboud Foundation sponsored the ESSSAT Research Prize and the ESSSAT Student Prize, the Counterbalance Foundation sponsored the ESSSAT Communication Prize. All three foundations did that not for the first time – our deep thanks to them.

Thanks also to Ulf Görman and Chris Wiltsher for their contribution to bringing this book to reality.

Finally we are again grateful to the staff of T&T Clark for the co-operation on this volume, the fourth in the series Issues in Science and Theology, of which previous volumes were titled *The Human Person in Science and Theology* (vol. 1), *Design and Disorder: Perspectives from Science and Theology* (vol. 2) and *Creative Creatures: Values and Ethical Issues in Theology, Science and Technology* (vol. 3). We hope that this new volume will contribute to the dialogue between science and theology as well as the former ones did. The reader who has enjoyed, or not enjoyed, 'drinking' from the streams of wisdom and knowledge presented here may decide for herself or himself – and may let the editors know, via www.ESSSAT.org, and may even continue the discussion started at the conference in Barcelona.

Abbreviations

GMO	Genetically Modified Organism
NIV	New International Version
PG	J.-P. Migne (ed.), Patrologiae cursus completus ... Series graeca (166 vols; Paris: Petit-Montrouge, 1857–83).
RSV	Revised Standard Version
SCG	Thomas Aquinas, *Summa Contra Gentiles*
ST	Thomas Aquinas, *Summa Theologicae*

Introduction

Mapping the Issues

Hubert Meisinger

The Hebrew Bible is full of wisdom, and two books are especially dedicated to that notion: Wisdom of Solomon and Proverbs. Without providing a thorough introduction to both books I would like to focus briefly on two verses which can be found in Prov. 2.10–11:

> . . . wisdom will come into your heart, and knowledge will be pleasant to your soul; discretion will watch over you; understanding will guard you; (RSV)

These two tiny verses offer invaluable insights into what will be discussed in this book: the consideration of science and theology, the nature of wisdom and knowledge and – above all – their interaction and interdependence.[1]

Of course, the writer of Proverbs did not know about science and theology and the dialogue between these two in our modern times. But what he writes about wisdom (חכמה), knowledge (דעת), discretion (מזמה) and understanding (תבונה) is enlightening.

First of all, it is important to notice that Hebrew thinking is relational. The four main notions of those two verses do not stand in sharp opposition with each other. Together they form a cluster of terms, of which each contributes from a different perspective to the field they jointly describe. Let us focus on the first two notions, translated as wisdom and knowledge.

Wisdom is connected with the heart. And in the Hebrew context heart can be understood as the centre of the human being. This notion seems to be accessible rather easily to modern common sense. Wisdom is something that has to do with our being in its depth. It cannot really be learned, but can only be acquired in a lifelong process. It transcends pure knowledge, and does not even need knowledge in every single circumstance in which it is applied or emerges. It characterizes people as wise because they seem to be different: they

---

[1] I am grateful to the Hebraist Otfried Fraisse, Darmstadt, who gave helpful advice on my interpretation of Prov. 2.10–11.

understand better, know more, or – to be even more precise or concrete – they have different ways of accessing understanding, knowing and feeling. Wisdom lights up, is combined with intuition and – at least in the Hebrew Bible – is always related to God who is its source. Wisdom is accumulated over thousands of years and written down to preserve its wealth for generations to come.

Knowledge is connected with the soul. It is a notion which is not as easily accessible by common sense as the first one and thus deserves an even closer look. What is meant by the soul? The most accepted understanding is that the notion of the soul points towards the human being in its fullness. In the creation story, God blows the breath of life into the human being to make his whole body alive. That knowledge is connected with fullness and liveliness does not seem to be too obvious for modern minds. From a contemporary viewpoint, knowledge seems to be much more constrained and limited in breadth. Knowledge has to do with dead facts to be learned, with thorough investigations to be carried out and clear conclusions to be drawn. Knowledge – like wisdom – also accumulates, but not *by* a lifelong process, but *during* a lifelong process. Nothing about fullness and liveliness. The modern common-sense meaning of 'knowledge' is what in Hebrew may more likely be meant by the word translated as 'understanding' above: intelligence of the mind. But knowledge in Hebrew is more, has to do with fullness and liveliness. It does carry aspects of wisdom, because both belong to the same word-field in which they only stress different but not separate perspectives. This preliminary and short discussion points towards at least the following two important insights for our ongoing discussion:

'Wisdom', at first glance, seems to be accessible to our common sense much more easily than 'knowledge', as the word is used in the Hebrew book of Proverbs. Wisdom is connected with the heart as the centre and depth of human beings. Knowledge is connected with the soul, pointing toward the fullness of human beings.

Knowledge is an equivocal notion; there is no single meaning of it. What can be understood as knowledge is highly dependent upon the context in which the notion is used, and another and even more appropriate word for context, here, is culture. What we understand by the word 'knowledge' is highly dependent upon the cultural context in which it appears. The Hebrew meaning differs from our modern meaning. Moreover, it is even a matter of translating within the word-field wisdom–knowledge–discretion–understanding and even more concepts which are highly interconnected.

'At first glance' was of course written intentionally. Is 'wisdom' really more easily accessible to modern common sense? Do we still share the concept of wisdom for which Wisdom of Solomon and Proverbs are such outstanding examples in the Hebrew Bible? Is the heart still the centre and the depth of a human being in a time where genes – in what is to my mind a reductionistic perspective – are likely to determine what human beings are? In a time where our brain is more often thought of as the centre of human nature than our heart – at least in certain modern academic discourses about brain research and God modules in the brain? The decade of the brain has passed not too long ago, but will there ever be envisaged a decade of the heart?

Although such questions are raised, challenging new insights have indeed arisen about what constitutes a human being, and our modern context is more or less totally different from former ones, when wisdom of the ages past was embodied in the great religious traditions. Wisdom, today, seems to be expected from science and technology, rather than from religion and theology.

But, to conduct a short exercise with you, the reader of this introduction and book: Where do you point to with your finger or hand, as it were, when you say 'It is me' or 'I'? Do you point towards your heart as centre of your being human or towards your head and brain? At least in my German context, pointing with a finger towards the head does not at all say 'I .... .'

Another aspect of this '*but*' is that the scientists who are called wise, the modern sages, are mostly those who have begun to philosophize about their field, transcend their pure or hard science and take a more holistic approach towards reality and human beings as part of it. People like Carl Friedrich von Weizsäcker, Hans-Peter Dürr, Ilya Prigogine, John C. Eccles and Erwin Chargaff belong to this group of modern sages. However, an erosion has also begun in that field. Reductionists like Edward O. Wilson, Richard Dawkins or Stephen Hawking also claim to be modern sages, and indeed are seen and accepted as such by the wider public, because the power of their written imagination influences cultural perspectives on what a sage is or is not.

Both wisdom and knowledge, then, seem to have run through a process which is not independent of cultural dynamics and in which their wealth of meaning and significance within an exciting word-field has become diminished. Therefore it is time to revisit the two notions mentioned above again, especially as they are connected in the too-easy formula: 'Religion and theology are about wisdom; science is about knowledge; and both science and theology shape our culture.' Is this really true?

No. On the one hand, religion and theology are not only wisdom: at least theology – understood as science (cf. Pannenberg 1976), though of course not as natural science – has gained and achieved a lot of knowledge since the Enlightenment, and this can no longer be neglected. Indeed, it should even gain more strength over against the growing fundamentalist movements which – according to David Lyon (2000) – are outcomes of our modern or even postmodern irritations with respect to our search for identity and certainty.

On the other hand, science – as natural science – does not only produce knowledge in a common-sense understanding of that notion, widely characteristic of the hard sciences. At least a new and broader (post)modern understanding of science can no longer be excluded from wisdom, in which knowledge is seen as relational, with social responsibilities – thus far more in line with the Hebrew understanding mentioned above, where knowledge also covers aspects of wisdom since both belong to the same word-field.

Nor is it only the streams of science and theology which shape culture. Culture has manifold other sources as well: art in its various forms, music, sport – to mention only a few of them. Thus cultural dynamics may arise partly independent of science and theology, but nevertheless with an impact on the meaning, the evaluation and the appreciation of science and theology – of each for itself and of their interaction – in a concrete cultural setting. It is a dynamic, reciprocal interplay with different feedback mechanisms, bottom-up and top-down influences that characterize culture and its components' respective dimensions.

In that view, within our cultural framework with its specific dynamics, both science and religion-and-theology contribute to the understanding of us as human beings and of our world and the cosmos, which is only partially accessible for us because of our limited senses and the constraints of time and space as shown in the theory of relativity.

Nevertheless, wise interpretations of scientific insights are still waiting to be developed, not to mention completed. But there are some first attempts. For example, a wise interpretation of the notion of a God module, or of evolutionary algorithms which try to explain religiosity, does not necessarily lead to the end of religiosity. On the contrary, argues the German biologist and theologian Caspar Söling[2], recipient of the ESSSAT Research Prize in 2004: religiosity seen as a basic constituent of human beings cannot on ideological grounds be ignored by science, but has to be taken into account in biological, psychological or pedagogical anthropologies. Thus, next to an evolutionary epistemology, an evolutionary ethics and an evolutionary aesthetics, an evolutionary theory of religion has yet to be developed. Such an evolutionary theory of religion should take into account the insights of both theology and science on religiosity, in order to become a factor able to shape our culture and to give rise to new cultural dynamics shaping the meaning of science and theology respectively.

The Contents of this Volume

Though the first part of this introduction with preliminary considerations has mainly dealt with the understanding of us as human beings with respect to science, theology and culture, this book is not about anthropology.[3] It is about the interaction of science, theology and culture in general and in different respects – ranging from viewpoints of philosophy, ethics, ecology,

---

[2] Söling 2002; cf. Söling 2004.
[3] Which for example is the focus of Hefner 1993.

hermeneutics, history and Eastern Orthodoxy, to a few selected practical issues.[4] Two powerful dimensions of human culture, science and religion-and-theology, and their dynamic interaction with each other and with culture, build the heart of this book.

Performing this task, the discussion about the relation of the three notions mentioned will be intensified in comparison with what has taken place so far. Wisdom and knowledge will be considered with respect to science and theology in their cultural setting, thus opening a wide horizon of thinking which goes far beyond a two-cultures thesis or a clash-of-cultures thesis. Our concern is much more that of mutually enriching the concepts of science and theology in a friendly,[5] critical and ambitious way, in the synchronic framework of modern culture, while taking into account diachronic insights. And it is syn-spatial and dia-spatial also in that European and Latin-American approaches toward the topic will become better known in a field where Anglo-American approaches prevail. Thus, we do not try to establish one culture for all of humankind, but dynamically show different aspects of different cultures and their contributions to the field that the triad science, religion and culture make up.

Taking these considerations as background, the contents of this volume and the individual papers are briefly described in what follows.

This fourth volume of the series Issues in Science and Theology (IST) bears upon material presented at the Tenth European Conference on Science and Theology, arranged by ESSSAT, the European Society for the Study of Science and Theology (www.ESSSAT.org) and held in Barcelona, Spain, in April 2004. The theme for this conference was 'Streams of Wisdom? Science, Theology and Cultural Dynamics', and its aim was to cast new light on questions such as those raised above. This book contains the plenary Templeton lectures given by Mariano Artigas, Celia Deane-Drummond, Lucio Florio, Peter Harrison and Walther Ch. Zimmerli as well as a selection of papers discussed in paper sessions given by Dirk Evers, Michael Fuller, Antje Jackelén, Alexei Nesteruk and Chris Wiltsher. Together the different authors give an important insight into the challenging relationship between science, theology and culture and allow the reader herself or himself to dive into the streams of wisdom and knowledge which were opened up throughout the conference. Roughly speaking there are four centres of gravity of the approaches: Evers, Artigas and Wiltsher talk about science, theology and culture in more general terms; Harrison, Nesteruk and Florio continue with respect to historical and

---

[4] In that respect it also differs significantly from other publications in the field of science–religion–culture: Brown (1986) sets out a more limited explanation of science – its history from medieval times to the present – to the public and locates the adventure of science in a wider cultural context. Gilbert (1998), as a historian from the University of Maryland, begins with the Scopes trial in 1925 and culminates in the 1962 'Space Age' World's Fair in Seattle. With respect to religion he fails to define it thoroughly, but on the whole speaks broadly about religion in America. He notices the many fundamentalist views which are not too helpful in the dialogue. Some of the science-embracing views discussed are not helpful either.

[5] Cf. Mortensen 1995: 262–77.

hermeneutical perspectives; Deane-Drummond, Fuller and Jackelén deal with ethical issues; and Zimmerli finally offers a philosophical gateway.

Dirk Evers argues in his essay in favour of a sapiential theology rather than a theology organized in analogy to the (natural) sciences. By means of the respective notions of progress he shows the significant difference between both types of human striving towards intellectual cognition, science and theology. He proposes wisdom as a possible connective link which allows for a qualified interaction between scientific and religious understanding. Finally, he explains how this qualified 'difference-model' can significantly contribute to the cultural dynamics of pluralist societies.

Mariano Artigas' paper deals with the reliability of science and its cultural impact. Though absolute certainty is impossible, scientific criteria enable us to reach a reliable knowledge which is even extrapolated into the ambit of religion and the humanities. Though these ambits should be distinguished from the scientific ambit, a fruitful dialogue can be maintained among them, particularily on the analysis of general presuppositions of science and the implications of scientific progress upon them: intelligibility or rationality of nature and natural order, human ability to know the natural order in scientific arguments, and the values being implied by scientific activity itself, which include the search for truth, rigour, objectivity, intellectual modesty, service to other people, co-operation, and related values. His argument is that scientific progress provides feedback on these presuppositions by retrojustifying, enriching and refining them. In the light of such feedback, the analysis of each of these presuppositions provides a clue to the philosophical meaning of scientific progress and to its theological relevance.

Chris Wiltsher explores the phenomenon that while science had earlier displaced theology, becoming the prime source of wisdom, at the start of the twenty-first century both theology and science have become displaced as sources of wisdom. He suggests that this has happened because in the eyes of many the pure streams of wisdom of science and theology have become polluted by the activities of the all-too-human theologians and scientists. This has changed public perception of science and theology, influenced especially by recent trends in biography.

Peter Harrison's concern is to show that the disjunction of wisdom and scientific knowledge underwrites the achievements of science and lies at the heart of modern Western culture. For medieval thinkers, he argues, both science and religion were primarily personal qualities. Thomas Aquinas for example thought science (*scientia*) to be first a habit of mind and only secondarily a method or body of organized propositions. Thomas also classified religion (*religio*) as a virtue, rather than a set of objectively identifiable beliefs and practices. And it was prudence (practical wisdom), he shows, which was the key virtue which provided the unity of the virtues. Partly as a consequence of Protestant critique of the Aristotelian/Thomist conception of virtue, both *scientia* and *religio* came to be understood not as bodies of knowledge. These developments had their counterpart in the realm of knowledge with the increasing specialization of academic disciplines. Together, he argues, these social transformations invested the modern West with its distinctive character.

Alexei Nesteruk discusses the problems of linking scientific wisdom with the issue of existence-as-communion, which forms the ultimate wisdom of creatio. He discusses the patristic contribution as a radically different approach to wisdom in comparison to contemporary treatment of wisdom as intellectual knowledge. He also links this to problems of personhood and communion in order to elucidate the problems in the context of contemporary science–religion dialogue. The problem of scientific wisdom is formulated by him in the form of the paradox of presence in absence, which demands for its comprehension a deep theological insight that he tries to deliver.

Lucio Florio approaches the debate about knowledge and cultures from the perspective of the personal subject, in whom the concrete confluence of experiences and knowledge is produced or not. He argues that, except for collectivist conceptions of the human being, for all philosophies and religions the individual person is the one who processes and synthesizes the assemblage of experiences, including those which arrive through the objective frames of culture. The actual human being is the one who knows, and Florio outlines some reflections which bear an integrative character. The individual person is a pilgrim who interprets his existence through the different hermeneutic horizons that culture offers him. Common knowledge, sciences, philosophies, arts, religions provide many dimensions of meaning to guide him in his particular history. Religions offer the traveller a personal and transcendental frame of comprehension. In particular, Christian revelation adds the face of a triune God who allows the traveller to understand his journey through the idea of communion.

The scientific context of Celia Deane-Drummond's approach is environmental science, drawing particularily on current research on climate change, which challenges traditional theological notions of divine providence and forces theologians to take the issue of the earth seriously by looking deeply into its traditions of wisdom and beauty. These traditions can serve as mediating concepts with science, while pointing to accompanying transcendentals of goodness and truth. Deane-Drummond argues for a recovery of holistic thinking expressed through a combination of contemplation on God with right action which involves a meeting of streams from Eastern traditions (Bulgakov) and Western traditions (Hans Urs von Balthasar and Thomas Aquinas). She argues for the need to reclaim both beauty linked with the virtue of temperance, and wisdom linked with the virtue of prudence, in the context of issues raised by climate change.

In his contribution Michael Fuller develops a link between ethics and the concept of wisdom. Discussing Francis Fukuyama's thesis that legislation be used to control biotechnological research, Fuller convincingly makes clear that legislation is indeed desirable to regulate biotechnological advances. He even suggests that bioethical investigations can provide a fruitful meeting-place for science and wisdom. But he neglects a positive answer to Fukuyama's question whether there is a secular ground for believing that human beings are entitled to a special moral status or dignity.

Antje Jackelén examines the questions of food justice and food safety as a test case for the dialogue between religion and science. Drawing upon the inter-connectedness of different types of knowledge she demonstrates that this dia-logue is relevant over the whole range from the bio-sciences, through various religious and cultural values to what children, women and men throughout the world find or do not find on their plates. For her, food is the ideal topic for a conversation that seeks to involve both religion and science, because it is a theme that not only is of practical relevance for everybody, but is central to human survival and culture. Its significance is existential, personal, social, political, religious and economical. She also makes clear that religious leaders must find more effective ways of promoting education and involving their communities in informed dialogue over the whole breadth of the issues involved, or else they will deprive the global community of essential resources needed to help it address some of the most urgent issues of our time.

Walther Ch. Zimmerli's basic thesis is that technology is the modern form of wisdom. Technology directly leads to wisdom, since technology urges us to handle with great care what we cannot fully understand rationally. Having discussed the notion of truth in general and of scientific truth in particular, he points out that true science is technology, intentionally shaping and changing our world. The driving force of investigations and technological actions, of knowledge in general, therefore, is identified as ignorance, and the task of technology, a new kind of magic, is the management of ignorance as the modern equivalent of traditional wisdom.

Our ambition with this volume is to contribute to and to enrich the ongoing discussion in science and religion with respect to the role culture plays in that triad. We hold it necessary to take science and theology into account when reflecting upon culture, and to take culture into account when reflecting upon science and theology.

References

Brown, R. H.
  1986   *The Wisdom of Science: Its Relevance to Culture and Religion* (Cam-
          bridge: Cambridge University Press).
Gerber, U. and H. Meisinger (eds)
  2004   *Das Gen als Maß aller Menschen? Menschenbilder im Zeitalter der Gene*
          (Darmstädter Theologische Beiträge, 10; Frankfurt am Main/Ber-
          lin and others: Peter Lang).
Gilbert, J.
  1998   *Redeeming Culture: American Religion in an Age of Science* (Chicago:
          University of Chicago Press).

Hefner, P.
    1993   *The Human Factor: Evolution, Culture and Religion* (Theology and the Sciences; Minneapolis: Augsburg Fortress).

Lyon, D.
    2000   *Jesus in Disneyland: Religion in Postmodern Times* (Cambridge: Polity Press).

Mortensen, V.
    1995   *Theologie und Naturwissenschaft* (trans. from Danish *Teologi og naturwidenskab* by Eberhard Harbsmeier; Gütersloh: Gütersloher Verlags-Haus).

Pannenberg, W.
    1976   *Wissenschaftstheorie und Theologie*, ET *Theology and the Philosophy of Science* (trans. Francis McDonagh; London: Darton, Longman & Todd).

Söling, C.
    2002   'Der Gottesinstinkt – Bausteine für eine evolutionäre Religionstheorie' (Dissertation, Naturwiss. Fachbereiche, University of Gießen; http://bibd.uni-giessen.de/ghtm/2002/uni/d020116.htm).
    2004   'Religiosität im Zeitalter der Gene', in Gerber and Meisinger 2004: 65–75.

Progress in Science and Theology

Dirk Evers

Introduction

In this essay I want to propose an alternative to some recent attempts to establish Christian theology as scientific theology[1] – a claim which rests on alleged structural, methodological and material analogies between theology and science. Instead I want to insist on the irreducible difference between explaining and understanding, suggesting a way of doing theology that could be called *sapiental* rather than *scientific*.[2] Though I am convinced that only the interplay of explaining and understanding can provide a meaningful foundation for any intellectual discipline, it seems evident to me that the natural sciences focus on explaining measurable effects from distinct causes while theology focuses on understanding, trying to elaborate the meaning of things and the state of affairs with reference to the relationship between God and human beings. While there can be no strict separation between looking for explanation and asking for understanding, because one presupposes the other, the intentions and the directions of interrogation are significantly different. This, I want to argue, becomes apparent in the different notions of progress with respect to science and to theology.

---

[1] The English word 'science' originally meant 'an organized body of knowledge, or an intellectual discipline' (McGrath 2001: 24). The German term *Wissenschaft* has kept this general denotation while in modern English the meaning of 'science' shifted to 'natural science' (*Naturwissenschaft*). To avoid misunderstanding it might be worthwhile noting that I use the term in the modern English meaning, except when indicated by single quotation marks. I do not question the general character of theology as *Wissenschaft* but only the attempt to develop it in analogy to the natural sciences. I also note that the German term *Naturwissenschaften* is most commonly used as a plural referring to the wide spectrum of natural sciences from geology, zoology, biology, chemistry, etc. to cosmology, physics and so on. Thus *Naturwissenschaft* is not envisioned as a monolithic body but rather as a (not exhaustive) plurality of sciences. Cf. below, note 10.

[2] Thus in a sense the old question dating back to Augustine whether theology is science (*scientia*) or wisdom (*sapientia*) isn't settled yet. I am trying to think roughly along the lines of Augustine: 'striving through science towards wisdom (*tendimus per scientiam ad sapientiam*)' (Augustine 1968: 417.2 (= XIII.19)).

In modernity cultural change and dynamics are conceived in terms of progress, and it is apparent that the sciences, their technical applications and their impact on our worldviews, are among the central forces that drive these cultural dynamics. The history of the natural sciences presents itself as a progression from darkness to light, from ignorance to knowledge, from obscurity to enlightenment in whose due course comprehensive theories emerged which explain the phenomena of our physical world, form the basis of our scientific worldview and are main resources for providing objective knowledge and technological know-how. The heliocentric solar system developed by Copernicus, Kepler and others, the Newtonian classical mechanics, the theory of electrodynamics and thermodynamics, the theory of evolution and molecular biology, the theory of relativity and quantum theory: there are many well-defined and well-founded complexes of scientific knowledge which can within their limits and constraints be considered as justifiably true, as objective scientific insights that it would be irrational to reject since it is highly improbable that they would be left behind by future scientific theories. These results of scientific progress can be considered as real knowledge in the sense of justified true belief, and science can be understood as the creative progressive process which accumulates this kind of knowledge.

In contrast to this intimate connection of progress, modernity and scientific enlightenment, religion and theology seem to have suffered from a severe loss of importance and meaning. They are not considered to be a central part of progressive modernity but rather regressive and among those obstacles that modernity has overcome. Religion and theology appear to be outdated and are more or less successfully struggling to catch up with modernity. And too often their accommodation to contemporary science and its worldviews does not look like active progress but rather like a somewhat overexerted attempt to salvage what in the views of many contemporaries is atrophied and about to perish. Insofar as they are committed to authoritative ancient texts, past revelation and handed-down traditions, religion and theology apparently have a problem with the notion of progress.

But at a second glance this distinction between science and religion with regard to progress blurs and is not as clear any more. The identification of science and progress on one side and religion and traditionalist regression on the other is counteracted by the growing awareness that modernity is not necessarily a straightforward progress from the worse to the better. The progress of modern culture and the progress of science itself has revealed ambivalences that are questioning the quality and the essence of the technological and cultural achievements of modernity. Freedom does not necessarily grow in proportion to the technological means developed, and while individual self-determination has become the central ideal of Western culture we are in danger of losing overall and obligatory aims and values. And above all, the dynamics of scientific and technological progress has gained momentum in such a way that it has developed strong self-reinforcing tendencies which cannot easily be controlled by intentional steering. Thus for example we are progressing in environmental exploitation and pollution against better insight, forced by the rule that standstill would mean death.

On the other hand although religion indeed refers to sacred texts and inherited tradition, at the same time these traditions call the believer to leave her or his previous ways and to start a new life. From the story of Abraham's exodus out of his country and his father's house to Jesus' call to prepare for and to proceed towards the kingdom of God, the Jewish-Christian tradition is full of appeals towards progress into the future. In Christian theology the history of mankind as well as the individual life of a human being was seen as the 'pilgrim's progress' from creation to consummation, from birth to death and resurrection.

So the clarification of a few points might be of use for analysing the relationship between science and theology as progressive forces of cultural dynamics: (1) What is progress in science and how is it shaped and warranted? (2) Is there a meaningful way of referring to progress in religion and theology? (3) Does theology participate in or interact with scientific progress? (4) Can a notion of 'wisdom' serve as a connective link between the two realms? (5) What then is the task of Christian theology in a modern pluralist society in contributing to the shaping and forming of its culture? While the following considerations that are arranged along the lines of these questions are developed from a Christian theological background and therefore focus on Christian religion and Western pluralist societies, they do not claim to make significant statements about religion and society *in general*, though they are hopefully open to further extension.

Progress in Science

That the history of the natural sciences shows an enormous progress in knowledge, theory and method can not seriously be doubted. But epistemologically the objective assessment of real progress is not so easily specified. On which grounds can the growth of scientific knowledge be justified as an advancing progress towards truth and objective reality? The answer of *traditional empiricism* was that all scientific knowledge is derived from experience and that all universal propositions which formulate natural laws are generalizations from a significant number of empirical data and are thus verifiable by reference to experience. As David Hume (cf. Hume 1999) convincingly demonstrated, the notion that scientific laws are empirical generalizations in some way finally confirmable by 'positive' experience is aporetical. Consequently one of the leading philosophers of science in the twentieth century, Karl Popper, has identified the interplay between conjectures and refutations as the essential means of scientific progress. Scientific theories are not inductively derived from experience but are conjectures to be tested in conceptualized experiments of which we can assume that they provide the appropriate testing of our theories. Thus even observation-statements are theory-laden and hence fallible. Scientific theories are not inferred from experience, nor is scientific experimentation carried out in order to verify or finally establish the truth of theories. Consequently Popper identified *falsifiability* as the criterion of demarcation for science and non-science. All knowledge appears to be provisional, conjectural, hypothetical. We can never finally prove our scientific theories, we can only provisionally confirm or most probably refute them. Scientific theories are thus selected according to their *corroboration*.

Although Popper's original concept of corroboration proved too narrow with respect to actual historic developments, the basic insights seem to me unrefuted: scientific progress can be explained roughly in evolutionary terms. Science, like other human and organic activities, can largely be envisioned as an art of problem-solving which is put to the test by confronting it with reality. Scientific progress can then be identified with reference to the corroboration of the respective theory as well as to the fruitfulness of its implication towards further conjectures.

Though we do not directly derive objective truth from reality and have no objective criteria for the identification or even quantification of scientific progress, according to Popper we can apply what he called the concept of truthlikeness or 'verisimilitude'. A better scientific theory shows a higher degree of verisimilitude than its rivals, and 'better' is understood as 'closer to the truth'. In this way Popper was able to overcome the pessimism of a Humean anti-inductivist philosophy of science which holds that no scientific theories can be *known* to be true so that truth-claims on scientific grounds are on the whole meaningless. With his concept of verisimilitude Popper was able to argue for a view of science that allows for legitimate claims of scientific progress. The scientific quest for objective truth could now be envisioned as progress *towards* the truth, and empirical corroboration could be interpreted as an *indicator* of verisimilitude (Popper 1972: 103). It is important to affirm that Popper later saw his concept of verisimilitude basically as a heuristic and intuitive principle that does not allow for formal definition. It cannot be quantified, and Popper explicitly rejects the idea that 'degrees of verisimilitude ... can ever be numerically determined, except in certain limiting cases' (Popper 1972: 59).

The discussion on the growth of scientific knowledge and its progress after Popper's project of critical rationalism did not question the notion of progress through science as such, but it threw doubts on the methodological principles which should demarcate, identify and promote scientific progress and on the assumption of an accumulative and continuous progress. Thomas Kuhn's view on paradigm shifts, for example, is still in consonance with the overall principle of progress towards truthlikeness, although the claim of a methodologically controlled and guaranteed continuous progress is given up for a discontinuous dynamics of scientific revolutions. Other strands of twentieth-century epistemology of science did not share the view of progress *towards truth* at all. As an extremist epistemological anarchist, Paul Feyerabend (1975) incriminated methodological principles as hindering scientific progress, in favour of an 'anything goes' principle of creative anarchy. But still the concept of progress as such was not doubted, although it could not be stated according to methodological principles or objective criteria. Indeed, the pragmatic notion of science as problem-solving and of scientific knowledge as corroborated though manifold testing according to the internal standards of the respective theory can be considered as a certain consensus, although the creative changes of paradigms and theory-design are apparently subject to other, non-objective and methodologically difficult dynamics.

As another consequence, scientific progress has to be understood as not exhaustive with regard to all possible knowledge. Already Kurt Gödel's famous theorems (cf. Gödel 1931) indicate that not everything that can be known can be represented in a single theory since the criteria for truth, validity or truthlikeness have to be taken from outside any theory and cannot be reintegrated by means of the theory itself. A theory of everything is an epistemological chimera, especially when scientific progress is conceded in a meaningful way! Science provides relatively solid ground for cultivating and accumulating predictively powerful and reliable means of explanation and problem-solving with respect to concrete human quests and experiences – nothing more but nothing less.

Theology and Historical Progress

In contrast to science, the notion of progress in Christian theology has its criterion in the relationship between God and human beings. It is at the same time intimately related to history as the venue of God's revelation and to the notion of conversion as the qualitative transition from unbelief to belief as the precondition of progress towards God. Let us take a very brief look at the development of the theological understanding of progress and its conflict with modern science.

Christian theology developed its concept of progress in dispute partly with the Stoic notion of individual progress towards wisdom and virtue, partly with the classical idea of the perennial cycle of becoming and destroying. Augustine's conception of a linear world-age (*saeculum*), beginning with creation and ending with the return of Christ as the world's judge, became especially influential for the development of Western theological thought. The ages from Adam to Christ and then from Christ to the hidden end of the world resemble the stages of a human being's life, so that the history of humanity as such as well as the history of each individual can be seen as a linear development from God through Christ to eternity, structured by God's revelation.

But Augustine also pointed to the ambiguities and divergences of our finite lives and human history, designating the fate and destiny of human beings outside of space and time, namely in God's eternity. Against the Stoic concept of ideal virtue he designated the progress of a Christian as a never completed striving towards eternity. Human beings as progressing are creatures still waiting and longing for their fulfilment. Thus from Augustine through

Thomas Aquinas[3] to modern times a Christian notion of progress was established that saw progress as the designation of the finite creature in its individual life as well as the human species finding its way through its stages either towards God or away from him. Progress in this perspective could be to the worse or to the better, with the latter as a movement from finite worldly existence towards divine infinity. History was the means of God's revelation and agency so that contingent historic events shaped the relation between God and human beings. At the same time nature with its physical and morally significant order provided the fixed realm in which every creature had to fill its assigned place.

With the rise of the natural sciences in the sixteenth and seventeenth centuries a new idea of qualitative progress was announced that brought about a qualitative leap and totally new perspective on human growth in knowledge and skills. The human mind proved able to penetrate the heavens and change the technical means at our disposal so that it transcends every traditional perspective and given natural potential. Consequently enlightenment saw progress, as a process of overcoming traditional prejudices by science and reason, as the emergence from immaturity. With the new science and the discovery of the capacities of reason guided by experience, the obstacles of authoritative prejudice should be removed so that light would be thrown onto all areas of human understanding. Having removed the hard shell from nature's mysteries, the path towards autonomy and ever growing progress with regard to intellectual, moral and technical growth seemed open. This also applied to religious matters or, as Immanuel Kant put it:

> As matters now stand, a great deal is still lacking in order for men as a whole to be, or even to put themselves into a position to be able without external guidance to apply understanding confidently to religious issues. But we do have clear indications that the way is now being opened for men to proceed freely in this direction and that the obstacles to general enlightenment – to their release from their self-imposed immaturity – are gradually diminishing. (1923: 35)

Only in the nineteenth century 'progress' became a political slogan and thus a value as such in opposition to conservative politics preserving the status quo. Thinkers of the upcoming industrial age like Auguste Comte (cf. Comte 1830–42) or Herbert Spencer (cf. Spencer 1860–77) gave the idea of progress a new meaning: instead of intellectual enlightenment and the perfection of decent morality, the growing domination of nature and its means through scientific-technical progress became the central perspective. This coincided with the discovery of evolution and the theory of Charles Darwin, which seemed to establish progress as the universal and in itself creative tendency of nature: 'All corporeal and mental endowments will tend to progress towards perfection' (Darwin 1982: 428). Thus an ever increasing humanization of society and its

---

[3] Thomas Aquinas spoke of the 'progress of the sinner (*progressus peccati*)' (Aquinas 1952: 707 (ST IIa IIae, q. 162, a. 4 ad 4)).

individuals was thought to be directly linked with technological progress, be it in Marxist-socialist or in capitalist terms, a presupposition which is highly questionable nowadays. But on the whole progress can be seen as the leitmotif of modernity. Progress is universal, cumulative and unlimited; standstill means death.

Confronted with progress as the all-penetrating principle of modernity, theology met a severe challenge. History was no longer the contingent place of God's authoritative revelation with its predestined stages of creation, fall, deluge, God's covenants, election of the chosen people, incarnation of the Christ, progress towards the final judgement. Since scientific-technological progress had trespassed any given limit, history itself was seen as human-made. And while human wit and knowledge can penetrate the mysteries of nature and overcome with technical means the boundaries and limits set by the natural order, nature is not normative any more. In the age of evolution and genetic engineering this includes the biological nature of plants, animals and even human beings themselves. Nature only represents the contingent status quo and thus the starting-point for technical and manipulative interference. Nature is a variable, it is unsuitable as a measure of the humane. Humanity itself as the decisive driving force has to determine the direction, pace and content of progress. Faith and religion with their sense for oral and written tradition, for sacred texts and historic revelation, seemed to be themselves obstacles to progress and were soon identified as such.

But Christian theology also tried to meet the standards of modern scientific progress. It integrated insights from the natural sciences and used the ideal of rationality developed by the Enlightenment for reformulating its doctrines. Dogmatic criticism, historic-critical exegesis, comparative religious studies, philosophy of religion, process theology, and theology in dialogue with modern cosmology and science, seem to indicate that theology itself is trying to catch up with modernity and that it participates in historical progress, leaving behind outdated theological concepts and embracing up-to-date ones. However, insofar as the relation to God is concerned the 'progress of theology' is not to be confounded with a 'theological notion of progress'. Theology as the critical and accountable explication of the Christian faith under historical conditions is basically a hermeneutical enterprise and no accumulative empirical science. Thus it can not secure its progress by methodological means. Still it shares in the standards and criteria for truth of its time and in many respects participates in the general progress of science and culture.

But at the same time its task is ever fresh and new. Theology, Karl Barth wrote in retrospect on his life as a theologian, is different in that it never can start with settled questions, compiled results or safeguarded achievements but must 'every day, even every hour, begin anew at the *beginning*' (Barth 1962: 181). Ever again theology has to take on the task of a complex intellectual, spiritual and ethical struggle in dispute with contemporary science and culture in the light of the Christian faith. As this hermeneutical and procedural intellectual discipline (*Wissenschaft*, cf. above, note 1), it significantly differs from the empirical sciences. Theology does not accumulate knowledge for the sake of knowing.[4] Its language is not mathematics, and theological propositions like the doctrine of justification or the doctrine of divine properties cannot be tested by standardized experiments. Its objects cannot be reduced to the means of their measurement. While the electron in physics is exactly what physical theory can know about it, God is neither data nor a theoretical term or axiom. And theological doctrine cannot be used for technical applications. The explication of faith in theology is not represented in formulas or a deductive or axiomatic formal system, just as preaching and teaching is not explaining or deducing theorems.

Furthermore, theology and religion need analogical and metaphorical language. They need history, parables and stories. They interpret reality through faith and values and seek orientation for human existence. Theology brings forth, one could say, *orientating* rather than *dispositional* knowledge. It does so in close relation to the historic progress of humankind so that theology brings forth progress only as a contingent historical phenomenon through its different traditions, ever anew dealing with the challenges that the individual, the Christian community and the society they live in encounter. While neither methodological criteria nor instrumental reasoning nor supernaturally authorized metaphysics can be considered as formal guarantors of a succeeding appropriation and application of the truth of faith, a mediating category is needed to describe the interdependence of scientific and theological thought. This is where wisdom comes in.

Wisdom

As indicated, science and theology are not strictly separate, but they interact. Insofar as the progress of science can only be defined according to pre-scientific criteria such as simplicity, relevance, rationality, universality, fertility with respect to further investigation, and so on, it shares in a hermeneutical task. And theology has to make explicit the relevance of Christian faith, referring to the most significant and up-to-date science and methods available, thus participating in the progress of general scientific knowledge. At this point a meaningful notion of 'wisdom' can be applied as a qualified description of this process of relating the significance of scientific progress with the relevance of theological thought.

Since antiquity, wisdom has been understood as the integration of theoretical knowledge and practical prudence with religious or orientating knowledge:

---

[4] 'In theology we are allowed to be ignorant of things (*In theologia licet nobis quaedam ignorare*)' – a comforting remark of an outstanding exponent of theological thinking (Luther 1926: 284).

wisdom is the knowledge of divine and human things.[5] Knowledge of natural laws and states of affairs, knowledge of practical skills, and both integrated with knowledge about human beings and their quest for meaning and purpose in their world, come together and become relevant through wisdom. There is no formal method leading to such an integration, so that according to Greek antiquity no individual can realize wisdom as such, but only the deity can be called in himself wise (Greek: *sophos*) while the highest that can be ascribed to a human being is to be striving towards wisdom, that is, being a friend of wisdom (*philosophos*). Sapiential reason is receptive rather than experimental, confidential rather than suspicious, confessional rather than sceptical, a matter not only of intellectual power but of character. Wisdom cannot be made or produced but has to happen and has to be acquired. And it is a matter of *kairos*, that is the right words at the right place and time reaching the right people, and thus it is closely linked to the spoken word in concrete encounter.

Modern culture lacks this integration of theoretical and practical knowledge with reference to human self-understanding. Science, common sense and ethical and religious value-systems are falling apart.[6] A new ideal of sapiential knowledge is needed that might be able to shape cultural dynamics. Otherwise technically oriented and instrumental parameters and criteria for progress will shape development, such as economic profit or technical accessibility.

Since wisdom by its very nature is no technical, formal or conceptual notion but rather a hermeneutical, discursive and semantic one, it is difficult to define it in a rigorous way. Therefore I will describe its meaning by compiling some of its main aspects with special reference to theological wisdom. In one sense wisdom has to do with the acquisition and communication of human knowledge in all of its forms. But while at the same time more knowledge does not necessarily mean more wisdom, it also includes the capability to deal with ignorance and to refine knowledge to its relevant aspects. While science ideally aims at the completeness of knowledge in certain fields, wisdom does not strive towards encyclopedic perfection but wants to know what is decisive and relevant. Wisdom thus is also the skill of dealing with the unknown, the unrecognizable and the inexplicable. It does not refer to everything that is known and can be known, but it concentrates and illustrates. Therefore it takes contexts and implicit truths for granted in order to point to what is important here and now. It is thus the capability of distinction and differentiation. It discriminates and identifies issues of lasting importance and issues of momentary urgency,[7] and in that way it incorporates remembrance and expectation into present challenges.

---

[5] Cf. the stoic definition given by Cicero: 'Wisdom, moreover, as the word has been defined by the philosophers of old, is the knowledge of things human and divine and of the causes by which those things are controlled (*Sapientia autem est, ut a veteribus definitum est, rerum divinarum et humanarum causarumque, quibus hae res continentur, scientia*)' (Cicero 1821: 15 (= II.5)).

[6] Cf. Charles Taylor's analysis of the fragmentation of modern societies due to the 'atomism' of the individual (Taylor 1991).

[7] For this distinction cf. Ritschl 1987: *passim*.

Its place of corroboration is the *Lebenswelt*, the world of direct lived experience, not the laboratory, the experiment or the field-study. In this sense Luther could also call theology 'experimental wisdom (*sapientia experimentalis*)'.[8] It integrates theoretical knowledge and practical prudence so that our knowledge, our experience and our ignorance can be processed according to certain guiding differences and distinctions closely linked to the convictions and beliefs at the basis of our self-understanding. In the Christian theological perspective these fundamental attitudes are owed to God by means of scripture, community and the Holy Spirit, which refer to Jesus Christ as the source of divine wisdom. Thus Christian theology as sapiential 'science' (cf. Hailer 1997) aims at something that is beyond its ultimate control, namely at the event of the good life among human beings and between human beings and God.

Theology works for wisdom without being wisdom itself. It refers to the existence of wisdom as the condition of its possibility but not as its product. Successful theology works as an eye-opener. It instructs to *discover* the truth rather than to infer it syllogistically. At some occasions it might appeal to consensus and intuition, at others it might challenge what is taken for granted, interrupt what is considered self-evident and confront it with biblical narratives and theological concepts. In any case, it does not promote neutral knowledge. Its addressees have to relate to it, be it in consent or in dissent.

To argue and to act in favour of such an open ideal of wisdom which at the same time presses towards obliging truth is to my conviction relevant especially in a modern pluralist society, to which the Christian community and its theology with its historical consciousness and its hermeneutical tools might significantly contribute. I want to explain that a little further in the next and last section.

Pluralist Societies and Cultural Dynamics

Modern societies have to integrate a plurality of concepts, theories and value-systems. No religion, no church and no science can possibly supply an overall, obliging, universally accepted interpretation of reality. Any attempt to counter the loss and decrease of the formative and orientating power of religion as such or Christianity in particular by claiming a definite and eventually superior subject, method or competence for theology will in my view rather increase the common understanding of the Christian community that it is in its exclusiveness just one particular and somewhat old-fashioned fraction of society which is now quite beyond its once triumphant heydays. And at the same time through this frustration it might provoke fundamentalist, dogmatist or irrational tendencies within religion as a counter-reaction. However, experimental science and disengaged reason alone cannot provide the common ground on which to build a civil, just and humane society. In our family bonds, in our relations between the generations, in our engagement for society and communal

---

[8] Luther 1893: 98. Cf. Bayer 1994: 49.

work, in our notions of fair co-operation and mutual respect we depend on more than theoretical knowledge and instrumental reasoning.

Postmodernity has led to a radicalization of pluralism which is challenging the historical consensus our Western societies agreed upon. The diversity of lifestyles, belief-systems and value-orientations is now so advanced that the compromise of Western liberalism mediating between individual autonomy and the neutrality of the state concerning worldviews seems no longer adequate. In retrospect the liberal separation of individual conviction and common political life appears to be part of a process of differentiation within largely homogeneous cultures and societies. In the western European countries as well as in the United States which are formed by Christian religion, science and enlightenment, a common basis had been found that was not too far from what the majority of the people could integrate into their individual and group values and that was compatible with the public and the economic system.

Under the conditions of what some already call 'post-secular' modernity this situation has altered. Alongside liberal demands for liberty and individual rights of freedom of conviction are emerging calls for the recognition of the cultural identity of different groups and for a publicly and politically relevant realization of common values which go beyond the liberal moderation of opposite group interests. Confronted with fellow citizens from very different cultural backgrounds having a strong group identity and with the challenge of shaping technological progress, not only towards the maximization of effect and profit, the suspicion arises that the liberal ideal of a state that remains neutral on issues of worldview is itself the expression of merely one particular cultural tradition. A society in which worldviews and values are matters of mere private personal conviction and in which religion is considered a hobby or a private recreational activity threatens to become hollow and meaningless and susceptible to particularistic interests and uncontrolled economic and technological dynamics.

In such a setting theology in its dialogue with the natural sciences has to insist on a concept of reason that allows for its enrichment by wisdom integrating practical and orientating dimensions of human life. The task of theology is to keep alive the quest for an aim, for a *telos* of human existence, to refute the monopoly of total explanatory competence claimed by the natural sciences, but also to criticize and challenge the ambiguities of religion. This can only be fulfilled by a theology that is not designed as the continuation of the natural sciences with other or more elaborate means or simply on a different field of knowledge. What is needed is not the claim of an amended accumulation of knowledge regarding transcendent objects and states of affairs. Therefore theology must leave behind the notion of a logically sound system of the propositional truths of faith (*articuli fidei*) based on scripture and tradition as the ideal representation of revelation. In cultural dialogue theology must consequently design and present itself as theology on the way (*theologia viatorum*). It must proclaim the freedom of a Christian (*libertas christiana*) as the focus of faith and as its critical principle. It must foster and promote a culture of communication which respects the hermeneutical interplay of understanding, perception, reflection and practice. Its location, its *Sitz im Leben* is discourse, conversation, dispute.

Theology therefore has to be elaborated as the art of interpretation, of understanding prior to and beyond explanation, of appropriate judgement, of dealing with error, doubt, temptation and heresy, not as an abstract theory but as *a hermeneutic art and skill* of moderation between the Christian faith of individuals, its public organized forms and our theoretical and practical knowledge concerning the world we live in.[9] Only through public pluralist discourse can a process of clarification regarding the importance and significance of religious beliefs eventually be initiated. Within such a setting theology should try to strengthen the assurance of Christian faith, its expressiveness and its power to form concrete communal and individual life. For that purpose theology has to relate critically to at least the following six systems of reference (cf. Dalferth 1991: 19):

1. the concrete historic and living *Christian faith* as grounded in scripture, creed, teaching, churches and congregations;
2. the contemporary contexts, the *Lebenswelt* of human beings in our pluralist, secular and capitalist societies with their biographical and conventional value-systems and practical reasoning;
3. the relevant and up-to-date theoretical and practical *knowledge* of theories and facts of the different natural and social sciences;
4. the forms and regulations of our *societies* in their juridical, economic and political respects;
5. the historic and contemporary reflections of *philosophical thinking* which apparently share the pluralistic fate of modernity;
6. the diversity of *religious and cultural traditions* of humankind, including arts, music, literature, etc.

It is obvious that this cannot be achieved by individuals. In this concept theology has to be a discursive, a dialogical, a manifold and a context-sensitive enterprise where divergent views and different methodological means are necessary, but where the directions of purpose and the reference to the spiritual and historic sources are also coherent. Insofar as the different systems and categories of reference are mutually irreducible, theology has to be 'combinational' (cf. Dalferth 1991). Such a theology can not be regarded as 'scientific'

---

[9] As a theologian thinking along these lines one could name Bernard J. Lonergan; cf. Lonergan 1972.

theology according to the standards of science in general.[10] And it can not claim to be a super-science which integrates the sciences by transcending them, but it can appeal to the great tradition of practical reason and wisdom upon which the sciences themselves depend and for which they are intended. Thus it might even contribute indirectly to the progress of science itself as an integral part of human culture.[11] For that purpose it must uncover and communicate the fundamental conditions of human existence which cannot be technically 'produced' but are prior to all human agency, namely sympathy, confidence, mutual respect, kindness, love and mercy, linking them to God as the beginning of wisdom (Prov. 9.10).

Acknowledgement

I am grateful to LeRon Shults for going through the text and suggesting improvements regarding language and style. The errors and shortcomings that remain are not his fault; he did his best to set my English straight.

References

Aquinas, Thomas. See Thomas Aquinas.

Augustine
    1968   *De trinitate libri 15*, in *Opera*, vol. 16.2 (CCSL 50a; Turnhout: Brepols).

[10] This puts my view in contrast to Alister E. McGrath's continuation of Thomas R. Torrance's project of a scientific theology (cf. Torrance 2001; McGrath 2001, 2002, 2003). Torrance sees strong parallels between progress in science and in theology. Natural science is as such 'a religious operation' through which 'the scientist as priest of creation' allows 'the basic design, the meaning, of the universe to become disclosed' (Torrance 2001: 111–12). This consequently shapes his notion of progress. The mentioned disclosure 'is a progressive operation, for the theory of model is progressively changed and refined in the light of what becomes disclosed' (Torrance 2001: 125). This also applies, *mutatis mutandis*, to 'Christological inquiry': it is 'an instrument for the progressive self-revelation of Christ to us' (Torrance 2001: 126).

[11] A quotation by the famous physicist and one of the founders of quantum theory, Erwin Schrödinger, may illustrate this point. Schrödinger regrets that 'there is a tendency to forget that all science is bound up with human culture in general, and that scientific findings, even those which at the moment appear the most advanced and esoteric and difficult to grasp, are meaningless outside their cultural context. A theoretical science, unaware that those of its constructs considered relevant and momentous are destined eventually to be framed in concepts and words that have a grip on the educated community and become part and parcel of the general world picture – a theoretical science, I say, where this is forgotten, and where the initiated continue musing to each other in terms that are, at best, understood by a small group of close fellow travellers, will necessarily be cut off from the rest of cultural mankind; in the long run it is bound to atrophy and ossify, however virulently esoteric chat may continue within its joyfully isolated groups of experts' (Schrödinger 1984: 478–9).

Barth, K.
1962   *Einführung in die evangelische Theologie* (Zurich: EVZ-Verlag, 2nd edn).

Bayer, O.
1994   *Theologie* (Gütersloh: Gütersloher Verlags-Haus Mohn).

Cicero, M. T.
1821   *De officiis* (Leipzig: Steinacker & Wagner).

Comte, A.
1830–42 *Cours de philosophie positive*, vols 1–6 (Paris: Baillière).

Dalferth, I. U.
1991   *Kombinatorische Theologie* (Freiburg i.B./Basel/Wien: Herder).

Darwin, C.
1982   *On the Origin of Species by Means of Natural Selection* (London: John Murray, 6th edn).

Feyerabend, P.
1975   *Against Method: Outline of an Anarchistic Theory of Knowledge* (London: NLB).

Gödel, K.
1931   'Über formal unentscheidbare Sätze der Principia Mathematica und verwandter Systeme I', *Monatshefte für Mathematik und Physik* 38: 173–98.

Hailer, M.
1997   *Theologie als Weisheit* (Neukirchen-Vluyn: Neukirchener).

Hume, D.
1999   *An Enquiry Concerning Human Understanding* (ed. T. L. Beauchamp; Oxford/New York: Oxford University Press).

Kant, I.
1923   'Beantwortung der Frage: Was ist Aufklärung?', in Königlich Preußische Akademie der Wissenschaften (ed.), *Kant's gesammelte Schriften*, vol. 8 (Berlin: de Gruyter).

Lonergan, B. J. F.
1972   *Method in Theology* (London: Darton, Longman & Todd).

Luther, M.
1893   *Randbemerkungen zu Taulers Predigten* (around 1516), in *Martin Luthers Werke: Kritische Gesamtausgabe*, vol. 9 (Weimar: Böhlau).
1926   *Die Zirkulardisputation de veste nuptiali* (1537), in *Martin Luthers Werke: Kritische Gesamtausgabe*, vol. 39/I (Weimar: Böhlau).

McGrath, A. E.
2001   *Scientific Theology*, vol. 1: *Nature* (Grand Rapids/Cambridge: Eerdmans).
2002   *Scientific Theology*, vol. 2: *Reality* (Grand Rapids/Cambridge: Eerdmans).
2003   *Scientific Theology*, vol. 3: *Theory* (Grand Rapids/Cambridge: Eerdmans).

Popper, K.
  1972   *Objective Knowledge: An Evolutionary Approach* (Oxford: Clarendon
           Press).

Ritschl, D.
  1987   *The Logic of Theology* (Philadelphia: Fortress Press).

Schrödinger, E.
  1984   'Are there quantum jumps? Part I' (1952), in *Gesammelte
           Abhandlungen*, vol. 4: *Allgemein wissenschaftliche und populäre Auf-
           sätze* (Vienna: Verlag der Österreichischen Akademie der Wis-
           senschaften): 478–92.

Spencer, H.
  1860–77 *System of Synthetic Philosophy*, vols 1–10 (London: George Man-
           waring/William & Norgate).

Taylor, C.
  1991   *The Malaise of Modernity* (Concord, Ontario: Anansi).

Thomas Aquinas
  1952   *Summa theologiae*, vol. 2: Pars IIa IIae (Turin: Marietti).

Torrance, T. F.
  2001   *The Ground and Grammar of Theology* (Edinburgh/New York: T&T
           Clark).

The Reliability of Science and its Cultural Impact

Mariano Artigas

The way to wisdom? Where it goes?
We can but guess:
we err and err and err,
but less and less and less.
(Karl Popper, undated manuscript)

When I consider how many and how wonderful are the things
understood, investigated, and done by men, I know and
understand very well that the human mind is one of the
most excellent works of God.
(Galileo Galilei: Finocchiaro 1997: 115)

The reliability of science plays a central role in our culture. It determines what we consider objective and subjective, what we are ready to accept as possessing a reasonable level of evidence and what should instead be considered as personal opinions. Jürgen Habermas wrote at the beginning of his most celebrated book:

If we imagine the philosophical discussion of the modern period reconstructed as a judicial hearing, it would be deciding a single question: how is reliable knowledge possible. (Habermas 1972: 3)

Speaking of the dialogue between science and religion, Ian Barbour began one of his books in the same vein:

The first major challenge to religion in an age of science is the success of the methods of science. Science seems to provide the only reliable path to knowledge. Many people view science as objective, universal, rational, and based on solid observational evidence. Religion, by contrast, seems to be subjective, parochial, emotional, and based on traditions or authorities that disagree with each other. (Barbour 1990: 3)

The problem is that we do not have yet a generally accepted explanation of the reliability of science.

1. Galileo's Dialogue and Urban's Argument

This problem can be traced back until the Galileo affair. In the seventeenth century the reliability of physical science was not very high. Galileo did not have decisive arguments to prove Copernicanism. Even worse, the argument of the tides, his favourite proof, was not valid. The authorities did not consider Galileo the father of a physical science that did not yet exist.

In those days 'science' stood for the 'demonstrative' sciences that studied the real causes of things: they were the different branches of philosophy. Other 'predictive' sciences existed that used mathematical tools, but they were supposed to provide only models useful for the prediction of natural phenomena: this was the case of astronomy. An astronomer was considered a second-rate scientist. The salary of Galileo as a professor of the University of Padua was much less than the salary of the professor of philosophy.

Galileo claimed that Copernicanism was a true description of nature. He would have faced no problem at all had he presented Copernicanism as a mathematical hypothesis useful to calculate the movements of the celestial bodies. Cardinal Bellarmine was explicit on this in his famous letter to Foscarini in 1615 (Finocchiaro 1989: 67–9). Cardinal Maffeo Barberini, Galileo's friend and admirer, also insisted on this point. When Barberini became Pope Urban VIII in 1623, Galileo thought that the moment had arrived to publish his defence of Copernicanism. But he also knew that Urban had a very personal view about physical theory. It can be named 'the divine omnipotence argument'.

'The divine omnipotence argument' runs this way. We work out theories in order to explain the phenomena that we observe in the natural world. But God is infinitely wise and powerful. Therefore, God could have produced the effects that we observe using causes hidden to us. If we do not admit this, we deny God's infinite wisdom and omnipotence. The conclusion is that we can never be sure that our physical theories are true. The only way to know this would be to show that no other explanation is possible, but a host of different explanations are always possible in principle.

Galileo was told that he should present Copernicanism as a hypothesis, and that he should include Urban's argument in his work. So he did. Unfortunately, he placed Urban's argument in the mouth of Simplicio, the simpleton Aristotelian who is always a loser in the *Dialogue*. It was not difficult for the enemies of Galileo to persuade Urban that Galileo had mocked him (this surely was not the case). Urban became extremely angry. He concluded that Galileo had deceived him. This was the beginning of the end. The personality of the actors played a most important role in the drama. Nevertheless, all of them faced a real philosophical problem, namely: How can we establish a scientific theory as well proven? Urban's answer was: We never can.

2. The Underdetermination of Theories

In the hands of Kepler, Galileo and Newton, a new science was emerging that combined theoretical demonstration and practical prediction. The impressive triumph of the new approach in the following centuries reversed the situation: the new science became more and more the paradigm of objectivity and reliability. Nevertheless, the shade of Urban's argument has always been present until today. This argument is a theological version of an important methodological problem. Today it is known under the name of 'the underdetermination of theories'.

In the section on 'underdetermination' in the *Routledge Encyclopedia of Philosophy*, Larry Laudan has written:

> The term underdetermination refers to a broad family of arguments about the relations between theory and evidence. All share the conclusion that evidence is more or less impotent to guide choice between rival theories or hypotheses. In one or other of its guises, underdetermination has probably been the most potent and most persuasive idea driving twentieth-century forms of scepticism and epistemological relativism. (Laudan 1998)

The difficulty is so strong because it depends on a purely logical point. Any amount of confirmation of a hypothesis does not suffice to establish its truth. We cannot exclude that contrary evidence may be found in the future. Instead, a single consequence contrary to the hypothesis shows that it is false. Karl Popper named this problem 'the logical asymmetry between verification and falsification'. Verification is impossible, falsification is the only way to progress. Knowledge progresses only through error elimination.

Popper identified the scientific attitude with the critical attitude. We should not seek for positive proofs. We should rather seek for counterexamples of our theories. Our knowledge is always conjectural, and this would be the basis for tolerance and respect. Instead, searching for certitude would lead to dogmatism, intolerance and stagnation. Popper labelled his doctrine 'fallibilism'.

3. Fallibilism: Soft and Strong

Fallibilism is widespread today. If by 'fallibilism' we mean that our knowledge is not perfect, that we can always err, that we should always be open to detect errors and change our views accordingly, all of us should be fallibilists. But sometimes fallibilism means something else, namely that certitude is out of our reach. Popper admits that in empirical science we seek for truth and sometimes we may reach it. He adds, however, that we can never know whether this is the case. We should abandon the quest for certitude. We can progress only by eliminating errors. I have chosen as a motto for this lecture a line written by Popper: 'We err and err and err, but less and less and less.'

I find this version of fallibilism too strong. In 1979 I published my first book. The subject was the philosophy of science of Karl Popper. I sent him a copy. I told him in the covering letter that we know for sure many things in empirical science. He sent me a lovely handwritten letter, where he wrote something that cannot be found in any of his published writings or in the 462 boxes of Popper's archives at the Hoover Institution. This is the central paragraph: 'I also think that many scientific statements are true. I also think that we can be pretty sure of the truth of some of them. But no theory was better tested than Newton's – and we cannot be sure of it' (original mine).

Peter Hodgson, a nuclear physicist of Oxford University, told me that 'pretty sure' is a British understatement, so that Popper meant 'completely sure'. But I am not sure about Popper's use of his Austrian English. In any case, 'pretty sure' obviously means some degree of certitude, something that Popper usually avoided as if it were the devil himself.

We find here a paradoxical situation. The natural sciences are considered as a very reliable kind of knowledge, but, if the strong kind of fallibilism is right, then we cannot reach any kind of certitude. Some people conclude that much less will we be able to reach certitude in other ambits of human experience. Thus they are led to relativism and scepticism. Popper would protest against this. He considered himself a realist. But he insisted that we should abandon the search for certitude or reliability. The problem is whether we can combine this with a realist perspective.

4. Criteria of Validity

In order to establish the validity of our theories, some criteria are usually employed in empirical science. Thomas Kuhn, who was accused of relativism, answered his critics saying that there are objective criteria that help us to choose among competing theories. He took for granted that everyone knows which these criteria are, and, from a number of them, he selected five, namely *accuracy, consistency, scope, simplicity* and *fruitfulness* (Kuhn 1977).

A theory is *accurate* if its consequences are in good agreement with the results of existing experiments and observations. It is *consistent* if, on the one hand, it does not lead to contradiction and, on the other, it is consistent with other accepted theories. *Broadness of scope* means that its consequences should extend beyond the particular data it was initially designed to explain. *Simplicity* refers to bringing order to phenomena that otherwise would be isolated. And *fruitfulness* refers to the capacity to promote new findings in scientific research.

However, according to Kuhn, those criteria are not sufficient to determine the decisions of individual scientists: 'My point is, then, that every individual choice between competing theories depends on a mixture of objective and subjective factors, or of shared and individual criteria' (Kuhn 1977: 325).

Therefore, different scientists will not arrive at the same decision, even though they use the same data and share the same criteria. For Kuhn, the criteria of choice function not as rules, which determine choice, but as values, which influence it. Scientists committed to the same values may make different choices, as there is some ambiguity in the application of values (Kuhn 1977:

331). In other words, interpretation plays an important role in empirical science. I think this is a very important point.

In a book published in 1990, Ian Barbour listed four criteria for assessing theories in normal scientific research: *agreement with data, coherence, scope* and *fertility*. They correspond quite well with Kuhn's criteria. The most important criterion is *agreement with data*, especially when it is linked with the prediction of novel phenomena not previously anticipated (Barbour 1990: 34).

In 1989, Barbour had not published his book and I had not yet read Kuhn's essay. Then I proposed in a book a list of five criteria: *explanatory power; predictive power; accuracy* of both explanations and predictions; *convergence of varied and independent proofs*; and *mutual support among different theories* (Artigas 1989: 135–42). I still think today that this is a good list. It is easy to compare the three lists and see that they are in good agreement.

I would like to point out an important property that is shared by the three lists. They show that in order to evaluate our theories we do not employ only quantitative criteria. There is a qualitative flavour in those criteria. The more these criteria are successfully applied to a hypothesis, the more we can rely on them, and this cannot be quantified.

These criteria are not a kind of algorithm that can be applied automatically. They include qualitative appraisals. This is why they can supplement purely logical reasons. It is not only the quantity of conclusions that matters, but how well the phenomena are explained, how accurate the explanations are, whether the theory makes really novel and important predictions, whether it is supported by proofs that come from disparate domains, whether and how well it can be combined with other well corroborated theories.

We apply these criteria also in other ambits, including ordinary life. The difference is that in empirical science we test our theories against experiments that can be controlled and reproduced by anyone, and we use, whenever possible, mathematical instruments.

5. Consilience and Reductionism

I would like to comment on my fourth criterion (quasi-identical with Kuhn's and Barbour's *broadness of scope*), namely *convergence of varied and independent proofs*. The fact that different phenomena, which can be measured in an independent way, are explained and predicted by one and the same theory, is a very good reason in favour of that theory.

There is no mystery in this. The same criterion is applied in judicial affairs. We acquire a strong certitude if several testimonies coincide that come from completely independent people. This is not perhaps purely formal logic, but is real strong logic, and is used very often in daily life and in empirical science as well.

In the nineteenth century William Whewell (1794–1866) coined the term 'consilience' to express an idea similar to the convergence of varied and independent proofs, and he considered it as the best proof that a scientific hypothesis can receive. In his classical work *The Philosophy of the Inductive Sciences*, Whewell wrote:

> The evidence in favour of our induction is of a much higher and more forcible character when it enables us to express and determine cases of a *kind different* from those, which were contemplated in the formation of our hypothesis. The instances, in which this occurred, indeed, impress us with a conviction that the truth of our hypothesis is certain. No accident could give rise to such an extraordinary coincidence. No false supposition could, after being adjusted to one class of phenomena, so exactly represent a different class, when the agreement was unforeseen and uncontemplated. That rules springing from remote and unconnected quarters should thus leap to the same point, can only arise from *that* being the point where truth resides. (Whewell 1996: 230)

In this case, Whewell spoke of a *Consilience of Inductions*. The term *consilience* has been used recently by Edward Wilson as the title of a book that has provoked strong discussion (Wilson 1998). Wilson's thesis is that a consilience progressing from the basic levels of the natural world to the upper levels could reach the levels of the humanities, including ethics and religion. Wilson would like to explain all kinds of human experience on the basis of the natural sciences. He frankly admits that this idea is a metaphysical programme:

> The belief in the possibility of consilience beyond science and across the great branches of learning is not yet science. It is a metaphysical world view, and a minority one at that, shared by only a few scientists and philosophers … Its best support is no more than an extrapolation of the consistent past success of the natural sciences. Its surest test will be its effectiveness in the social sciences and humanities. (Wilson 1998: 9)

Stephen Jay Gould has strongly criticized Wilson's perspective. Gould declares himself as a 'materialist in practical scientific work and as an agnostic in religious matters'. He agrees with Wilson 'that mental processes have physical groundings and, if knowable at all, must be consistent with the natural sciences' (Gould 2003: 232–3). But he criticizes Wilson's proposal.

Gould's first argument is 'that reductionism will not suffice even within its potentially applicable domain of subjects traditionally assigned to the natural sciences', and he adds: 'the "higher" we mount, the less we can rely on reductionism for the twinned reasons of (1) ever greater influence of emergent principles, and (2) ever greater accumulation of historical accidentals requiring narrative explanations as contingencies' (Gould 2003: 233, 227–8).

Gould's second argument against Wilson is more radical. It refers to the different nature of empirical science and the humanities: 'the argument that, by the logic of its enterprise and the nature of its fundamental questions, the concerns of traditional subjects in humanities (and also in ethics and religion) cannot be addressed and resolved by the methods of scientific inquiry, reductionistic or otherwise' (Gould 2003: 233).

6. Reliability and Patterns

Gould defends the thesis that science and religion constitute two *Non Over-lapping Magisteria* (NOMA) (Gould 2000). I do not agree with all the details of Gould's view. Nevertheless, I agree that there exists a gap between the perspectives of the natural science and the humanities, including religion. The methods used in empirical science are reliable as far as they are used to study the material world of factual reality, but cannot be extended to other fields.

The natural sciences study 'the material world of factual reality' (in Gould's terms), and they do this in a very specific way. The natural world does not speak our language, it only speaks with facts. Therefore, in order to obtain answers from our mute partner, we must build models and test them against experiments. Only those theories are accepted that can lead to empirically testable consequences. This is a first requirement that any theory must fulfil to be acceptable in empirical science.

Intersubjectivity is, first of all, a requirement, a password necessary to enter through the door of empirical science. The arguments we use in empirical science must be expressed in a language that can be used by any partner, and must include well-established references to empirical facts.

The success of empirical science shows that we are able to build this kind of language. But this also tells us something about the natural world. In fact, repeatable experiments that always produce the same results indicate that there exists a natural order, a net of stable relationships between the different features of the natural world.

Natural order can be considered a presupposition of empirical science that is retrojustified, enlarged and refined by the progress of science. As the fisherman must suppose that there are fishes in the lake or the sea, scientists must suppose that there exists an underlying order that they can discover. Success is not guaranteed in advance, but when it exists it confirms that the presupposition was right, and provides us with a better knowledge of the natural order. Further progress indicates more orderliness.

The reliability of empirical science depends ultimately on the existence of patterns in nature and on our ability to find them. No wonder that when we study aspects of the reality in which the spiritual and cultural dimensions intervene, we cannot reach the same kind of reliability.

We should not be surprised that in other ambits we do not reach the kind of intersubjectivity that we reach in empirical science. The peculiar reliability of empirical science is an advantage for many purposes, but it is limited only to those dimensions of reality that can be submitted to empirical control. This kind of approach is insufficient and inadequate when we study the spiritual dimensions of human beings and other metascientific issues, as the nature and scope of science itself.

It is not difficult to integrate the perspectives of empirical science and the humanities, including religion, if we consider them as separate and complementary ambits that can coexist in the same person. The question is: Can we go further on, establishing some kind of dialogue and collaboration?

7. Bridging the Gap

According to the warfare model, popularized in the nineteenth century by John William Draper (1811–82) and Andrew Dickson White (1832–1918), science and religion are antagonistic enterprises that cannot coexist. Gould has criticized this view:

> I cannot emphasize too strongly that the old model of all-out warfare between science and religion – the 'standard' view of my secular education, and founded upon two wildly successful books of the mid- to late nineteenth century (Draper, 1874, and White, 1896 . . .) simply does not fit this issue, and represents an absurdly false and caricatured dichotomy that can only disrespect both supposed sides of this nonexistent conflict. 'Religion', as a coherent entity, never opposed 'science' in any general or comprehensive way. (Gould 2003: 29)

Most people today agree that the conflict thesis does not correspond to the historical record (Russell 2002; Wilson 2002), and also admit that there exists a methodological gap between science and religion. The question is: Can we bridge this gap? Can we go further on, establishing some kind of dialogue and collaboration? Now I am going to briefly explore a particular bridge, which I have developed in my book *The Mind of the Universe* (Artigas 2000).

First of all I must confess that I do not trust too much in the so-called 'boundary questions' that according to John Polkinghorne 'are questions which arise from science and which insistently demand an answer, but which by their very character transcend that of which science itself is competent to speak' (Polkinghorne 1990: 88). I think that if they cannot be solved by scientific means, they should not be considered as scientific questions. They could be called 'subjective connections'. As the scientist and the human being are the same person, an astrophysicist studying the origin of the universe can pose the question of creation in a metaphysical sense, but not as a scientist. This is already metaphysics.

My proposal focuses on one particular kind of boundary question: *the general presuppositions of empirical science, and the feedback of scientific progress on them.* I speak here of the *general* presuppositions of empirical science, which can be considered as necessary conditions for all branches of empirical science.

There are three kinds of such presuppositions. The first refers to the intelligibility or rationality of nature: it can be labelled as ontological, and is closely related to natural order. The second refers to the human ability to know the natural order: it can be labelled as epistemological, and includes the different forms of scientific argument. The third refers to the values implied by the scientific activity itself: it can be labelled as ethical, and includes the search for truth, rigour, objectivity, intellectual modesty, service to other people, co-operation and other related values.

Moreover (and this is the central point in my argument), there is a feedback from scientific progress on these presuppositions, because the progress of science retrojustifies, amplifies and refines them. These presuppositions are necessary conditions for the existence of science; therefore scientific progress is a sufficient condition for their existence, and enables us to determine their scope.

Seen under the light of that feedback, the analysis of those presuppositions can provide a clue to the philosophical meaning of scientific progress and, therefore, to its theological relevance. We can show that scientific progress is most coherent with a theistic and spiritualist perspective.

I have developed this proposal in my book, and have published shorter versions elsewhere (Artigas 2002). Now I will limit myself to a few hints, underlining how this proposal is related to the reliability of science.

8. Self-organization, Scientific Creativity and Scientific Values

Scientists must presuppose that the natural world is not chaotic, but ordered. Order is often equated with the 'rationality' or the 'intelligibility' of the world.

I dare say that *now, for the first time in history, we have a scientific worldview which provides a complete and unified picture of the world*, because it includes all natural levels (micro- and macro-physical, as well as biological), their mutual relations and their evolution. I do not mean that we know everything about the world. But we already know some basic features of the different natural levels and their mutual connections.

The new worldview is centred on four basic ideas: *natural dynamism, patterning, information* and *self-organization*. Inert and passive matter does not exist. Natural dynamism is deeply intertwined with spatial and temporal structures. It is stored, coded as it were, in spatial structures, and is deployed following specific rhythms. It is a directional dynamism that, moreover, tends to co-operate, forming new structures or patterns. Patterning, or the creation of new patterns, is a basic feature of the natural world.

In this new worldview the concept of information plays a relevant role. I want to say that information is 'materialized rationality'. It guides the successive formation of increasingly complex patterns. Information is stored, displayed, integrated, coded and decoded in the different natural systems and processes. In this perspective we can say that an electron 'knows' physics and chemistry much better than we do, as it will act in different circumstances according to the immensely varied potentialities it contains.

The natural world can be seen, therefore, as the result of a dynamic process of self-organization. Our world is the result of the deployment of a dynamism that produces different natural levels with new emergent characteristics.

This new worldview provides a good base for reflection on anthropology and natural theology. Seeing that nature is full of organization, directionality, synergy (co-operativity) and very sophisticated activities, is most coherent with the existence of a 'continuous' activity of divine wisdom. The corresponding idea of God is that of a Creator who has conceived the natural dynamism, and uses it to produce, according to the natural laws created by Him, a world of successive levels of emerging novelties.

The key metaphor of this worldview is self-organization. The curious thing is that this is explicitly contained in a definition of nature provided by Thomas Aquinas, which is surprisingly modern. Commenting on Aristotle, Aquinas surpasses him and writes: 'Nature is nothing other than the ratio of a certain art, namely, the divine, inscribed in things, by which things themselves move to a determinate end: just as if the master shipbuilder could impart to the wood something from which it could move itself to taking on the form of the ship' (Aquinas 1965: 268). Now we can say that God acts this way and we can provide many striking examples.

Scientific progress retrojustifies, enriches and refines the ontological pre-suppositions of science, turning order into self-organization, and helps us to consider the central role that natural and divine creativity play here. All this means progress in our religious understanding. We can realize this better if we consider the early reactions provoked by the theory of evolution. On 25 May 1878, Tommaso Zigliara, one of the most important theologians in Rome at the time, signed a report ordered by the Congregation of the Index in the Vatican. His first conclusion was that 'the Darwinian system on the primitive cells and their successive evolution and transformation ... is nothing else than the material part of absolute evolutionism, which is Hegelian pantheism' (Zigliara 1878: 18).

One could object that evolution could proceed moved by the divine action. This was the reasoning of Roman Catholic supporters of evolution, such as Dalmace Leroy, John Zahm and others. Nevertheless, evolutionism was easily considered as a materialist and atheist doctrine. The worldview centred on self-organization, and the corresponding theological reflections represent a very important paradigm shift.

We cannot use science to prove metascientific theses. It cannot be used, under the form of anthropic principles, as a substitute for metaphysical and theological reasoning. But the new worldview shows that our world is full of directional dimensions, of tendencies and synergy, of rationality. It introduces information, which is materialized rationality, as a concept that plays a central role in explaining our world. It represents our world as the result of a gigantic process of self-organization, where successive specific potentialities have become actualized, producing a series of increasingly organized systems that have cul-minated in the human organism, which provides the basis for a truly rational existence. Therefore, the present worldview amplifies the basis for teleological reasoning, which is one of the main bridges that may be used to connect the natural and the divine.

Something similar happens with the two other general presuppositions of science in their respective levels. Scientific progress clearly shows the singu-larity of human beings. We are natural beings that, at the same time, transcend the natural level. Creativity, argument, interpretation and criticism are essential components of empirical science, and they are a proof of our singularity. They show that we possess dimensions that transcend the natural ambit and can be labelled as spiritual. The very existence and progress of the natural sciences is one of the best arguments that show our spiritual character. But, at the same time, the success of scientific method shows that our spiritual dimensions related to creativity and argument are intertwined with our material dimensions, so that we are a single person constituted by both aspects. All this is coherent with the view that man is a co-creator who participates in God's plans, and has the capacity of carrying the natural and the human ambits to more and more evolved states. Therefore, also on this level we can appreciate that scientific progress retrojustifies, enriches and refines the epistemological presuppositions of science. Thanks to this progress, we know better our own capacities, and are able to develop them in a line of an increasing creativity that corresponds to God's plans.

Finally, the meaning and relevance of science reach their highest peak when we consider its ethical presuppositions. Empirical science is, above all, a human enterprise directed towards a twofold goal: a kind of knowledge of nature that can be submitted to empirical control and, therefore, can provide a dominion over nature. Therefore, the meaning of science is also twofold: the pursuit of truth and service to humankind. In this case, it is obvious that scientific progress retrojustifies, enriches and refines these goals, and provides better means for their implementation.

Besides, scientific work requires an entire set of values, such as love for truth, rigour, objectivity, intellectual modesty, co-operation, interest in solving practical problems (medical, economic and so on), so that scientific progress contributes to the spread of those values.

I consider the pursuit of truth as a value essential to the scientific enterprise. Karl Popper said: 'The fact that science cannot make any pronouncement about ethical principles has been misinterpreted as indicating that there are no such principles; while in fact the search for truth presupposes ethics' (Popper 1987: 141).

This is very important. Empirical science is meaningful above all as a search for truth, and truth is a central ethical value in human life. Pope John Paul II, in a few words full of philosophical meaning, has written: 'One may define the human being, therefore, as *the one who seeks the truth*' (John Paul II 1998: n. 28).

There is another passage of *Fides et ratio*, which can easily remain unnoticed, but is most important for my purpose. In the very beginning of the encyclical we read:

> In both East and West, we may trace a journey which has led humanity down the centuries to meet and engage truth more and more deeply. It is a journey which has unfolded – as it must – within the horizon of personal self-consciousness: the more human beings know reality and the world, the more they know themselves in their uniqueness, with the question of the meaning of things and of their very existence becoming ever more pressing. (John Paul II 1998: n. 1)

This coincides with my accent on the anthropological feedback of scientific progress on human self-knowledge (Karol 1999).

I do not mean that my proposal is the only possible bridge between science and religion. But I think it is a serious candidate that can be used in the three fields of ontology, epistemology and ethics. In my book *The Mind of the Universe* I have explored a number of issues belonging to this perspective, and I have also pointed out a number of issues that could be explored further. I only wish that this proposal might serve to promote new reflections on this important topic.

References

Aquinas, Thomas. See Thomas Aquinas.

Artigas, M.
> 1989   *Filosofía de la ciencia experimental* (Pamplona: Eunsa).
> 2000   *The Mind of the Universe* (Philadelphia: Templeton Foundation Press).
> 2002   'The Mind of the Universe: Understanding Science and Religion', in A. Ramos and M. I. George (eds), *Faith, Scholarship, and Culture in the 21ˢᵗ Century* (Washington: Catholic University of America Press): 113–25.

Barbour, I.
> 1990   *Religion in an Age of Science* (San Francisco: Harper).

Ferngren, G. B. (ed.)
> 2002   *Science and Religion: A Historical Introduction* (Baltimore: Johns Hopkins University Press).

Finocchiaro, M. A. (trans. and ed.)
> 1989   *The Galileo Affair: A Documentary History* (California Studies in the History of Science 1; Berkeley: University of California Press).
> 1997   *Galileo on the World Systems: A New Abridged Translation and Guide* (Berkeley: University of California Press).

Gould, S. J.
> 2000   *Rocks of Ages: Science and Religion in the Fullness of Life* (London: Jonathan Cape).
> 2003   *The Hedgehog, the Fox, and the Magister's Pox* (New York: Harmony Books).

Habermas, J.
> 1972   *Knowledge and Human Interests* (trans. J. J. Shapiro; London: Heinemann).

John Paul II
> 1998   *Fides et ratio* (encyclical from 14 September 1998).

Karol, M.
> 1999   ' "Fides et ratio" n° 1: ¿cuál es el texto correcto?', *Anuario Filosófico* 32: 689–96.

Kuhn, T. S.
> 1977   'Objectivity, Value Judgement, and Theory Choice', in T. S.

Kuhn, *The Essential Tension* (Chicago: University of Chicago Press): 320–39.

Laudan, L.
1998 'Underdetermination', in E. Craig (ed.), *Routledge Encyclopedia of Philosophy*, vol. 9 (London and New York: Routledge): 527.

Polkinghorne, J.
1990 'A Revived Natural Theology', in J. Fennema and I. Paul (eds), *Science and Religion: One World: Changing Perspectives on Reality* (Dordrecht: Kluwer): 87–97.

Popper, K. R.
1987 'Natural Selection and the Emergence of Mind', in G. Radnitzky and W. W. Bartley (eds), *Evolutionary Epistemology, Rationality, and the Sociology of Knowledge* (La Salle, IL: Open Court): 139–55.
[Undated] Undated manuscript, in Popper's archives, Hoover Institution (Stanford University), box 13, folder 2.

Russell, C. A.
2002 'The Conflict of Science and Religion', in Ferngren 2002: 3–12.

Thomas Aquinas
1965 *In octo libros Physicorum Expositio* (Turin: Marietti).

Whewell, W.
1996 *The Philosophy of the Inductive Sciences*, with a new introduction by Andrew Pyle (London: Routledge/Thoemmes Press). (Original 1840.)

Wilson, D. B.
2002 'The Historiography of Science and Religion', in Ferngren 2002: 13–29.

Wilson, E. O.
1998 *Consilience: The Unity of Knowledge* (New York: Knopf).

Zigliara, T.
1878 'Report', in Archive of the Congregation for the Doctrine of the Faith, Index, *Protocolli 1878–1881*, fol. 18.

'Don't Drink from that Dirty Stream!'

The Decline of Science and Theology as Sources of Wisdom in Europe

Chris Wiltsher

Introduction

'Where shall wisdom be found?' asked the writer of the book of Job some three thousand years ago. Many answers would be offered in the Europe of today, but few Europeans, I suggest, would include science or theology among the more important sources. Yet for nearly two hundred years scientists have been regarded as sages in Europe, and for nearly two thousand years Europeans have looked to their theologians for wisdom. What has happened? My tentative suggestion is that the position of science and theology as sources of wisdom has been undermined by the development in recent decades of a public perception that scientists and theologians cannot be trusted as sages.

Implicit in this suggestion is the claim that theology and science can be seen as sources of wisdom, and theologians and scientists can be accepted as wise men and women. Stated baldly and read quickly, such a claim might seem trivially true to some and trivially false to others. Many theologians, and religious believers more generally, take it for granted that the study of theology yields wisdom; many professional scientists, while not describing their work as a search for wisdom, seem to believe that the insights flowing from their work yield wisdom. On the other hand, many who are sceptical of religious claims would reject the idea that theology can yield wisdom, and many within and without the scientific field see science as yielding knowledge, not wisdom.

One issue here is the distinction between wisdom and knowledge or understanding. Both science and theology offer systematic accounts of the world in which we live which are claimed to yield knowledge and understanding: but do these amount to wisdom? Scientists and theologians may be trained and learned people, acquiring deep understanding: but does that make them sages?

These questions lead to broader questions about the very nature of wisdom, and how wisdom is recognized, and how wise men and women are recognized. It is clear that in every age some men and women have been regarded as wise, but it is not clear how they have achieved that status, nor what they have in common.

This paper offers some preliminary reflections on these issues, using the role of science and theology in European culture as a way in. The choice of science and theology as a focus is dictated in part by the origins of this paper in a contribution to the workshop programme of the Tenth European Conference on Science and Theology, which had the title 'Streams of Wisdom? Science, Theology and Cultural Dynamics'. The conference title points to and questions assumptions about the relationship between wisdom, science, theology and culture. It also points to the central role played by science and theology in European culture, a role which makes these areas of intellectual endeavour a particularly appropriate focus for this discussion.

Even a cursory glance at the history of Europe shows that science and theology have played major roles in the development of European culture. Theological ideas drawn from Christianity, Islam and Judaism underpin our varied ethical traditions, influence our systems of justice and provide the basis for our understanding of human relationships. European languages are full of words and idioms which can be directly traced to the holy books of the three religions, while European architecture, literature, music, painting, poetry and sculpture all bear witness to the influence of these religious streams.

Similarly, science has had an enormous influence on European culture. It has changed our vocabulary, broadened our horizons, given us new ways of seeing the world and added significantly to the discussion of the meaning of life. Through its espousal of observation and experiment as methods of obtaining knowledge, science helped to change European approaches to authority, replacing reliance on oral and written authorities with an experiential test, and so altering the very way we think.

In achieving these cultural effects, science and theology impinged on the lives and consciousness of all Europeans, and popular conceptions developed of science and theology, or perhaps more accurately, of scientists and theologians. It is these popular conceptions which provide the starting-point for my discussion. I want to explore the suggestion that in the past eminence in science or theology was popularly taken to be a strong indicator of wisdom. A person recognized by professional peers as a leader in science or theology was seen by the public at large as being likely to have the characteristics required of the sage. Now, I suggest, leading scientists or theologians who are regarded as wise have reached that status independently of, even in some cases in spite of, their eminence in their chosen field.

The discussion in this paper is a tentative sketch, limited to Europe, and to those eminent in science and theology. This latter restriction is necessary to keep the topic manageable, but we should note that eminence and wisdom do not necessarily go together. Many eminent people would not popularly be regarded as wise – for example, many leading political figures – while many people popularly regarded as wise do not stand out in any field of human endeavour.

An advantage of restricting the focus to eminent men and women is that it is fairly easy to establish that some were regarded as wise. Figures as diverse as Hildegard of Bingen, Marie Curie, John Knox and Albert Einstein had established reputations in their fields of expertise but were also consulted widely on matters far beyond those fields. It is indisputable that in the past men and women of eminence in science and theology were popularly respected as sages.

It is much more difficult to suggest eminent scientists or theologians of the present who would be widely regarded as wise, as distinct from learned, knowledgeable, influential or telegenic. The difference between past and present demands attention and provides a starting-point for reflection: my suggestion is that the reputation for sagacity, or otherwise, of scientists and theologians is intimately connected with popular perceptions of science and theology. It is convenient to begin exploring that suggestion with a brief consideration of the nature of wisdom.

Wisdom

Wisdom may be defined as the capacity to make sound judgements about living. The wise are people to whom others turn for advice about what to do, often what to do in difficult circumstances; they are people who are recognized as combining knowledge, experience and insight to produce balanced judgements. It is not possible in this paper to analyse wisdom in any depth, but there are some characteristics of wisdom and the wise which are particularly interesting.

It is useful to note first that the wise are not self-selected or self-accredited: they are recognized as wise by others. How that recognition comes about, especially at a local level, is a fascinating question which cannot be explored here. However, the role of public perception in the recognition of wisdom is important. Public perceptions are formed from truths and half-truths, and lack subtle nuance, but they do show us what the public at large regards as significant. Public perceptions also change, sometimes radically, and it is a change in public perception to which I want to draw attention.

Another interesting aspect of wisdom is that wisdom is associated with individuals, those who are regarded as wise men and women. We may on occasions refer to 'traditions' of wisdom, but then we mean the accumulated and recorded utterances of wise people over long periods.

One major reason for this focus on individuals is that when we seek wisdom we are seeking judgements about what to do in the present or future. The wisdom of the past may give us insight, but it cannot be applied directly to our present situations. For that we need sages in the present. They may draw on the wisdom of the past, but they will bring to bear their own understanding of the present, their own insights into the way the world is changing. Because human life is dynamic, balanced judgements about how to live must also be dynamic. In particular we expect the wise to notice and take into account subtle changes and nuances which escape most of us: this is part of the difference between an advisor and a sage.

A further difference between an advisor and a sage is that the sage demonstrates a profound understanding of the world and of the human condition. Such understanding requires knowledge, a wide range of knowledge which encompasses the phenomena of the world and the intricacies of human personality and human relationships. In the wise, such knowledge is enhanced by deep reflection to produce an interpretation of events which reveals how the world works at deep levels and suggests how it will work in the future. To achieve the necessary level of insight, the wise must be deep thinkers and also what we might call lateral thinkers, able to make connections which others miss and draw a wide range of elements together to produce an integrated vision.

On the basis of subtle and nuanced interpretation, supported by knowledge and reflection, the sage is able to make balanced judgements and offer advice. A reputation for wisdom must be related in some way to the efficacy of the advice given: only those who are known to give sound advice will be regarded as wise. But what counts as 'sound' advice? It would be easy to assume that the advice will be regarded as sound if following it brings benefit: but sometimes the sage will give sound advice which does not lead to benefit for the recipient. Presumably then the advice is accepted as wise because it sets events in a wider context and offers some kind of satisfactory explanation for them. It seems that rather than using a kind of utilitarian calculus to assess the soundness of advice, we resort instead to some deep-seated sense of 'rightness': the sage's advice brings about outcomes which suggest that the workings of the world at the deepest level are harmonious and beneficial, whatever is apparently happening on the surface.

To offer sound advice, so construed, sages must not be influenced by human concerns which might unbalance their judgements. The judgements of the wise must not be affected by their own emotional attachments or their own interests or fears about the consequences of their speech. The wise must tell the truth, as they see it. Being wise, and therefore sensitive to human reactions, they may not always tell the whole truth, for that may be more than the recipient is able or willing to receive. Nevertheless the wise are not afraid of human reactions, nor are they seduced by the potential of worldly rewards for their advice.

Being indifferent to reaction, the wise are also not bound by laws, implicit or explicit. Their law is a 'higher' law than any human law, and human rules and regulations are simply factors in making a judgement. So are social expectations, such as respect for authority or social position: aristocracy and peasant, rich and poor are treated alike by the true sage, and sagacious advice is not fashioned to suit a recipient's view of the situation.

The wise person then needs deep knowledge and understanding, an ability to interpret the world, noticing connections and nuances which have escaped others, and an ability to make balanced judgements unaffected by human interests, including their own interests. These characteristics will be demonstrated through advice which produces outcomes resonating with our feelings of 'rightness'.

These characteristics take time to develop, which is one reason why we expect the sage to be a person of experience. They will develop more quickly and readily in certain kinds of environment. Environments which enable access to knowledge in depth, which encourage deep reflection, which nurture attitudes of honesty and lack of self-interest, which develop skill in interpretation and balance in judgement: environments such as these are likely to nurture sages. And environments which nurture sages are also likely to be environments in which wisdom can be found. Here, I suggest, is a link between wise men and women and streams of wisdom: streams of wisdom nurture wise men and women who articulate the wisdom they have found; wise men and women give voice to the wisdom of the streams which have nurtured them.

The link is reciprocal, but not necessary. Nurture in a particular stream of wisdom does not of itself make someone wise, but it may be a prime indicator of a potential sage. The recognition of wise people nurtured within a particular environment does not of itself indicate that the environment contains wisdom, but it may be a good indicator. Conversely, if the most eminent people nurtured in a particular environment are found wanting in wisdom, it may be that that environment is not a good source of wisdom.

In the light of these considerations, I return to my focus on science and theology as sources of wisdom in Europe. My suggestion is that in the past, public perceptions of science and theology and the systems of nurture provided by science and theology led to public expectation that eminent scientists and theologians were highly likely to be wise men and women, and to their acceptance as sages without further examination. In the present, I suggest, close scrutiny of scientists and theologians has combined with growing public scepticism about the basis, methods and results of study in science and theology to suggest that the environments of science and theology are highly unlikely to produce wise men and women; and in consequence that science and theology are unreliable sources for wisdom.

To explore this further, I turn to perceptions of theology and science in the past, taking them in that order for historical convenience.

Wisdom Past: The Pure Stream of Theology

For the purposes of this discussion, theology can be understood as reflection on the world in the light of belief in God as understood within the theistic family of Judaism, Christianity and Islam. Theologians in these traditions attempt to interpret this world from an extra-worldly perspective. Public perception of this task in the past in Europe was shaped by the dominance of forms of Christianity and acceptance of their claims.

In medieval Europe the main theological stream of wisdom flowed from study of the Bible. Here was a book, or collection of books, regarded as divinely inspired and revelatory. The Bible contained information on how human beings should live in the world created by God, rules to help them live in the required way, and ways of recovering from error. The Bible was thus an unparalleled source of material to feed the reflections of the wise. Moreover, being the record of a divine creator, it was pure, unsullied by human error.

The Bible was difficult to read and understand, so organized Christianity provided interpreters. These people spent their time poring over the Word of God, examining the interpretations offered by others and engaging in vigorous discussion. It was important that these interpreters were people of faith as well as people of learning: through their faithful study, they were able to discern divine truths through the fog of human concerns. Further, as people of faith they were able to invoke the aid of the divine in making their interpretations: prayer was an integral part of the theological task.

Faith and piety combined also to elevate the deeply committed student of theology above the pulls of human interests. Being totally dedicated to the service of their God, theologians had no need to fear anyone, and they were indifferent to the worldly rewards on offer to trusted advisors, being content with simplicity, even austerity, in their daily lives.

Thus the study of theology provided an environment which could readily nurture the characteristics of the wise noted above. Those recognized for their eminence in theology were likely to have the rich understanding which would enable them to interpret events in the world and make judgements which would be in keeping with the judgements of God. Moreover, the advice offered by these theological sages could be tested in practice.

The study of theology required skill in reading and writing, and those trained in these arts were in demand as scribes, record keepers, accountants and professional managers. Great lords ruled, but they relied on clerks – clerics – for their administration, particularly their financial administration. Inevitably, administrators became advisors to perplexed magnates; and their training in theology enabled the best advisors to become sources of practical wisdom for their earthly masters.

However, the wise, as distinct from the merely crafty or cunning, never forgot their heavenly master. Their advice was tempered by considerations of justice and goodness, and they were not afraid to rebuke the powerful or stand up for the weak. They did, of course, have the advantage that the results of following their advice could always be claimed to be the will of God, inscrutable to human eyes and beyond human judgement.

It is a mark of the high esteem in which religious sages were held that people would travel great distances to consult them, even those of high status in society being willing to make arduous journeys to visit a recognized sage. However, we should note that the high position of some theologians as sages was independent of people's daily experience of religious officials. Drunken, lecherous or incompetent priests were the subjects of countless tales and the butt of thousands of jokes. Powerful prelates were seen as men of the world, not necessarily as trusted men of God. Nevertheless, the utterances of personages such as Hildegard of Bingen and John Knox were listened to with respect. Here were people who had looked long and hard into the mysteries of life, and their considered thoughts were nourished in a stream of wisdom untainted by prejudice or self-interest – or so it seemed to their contemporaries. Whatever deficiencies we might see with the benefit of hindsight, there can be little doubt that theology was seen for centuries as a pure stream of wisdom contributing positively to the dynamics of European culture.

Wisdom Past: The Pure Stream of Science

As the Renaissance and the Reformation came and passed into history, the Bible was gradually replaced by the Book of Nature as the principal source of knowledge about the world, and the interpreters of the Book of Nature became the new wise men and women. Later still, the 'human sciences' and 'social sciences' offered further insights into human behaviour, which became part of the material feeding the new sages.

That the sciences, especially the natural sciences, produced knowledge was taken for granted, by the public at large and by many professional scientists. No matter how often it was pointed out that science worked by hypothesis and was always open to change, some of the results of science were guaranteed to endure, and on them men and women built a new world. In the public perception it followed that those who peered furthest into the unknown in search of knowledge, those who had the insight to see what had not been noticed before, would develop a profound understanding of the world in which humans live.

One guarantee of the accuracy of the knowledge gained through the sciences was the method used to acquire knowledge, a method of observation and rigorous testing in an objective fashion. This method was allied to a fearless openness in which scientists published their results for all to see and test. Thus the methodology of science, in public perception, guaranteed not only the integrity of the knowledge but also the objectivity of the knowledge seekers. These seekers, these scientists, were trained in disinterestedness. Governed entirely by 'the facts' scientists were able to stand back from the detail, to avoid the snares of emotional involvement, and seek only the truth.

These popular images coexisted with ideas of mad scientists and those who broke ranks, became charlatans, or used their science for questionable purposes. Such people were seen as flawed scientists, while scientists of the highest calibre were assumed to be pure and untainted. The utterances of such as Charles Darwin, Marie Curie or Albert Einstein were listened to with respect, and their views on matters far beyond their scientific expertise were eagerly sought.

One factor in this was the assumption that scientists would have in view the best interests of humanity at large. Their aim, apparently, was to understand the world in order to harness its resources to improve life for all. The results could be seen in widespread technological advances bringing release from drudgery and untold comfort, in medical advances which extended life expectancy and enabled human beings to enjoy their longer lives more, and in the stretching of human horizons to the frontiers of space.

Thus science was seen as providing knowledge, training its best practitioners in understanding, guaranteeing their integrity, and producing beneficial results from their advice. As eminent scientists peered further and further into the mysteries of the cosmos, they, like the theologians of earlier times, were seen to be tapping a stream of pure wisdom. The study of science joined, and in some eyes replaced, the study of theology as a means of nurturing wise men and women.

Polluted Streams?

One of the hallmarks of the late twentieth century in Europe is the attention paid to personalities. The human sciences have taught us that few, if any, human actions are totally pure in motivation, while the huge growth in means of acquiring and processing information has allowed us to investigate the lives of individuals in unprecedented detail. One result of this focus on personalities is a change in public attitudes to scientists and theologians. In modern Europe religious and scientific leaders and spokespersons are seen first as human beings, subject to all the limitations of human being. Being subject to those limitations, the argument runs, they are no more reliable as sources of wisdom than any other claimants to the title sage. This has a direct bearing on the decline in appreciation of science and theology as sources of wisdom.

Using a very broad-brush approach we can distinguish at least three closely related elements in this erosion of public confidence in scientists and theologians. One is a widespread scepticism about the basis and methods of both science and theology, producing negative public perceptions of the knowledge, understanding and interpretative skill of scientists and theologians. Another element is a deep unease about the judgements made by scientists and theologians, as evidenced by the effects of their studies. A third element is the recognition of the human interests of scientists and theologians, leading to questions about their ability to make balanced judgements.

Scepticism about knowledge, understanding and interpretative skill began for theology with the challenge to interpretation of Christian scriptures. Once the Christian holy books, and those of other religions, became subject to critical study in the same way as other books, the claims of official interpreters were often found wanting. Further, it is clear that there are many questions about living which the holy books cannot answer directly and should not be expected to answer directly, being historically constrained. However, if the writings are historically constrained, to what extent can they reveal timeless truths? Moreover, the information provided by the holy books and their interpreters is often at odds with information from other sources, such as science, and the non-theological interpretations seem to provide a more comprehensive and complete view of the world. In public perception, the claims of theologians to knowledge, understanding and skill in interpretation have become suspect.

For scientists the methodological scepticism began with questioning from philosophy and sociology which exposed the thin justification for the claims to knowledge of so-called empirical science, and the role of human interest in the creation and support of scientific ideas. For a European public largely ignorant of scientific detail, scepticism is fuelled by disputes between leading scientists about fundamental matters: if the scientists cannot agree on the facts, why should anyone listen to their theories?

For both scientists and theologians, the rapid growth of disciplines and sub-disciplines poses a further problem for public perception. Increasingly in both science and theology, expert talks to expert, and only to expert, thus increasing suspicion that they have nothing to say of significance to the wider public.

Forms of methodological scepticism are closely linked to the second element, public unease with the results of science and theology. For science, this arises from public reaction to such things as pollution of the environment, medical 'mishaps' and the horrors of nuclear war, allied to fear of the unknown and the possibility of being 'controlled' in unacceptable and unpleasant ways. The public reaction is often ill-informed, often based on media reports which treat scientific theories as 'fact' and draw global and unwarranted conclusions from carefully qualified reports of research in progress. Nevertheless, the question arises: Can we trust the judgements of people whose work leads us down these roads to disaster, whether or not they accept responsibility for the applications of their research?

For theologians the situation is no better. Many in Europe question religious teachings on issues such as sexuality, the role of women or human 'domination' of nature. Such teachings are often seen as imposing unwarranted constraints on the development, self-expression or fulfilment of particular segments of society, or as buttresses for arrogant exploitation. Can those whose teachings support such malign results offer us wisdom?

Dislike of the effects of science and theology is linked to the third element, questions about personalities. These arise in part from the current media fashion for seeking a 'human angle' in every story, and its more extreme manifestation in the obsession with 'celebrity'. Any story in the media about science now must include something about the scientist, preferably illustrated by a picture if the scientist in question happens to be young and female. Similarly, stories with a religious focus concentrate on the individuals involved rather than the theological claims. Whether they like it or not, science and theology are drawn into the 'personality' game.

Since discord is always more newsworthy than harmony, the focus on personalities is accompanied by a deliberate concentration on their perceived or alleged failings. European thought has always had an iconoclastic streak, which is manifested in our time by a delight in 'dishing the dirt' on celebrities. The doings of the rich and famous, the cultural icons of our time, are recorded at length in the media; their misdeeds are recorded in even more detail. It should not be surprising that the same treatment is given to religious and scientific icons.

For a religious example, we can turn to Mother Teresa of Calcutta. Mother Teresa is widely revered in religious circles and beyond as a 'saint', and there are formal moves within the Roman Catholic Church to give her the status of Saint. But in the later years of her life, she was dogged by critical accounts of her contacts with dictators and figures who were not notably religious. Doubt was cast, often by innuendo, on her judgement and integrity, and this led to some very critical analyses of her life and work.[1] Could such a flawed person offer us wisdom?

Similarly, a man widely acknowledged as a scientific genius, Albert Einstein, has been the subject of 'revisionist' biography, in which as much attention is paid to his marital problems, his affairs and his alleged illegitimate children as to his scientific work.[2] The suggestion seems to be that this 'human face' of the scientist makes him less of a genius, less wise.

This iconoclasm extends beyond individuals with high profiles to others who are seen as representative figures. Gay clergy in the Church of England are attacked as 'hypocrites' because they do not challenge their Church's stance on homosexuality. Roman Catholic priests and nuns are accused of serious child abuse. Rabbis are pilloried for suggesting the creation of special areas where Orthodox Jews may observe the Sabbath in their own way. Imams are 'exposed' as 'inciters' of terrorism. In every case, a few individuals are held up as representative of the whole, and their alleged failings are implied to be failings of all. The result is the erosion of confidence in the integrity of those who hold official positions in religious institutions. The same effect is seen at an institutional level with attacks on the role of the Vatican in relation to Jews during the Second World War and the role of the Russian Orthodox Church during the rule of Stalin and his successors.

In relation to science, 'animal rights' groups 'expose' (and threaten) scientists who experiment on animals; others vilify those who carry out research on genetically modified crops. There is widespread distrust of results published by professional scientists employed by commercial organizations. The claims of a scientist to have cloned a human being are used to raise the spectre of 'scientists playing God'. Some scientists are found developing new drugs to enhance athletic performance, and the whole scientific community is accused of 'aiding the cheats', or of administering untested drugs without due regard for the possible long-term effects on the users. Again, the contested activities of a few individuals are used to pillory the whole body of scientists, thereby undermining confidence in science as a source of wisdom.

For my purposes it does not matter whether or not the attacks made on science and theology, scientists and theologians, are justified. My point is simply that these kinds of attack have created a climate of widespread

[1] See for example Hitchens 1995.
[2] Highfield and Carter 1993.

scepticism about scientists and theologians as trustworthy sources of wisdom in modern Europe. If the purveyors of wisdom are tainted, if their methods are suspect and the outcome of their endeavours malign, why should they be treated as wise? It is of no avail for scientists and theologians to point out the confusion between the practice of individuals and the wisdom of the whole. Nor does it help to protest that public scepticism is based on very superficial retailing of unexamined 'evidence', or that stories in the media are often slanted with the intention of questioning, even damaging, science or theology. Many, perhaps most, people in Europe now simply accept, rightly or wrongly, that the streams of wisdom offered by theology and science are irredeemably polluted, and that no sensible person should drink deeply from them.

Wisdom Future

'Where shall wisdom be found?' – Among the candidates in twenty-first-century Europe are: New Age 'religious movements'; self-proclaimed 'gurus' of 'personal fulfilment' with their collections of writings combining esoteric ideas from all over the world in floods of purple prose; stars of cinema and music and sport who are as famous as their last performance or as infamous as their last bout of misbehaviour; and old favourites such as astrology and tarot readings. Science and theology appear at the margins, for those of older generations, if they appear at all.

It might be argued that the change in status of both science and theology is just one part of a general change within European culture, a change in which authority of all kinds is questioned. The questioning of authority leads to scepticism about knowledge claims, to scepticism about the motives of those claiming authority, and to scepticism about the proclaimed effects of the advice offered.

However, the questioning of established authorities has not diminished the search for wisdom. People still seek sound advice in difficult circumstances. It is where they go for that advice which has changed. There are many stalls in the wisdom market-place, and some of those long established are ignored. My suggestion is that science and theology are among those that are now ignored, not because of the rejection of their authority, nor because of a lack of interest in science or theology (science fiction, pseudo-science and New Age religion all attract significant interest), but because their eminent representatives are seen as offering bad advice, not wisdom.

In spite of this, I do not suggest that there is any danger of science and theology disappearing from the sources of wisdom for Europe. Not only are they too deeply embedded in current culture to vanish quickly, they continue to search for and proclaim wisdom. Theologians and scientists continue to provide insights into how human beings should live. Scientists wrestle with new discoveries about the world in which we live and try to make sense of the implications of those discoveries for present-day humanity and its successors. Theologians struggle to bring the vast accumulation of human knowledge into dynamic interaction with fundamental theological claims to yield fresh insight into living in the light of eternity.

In modern Europe the insights offered will be valued as wisdom because they are seen to have positive effects and felt to be 'right', not because they are offered by scientists or theologians. The test is: Is this practical, beneficial, sound advice? This means that those speaking for science or theology must be more modest in their claims, more willing to have their claims contested, and more willing to defend their claims in public. Theological apologetic is more important then ever, and scientific apologetic, the defence of scientific claims, will become increasingly important.

In my view, this is good for both science and theology. Removed from the expectations heaped on cultural icons, the exponents of science and theology have time and space in which to analyse more carefully what they offer as wisdom. Removed from the glare of publicity, scientists and theologians can afford to spend time in dialogue with those who do not share their pre-suppositions. Drawing on other streams, more critical of their own streams, they can offer a deeper, more nuanced wisdom.

There is one important caveat to be noted. This discussion has a strictly European context and focus. In other parts of the world, the situation may be different. Certainly in some places religion is still highly regarded as a source of wisdom, and in some places science has yet to have its feet of clay exposed. Since we live in a 'global village' with considerable interchange between cultures, it is very likely that my description of Europe will need modification in the light of continued interchange with non-European cultures. This can only add to the rich pool of wisdom on which Europeans draw.

This contribution has touched on many issues, all of which deserve exploration in greater depth. One thing highlighted by this discussion is the difficulty of saying exactly what counts as wisdom and how it is recognized. Another area for fruitful study is the link between wisdom and spirituality, broadly conceived: according to my argument, sages steeped in science and theology were helped by their nurture to become persons recognized as wise. Yet there were many others seen as sages, who were outside the training systems of science or the Church: what gave them their profound insights? My suggestion is that some form of personal spirituality plays a large part in their sagacity, and this is reflected in the nurturing of scientists and theologians. There are fascinating cultural issues here, whose study must be postponed.

'Where shall wisdom be found?' – In Europe in the early years of the twenty-first century, wisdom is to be found in the pooling of many streams, of which theology and science are but two, and not the most influential. Scientists and theologians who become acknowledged as sages will be those who draw on many streams, and commend themselves in part for their blending of those many streams. Nevertheless, there will be scientists and theologians who are recognized as wise men and women: for there will be those in the present and future, as in the past, nurtured in science and theology, who have the capacity to understand what it is to be human now.

References

Highfield, R. and P. Carter,
   1993   *The Private Lives of Albert Einstein* (London: Faber & Faber).
Hitchens, C.
   1995   *The Missionary Position: Mother Teresa in Theory and Practice* (London: Verso).

Disjoining Wisdom and Knowledge

Science, Theology and the Making of Western Modernity

Peter Harrison

Few would argue today that the possession of scientific knowledge is, in itself, a mark of wisdom. This is partly because 'wisdom' has become an unfashionable category, but partly also because inasmuch as it has retained currency in the twenty-first century, wisdom has come to denote a holistic, non-technical, mode of knowing – a human quality that combines knowledge of the world with practical experience and, crucially, a set of moral commitments. In certain respects, then, it has become the antipathy of scientific knowledge. This is borne out by the fact that the narrow technical expertise of the West is often contrasted with the 'wisdom' of traditional societies. By implication, if the former has delivered impressive material and technological benefits to its possessors, this has been accompanied by a certain loss of moral perspective that characterizes the latter.

Of course, it was not always so. Some periods of Western history witnessed an intimate connection between science and wisdom. My concern in this paper is to provide a brief history of wisdom in the West, particularly in relation to science and theology, with a view to tracing the gradual dissociation of wisdom from both theology and the natural sciences. This is admittedly a rather ambitious undertaking, and in order to make the task more manageable I propose to focus on four distinct phases of this relationship in the West and deal with them in chronological order: (1) Early Christian and patristic views that oppose heavenly and earthly wisdom, and which identify classical science with the earthly wisdom. (2) Thomas Aquinas's thirteenth-century adaptation of Aristotle's classification of the sciences, according to which both theology and the study of nature (natural philosophy) count as sciences and as virtues. In a sense, both are forms of wisdom, with the earthly wisdom of the sciences not being opposed to the heavenly wisdom of theology, but rather providing a path to it. (3) The early modern rejection of the Thomist notion that science (*scientia*) was a virtue, and the tendency to regard both theology and natural science as activities related to propositions. (4) The final stage of the dissociation of wisdom and science that came with the professionalization of science in the nineteenth century, when both moral and theological issues are explicitly excluded from the scope of the natural sciences. I shall follow this with some concluding remarks about what all of this might mean for our current understandings of the relationships between science, religion and wisdom.

1. Earthly or Heavenly Wisdom?

In the famous trial held in the year 399 BC, Socrates announced to his fellow Athenians that 'real wisdom is the property of God' and that 'human wisdom has little or no value'. He went on to announce to his audience that 'the wisest of you is he who has recognized ... that in respect of wisdom he is really worthless' (Plato, *Apology* 22c–23b).[1] Informing a jury of one's peers that they are worthless has little to recommend itself as a defence strategy. Not surprisingly, perhaps, Socrates was found guilty and sentenced to death, becoming the first martyr to the cause of philosophy. The relevance of the achievements of Socrates for the Western tradition of wisdom is fourfold. First, Socrates taught that the aim of the fulfilled philosophical life is the attainment of wisdom. Second, he diverted the course of Greek philosophy away from the study of the natural world and refocused attention on human affairs and moral values (Plato, *Phaedo* 96a–100a). Wisdom was to be found, he insisted, not in the study of nature, but in the moral sphere. Third, Socrates taught that wisdom was not something that could be possessed, but rather it was to be sought after and loved. 'Philosophy', then, in the Socratic scheme of things was, as its etymology implies, 'love of wisdom', and the true philosopher one whose life was devoted to its pursuit (Plato, *Republic* 376b). Fourth, as we have already seen, true wisdom was located beyond the mundane sphere of ordinary human knowledge, in the realm of the spiritual and divine. It was to be sought after in the present life, but could not be fully attained until the life to come. Subsequently Plato (427–347 BC) was to formalize this programme, dividing reality into the spiritual and material worlds, and firmly insisting that seekers after wisdom ignore the distractions of the material world, and focus their efforts on transcendental and eternal realities.

The views of Socrates and Plato on the nature of true wisdom have echoed down through Western thought ever since, receiving a particular impetus from Judaeo-Christian thought. In an influential passage in his letter to the Corinthians, St Paul thus disparaged the 'wisdom of the world', in light of

---

[1] Genuine wisdom was to be achieved only in the next life: 'the wisdom which we desire and upon which we profess to have set our hearts will be attainable only when we are dead, and not in our lifetime' (*Phaedo* 66e).

which the Christian gospel seemed like mere folly (1 Cor. 1.18–25).[2] In certain respects this resembles the position of Socrates and Plato, contrasting heavenly and earthly wisdom. The great fifth-century Father of the Latin West, Augustine (354–430), subsequently made an informal distinction between wisdom (*sapientia*) which pertained to theological truths, and knowledge (*scientia*) which pertained to 'scientific' truths. Wisdom ranked before knowledge.[3]

But the Greeks were by no means the sole influence on these patristic understandings. Early Christian writers had at their disposal not only the pronouncements of Greek philosophers, but the Wisdom literature of the Hebrew Bible, in which the vanity of merely human knowledge is a recurring theme.[4] Moreover, while the thought of Plato seemed to many of the Church Fathers a helpful, if flawed and fragmentary, adjunct to Christian theology, the question had to be posed whether Greek philosophy might not itself be regarded as the 'wisdom of the world' – a wisdom that was not so much to be subsumed into Christian thought, but rather be repudiated as dangerous and potentially heretical. While the Alexandrian Fathers tended to answer this question in the negative, many in the Latin West took a different view. The North African apologist Tertullian declared that 'philosophy is the material of the world's wisdom, [of] the rash interpreter of nature'. Famously, he went on to ask: 'What indeed has Athens to do with Jerusalem? What has the Academy to do with the Church? ... Our instruction comes from the porch of Solomon' (*De praescriptione haereticorum* 7).

A significant dimension of the patristic attitude towards Greek science was the moral disapprobation associated with the investigation of nature. Scientific proclivities were not innocent pastimes. Rather more insidiously, they were expressions of the intellectual vice of curiosity (Harrison 2001). Virtually all of the Fathers counselled against curiosity in investigating the things of nature, many explicitly linking it to the Pauline notion of worldly wisdom.[5] Augustine wrote at length on the nature of curiosity, describing it as 'a lust for

---

[2] Cf: 'Beware lest anyone cheat you through philosophy and empty deceit, according to the tradition of men' (Col. 2.8); 'Avoid the profane and vain babblings and contradictions of what is falsely called knowledge' (1 Tim. 6.20; see also 1 Cor. 2.1f.; 8.1; 2 Tim. 3.13–16).

[3] 'If then this is the correct distinction between wisdom and knowledge, that wisdom is concerned with the intellectual cognizance of eternal things and knowledge with the rational cognizance of temporal things, it is not hard to decide which should be preferred and which subordinated to the other' (Augustine, *The Trinity* XII.25 (1996: 336)). But cf.: 'Nor of course should we take these two as if we could never call this one that is concerned with human affairs wisdom, or that one that is concerned with divine things knowledge. In a broader manner of speaking each can be called wisdom and each knowledge' (XIII.24 (1996: 364)). Augustine links this distinction to that between the active and contemplative lives – active knowledge, but contemplative wisdom (VIII.6). On the significance of this Augustinian position see Serene 1988: 498–504.

[4] 'I set my heart to know wisdom ... and perceived that this also is grasping at the wind' (Eccl. 1.17; see also 12.12 and *passim*; Esdras 4.23; 13.52; Ecclesiasticus 3.21–3).

[5] See e.g. Origen, *Against Celsus* VII.iv; Tertullian, *De anima* ii; Basil, *Hexaemeron* I.8–11; Peter Chrysologus, *Collectio Sermonum* 11; John Cassian, *Colationes* XIV.xvi; Basil, *Hexaemeron* I.9. Cf. Job 38.6; Jerome, *Commentarius in Epistolam ad Ephesios* 4.17.

experimenting and knowing', 'a diseased craving', a 'vain inquisitiveness dig-
nified with the title of knowledge and science' (Augustine, *Confessions* X.xxxv).[6]
Curiosity almost inevitably gave rise to the first of the deadly sins – *superbia*,
pride.[7] Here the proof-text came from St Paul: *'scientia inflat caritas vero aedificat'*
– knowledge puffeth up, but charity edifieth (1 Cor. 8.1). Subsequently, Paul
was to elevate the virtue of charity above all else, including knowledge: 'If I
understand all mysteries and all knowledge . . . but have not love, I am nothing'
(1 Cor. 13.2). To the contrast between worldly and heavenly wisdom, then, can
be added a related distinction – that between knowledge and virtue.

In sum, three aspects of the treatment of wisdom in the Greeks and the
Fathers are noteworthy. First, the distinction between earthly wisdom and
heavenly wisdom. Second, the tendency of the Latin Fathers to identify earthly
wisdom with 'scientific' knowledge. Third, the attribution of negative moral
qualities to those involved in the pursuit of natural knowledge – the virtue of
charity is opposed to knowledge that 'puffs up' with pride. Knowledge was
contrasted with virtue.

2. *Scientia*, Wisdom and the Virtues

From the twelfth century onwards, with the gradual introduction of Aristotelian texts into the West, a more positive attitude towards natural knowledge developed in the universities, not least owing to the efforts of Thomas
Aquinas. If the contrast between 'worldly' and 'heavenly' wisdom was a common motif in earlier efforts to relate science and Christian faith, Aquinas
accorded wisdom a central place in his effort to bring about a rapprochement
between pagan and Christian learning. Accordingly, his major apologetic work
– *Summa Contra Gentiles* – commences with a discussion of the 'office of the wise
man' (I.i). Here Aquinas sets out the Socratic ideal of the pursuit of wisdom as
the highest goal of human life and attempts to show that the truths of Christian
theology represent the unfulfilled goal of pagan philosophy.[8] Aquinas sought to
show, moreover, that Christian theology not only provides the answers to
questions of the philosophers, but also fulfils the criteria of the highest science
according to the standards of the classical tradition itself (Aquinas 1961: I, bk.
1, lsn. 3, sct. 56).[9]

In order to understand this we need to recall Aristotle's division of the

---

[6] For Augustine's treatment of curiosity, see Blumenberg 1961, 1962; Daston 1995. For the
association with original sin see *Confessions* X.xxxv.

[7] For the link with pride, see *De moribus Ecclesiae Catholicae et de moribus Manichaeorum* 21; *De
agone Christiano* 4.4; *De Trinitate* XII.9; *City of God* XIV.28; *In Supra Genesi contra Manichaeos*
II.18.27.

[8] This echoes, in some respects, the Pauline sentiment that the 'unknown God' whom the
Athenians worshipped was in fact the God of the Christian proclamation (Acts 17.23).

[9] On this point and for a helpful comparison of the positions of Aquinas and Ockham, see Alfred
Freddoso (1999).

sciences into speculative, practical and productive. The speculative sciences included *mathematics*, which dealt with unchanging, immaterial objects that were dependent on the human mind; *natural philosophy* that was concerned with changeable material objects that were independent of the human mind, and the '*divine science*' or metaphysics, which dealt with unchangeable, immaterial objects that were independent of the human mind (Aristotle, *Metaphysics* 1025b–1026a; *Topics* 157a6–13; cf. Plato, *Republic* 509–11).[10] In spelling out his understanding of wisdom, Aristotle argued that wisdom pertained to all the sciences, but pre-eminently to 'the divine science' or metaphysics (*Metaphysics* 982a–b, 996b).[11] Aquinas was to follow Aristotle's divisions of the speculative sciences, identifying Aristotle's 'divine science' with Christian theology (1986: q. 5, a. 1, obj. 1).[12] This subtle equivocation was justified on the basis of the assumption that Christian theology was in fact what Aristotle had been unknowingly questing after. This identification of Christian theology as the highest wisdom also explains Aquinas's well-known assertion that philosophy serves as a handmaiden to theology.[13] Having said this, Aquinas did not wholly abandon the earlier oppositional schema of earthly and heavenly wisdom, but instead viewed earthly wisdom in a far more positive light: 'For wisdom is twofold: mundane wisdom called philosophy, which considers the lower causes, causes namely that are themselves caused, and bases its judgements on them: and divine wisdom or theology, which considers the higher, that is the divine, causes and judges according to them' (1932: bk. 1, q. 1, a. 4, Body).

Critics of Aquinas were not slow to point out the apparent discrepancy between the sanguine synthesis of Thomas and the earlier, more oppositional, views of Augustine. There was also disagreement about whether theology was a speculative science devoted to knowledge, as Aristotle and Aquinas held, or a practical one focused on action. A number of Franciscan theologians, including John Duns Scotus, were to argue that since the goal of theology was to grow to

---

[10] Aristotle's division of the sciences was widely adopted in the Middle Ages. See e.g. Boethius, *De Trinitate* 2; Aquinas 1986: q. 5, a.1.

[11] But Aristotle notes that 'To judge from our previous discussion of the question which of the sciences should be called wisdom, there is reason for applying the name to each of them' (*Metaphysics* 996b1–25 (1984: II.1574)). The divine science, however, is fundamental to each of the other sciences, and hence wisdom is associated primarily with it.

[12] The specific content of 'metaphysics' is not entirely clear even in Aristotle. It becomes even more complex when the issue of its relation to sacred theology is introduced. See e.g. Lohr 1988.

[13] 'Hence (the teaching of faith) should be called the greatest wisdom, since it considers the highest cause, according to the saying of Deut. iv. 6: For this is your wisdom and understanding in the sight of nations. Wherefore human philosophy is a handmaid to her as mistress. For this reason sometimes divine wisdom argues from the principles of human philosophy: since also among philosophers the First Philosophy makes use of the teachings of all sciences in order to establish its purpose. Hence again both teachings do not follow the same order. For in the teaching of philosophy which considers creatures in themselves and leads us from them to the knowledge of God....' (*SCG* II.4; cf. *ST* Ia, q. 1, a. 5; Aquinas 1961: II, bk. 11, lsn. 4, sct. 933).

love God, it was not a speculative, but a *practical* science (Duns Scotus 1950–: 1, 207f., 217; Cross 1999: 8f.; Inciarte 1996; Harris 1927: I. 90–100).[14] William of Ockham (*c.*1288–1347) went still further, denying that theology was a science at all, at least in the Aristotelian sense. Adoption of these viewpoints would give rise to quite a different relationship between what we would now call 'theology' and 'science'. For Aquinas, the conversation between theology and the other sciences is premised on the fact that both are concerned with the intellect, and hierarchically ordered to the same end – knowledge. On the understanding of the Franciscans, however, theology would not be at the pinnacle of the speculative sciences.

It is worth taking time out at this juncture to see how these various options might have some relevance to our contemporary understandings of the relationship between science and religion. Ian Barbour's well-known typology classifying the relations between science and religion suggests that the relationships between science and religion can be placed in one of four distinct categories: Conflict, Independence, Dialogue, Integration (1990: 3–92). If, for the purposes of the exercise, we accept this typology, the Pauline/Augustinian view is essentially one of Conflict. Aquinas's position comes close to integration in certain respects, but is better characterized as 'subordination' – a category not represented in Barbour's typology. Ockham's position is more complex. He asserts the independence of Christian theology from the Aristotelian understanding of science, yet allows for the possibility of conflict between classical science and Christian theology. I will say more about possible implications of these positions in my concluding remarks.

In all this it is important to understand that in asserting the speculative nature of theology, and indeed of mathematics and natural philosophy, Thomas did not seek to over-intellectualize these activities and isolate them from moral, affective and volitional aspects of the human being. A basic premise of Thomas's epistemology is that to know something is to become like it. Hence, in coming to know God, in contemplating the divine nature, we become like God: 'when any created intellect sees the essence of God, the essence of God itself becomes the intelligible form of the intellect'. As a consequence, 'the rational creature is made deiform' (*ST* Ia, q. 12, a. 5). To be sure, this ultimate transformation is not possible in the present life. Nonetheless through the infusion of the theological virtues the justified individual begins to progress towards the likeness of God. The just thus possess, to use Thomas's own expression, 'a certain rectitude' (*ST* Ia IIae, q. 60, a. 5; Ia. IIae, q. 57, a. 2; cf. Aristotle, *Nicomachean Ethics* 1143b).

At one level, then, it can be said that for Aquinas knowledge of God is

---

[14] Other theologians such as Bonaventure were to suggest that theology was both speculative and practical: 'Theological science is an affective habit and the mean between the speculative and practical, and for (its) end it has both contemplation, and that we become good, and indeed more principally, that we become good' (Bonaventure 1882–1902: I. 13; see also the discussion in Aquinas, *ST* IIa IIae, q. 8, a. 6).

associated with a transformation that confers on the human being a set of *virtues*, understood as dispositions or habits. It was this understanding of the process of justification – according to which the Christian comes to possess certain virtuous habits – that was later to become a central issue in the Protestant Reformers' criticisms of the scholastic view of justification. Before we consider the momentous consequences of this Protestant critique, we must consider the status of the other virtues and their relation to knowledge. For Aquinas, the theological virtues were accompanied by moral virtues (prudence, justice, temperance, fortitude) and intellectual virtues (wisdom, science and understanding) (*ST* Ia IIae, q. 60, a. 5; Ia IIae, q. 57, a. 2; cf. Aristotle, *Nicomachean Ethics* 1143b). Understanding is the habit concerned with the grasp of self-evident principles; science is concerned with truths derived from those principles; wisdom with the highest causes, including the first cause – God (*ST* Ia IIae, q. 57, a. 2; Aquinas 1964: VI.iii.4–6; Aristotle, *Nicomachean Ethics* VI.3, 6–7; *Metaphysics* I.1). If we consider the intellectual virtues, it can be seen that both science and wisdom refer not merely to sets of propositions, but to particular mental habits (*ST* Ia, q. 89, a. 5; Ia IIae, q. 50, a. 4; q. 52, a. 2; q. 53, a. 1; *SCG* I.61; II.60; II.78; Aquinas 1951: a. 7, obj. 1). Strictly speaking, then, *scientia* is not merely, or even primarily, an organized body of knowledge, but rather an acquired habit of mind. Together, the intellectual habits perfect the intellect, in much the same way that the moral habits perfect the will (*ST* Ia, q. 82, a. 3; Ia IIae, q. 57, a. 1; Aquinas 1952: III, q. 22, a. 11). It need hardly be pointed out that this conception of *scientia* as a virtue is somewhat different from our modern notion of 'science'.

While it must be acknowledged that science, and hence the science of theology, is one of the *intellectual* virtues, these nonetheless have something in common with other virtues inasmuch as they are habits. Moreover, for Aquinas, wisdom plays an important role in linking all of the virtues – theological, practical and speculative. Practical wisdom (*phronesis*, *prudentia*) links the intellectual with the moral virtues, inasmuch as it informs action. In addition, wisdom is one of the 'spiritual gifts'. With this understanding of wisdom, Aquinas is able to approach the classical ideal of the ultimate unity of the virtues (*ST* Ia IIae, q. 57, aa. 4–6; Ia IIae, qq. 47–9, 51; cf. Aristotle, *Nicomachean Ethics* 1144b–1145a; Aquinas 1964: VI.x).[15]

Before moving on to consider the demise of this notion of *scientia* as a kind of virtue, it is worth pointing out that for Aquinas, 'religion' (*religio*) is also a virtue.[16] Interestingly, unlike *scientia*, the virtue of *religio* has no corresponding propositional component, no doubt because it is classified as a moral virtue,

---

[15] On the unity of the virtues see Annas 1993: 73–84. For an account of the development of conceptions of practical wisdom to the time of Duns Scotus, see Ingham 1996.

[16] '. . . a virtue is that which makes its possessor good, and his act good likewise, . . . Since then it belongs to religion (*religio*) to pay due honour to someone, namely, to God, it is evident that religion is a virtue' (Aquinas, *ST* IIa IIae, q. 81, a. 2).

and indeed as the pre-eminent moral virtue.[17] Over the course of the sixteenth and seventeenth centuries, *scientia* will cease to be a virtue in any significant sense, and so will *religio*. Both are reconceptualized as sets of beliefs and practices, with momentous consequences for how the relationships between science, theology and religion were subsequently conceptualized. One of the chief motive forces behind the early modern revision of conceptions of science and religion was, of course, the Protestant Reformation.

3. From Virtues to Method

Numerous attempts have been made to draw connections between the Protestant Reformation and the rise of modern science (see e.g. Harrison 1998: 5–8; Harrison 2003). Time forbids an enumeration of the various arguments relating to this issue. In the present context I want to suggest that two aspects of Reformation thought, and of Calvinism in particular, were of major significance in demolishing the prevailing Aristotelian conception of science and, along with it, a widespread understanding of the relationship between natural philosophy and theology.

First it must be said that both Luther and Calvin were far more conservative in their assessment of the capabilities of the human intellect than were their scholastic predecessors. Following the Fall of Adam, the Reformers argued, the mind was wounded both in its moral and intellectual capacities. It followed that reason – or 'the light of nature' as it was known – was a most unreliable guide. Its unreliability was not restricted to theological matters moreover, but extended to the other sciences as well. Luther thus contended that because of the Fall, 'the will is impaired, the intellect depraved, and the reason entirely corrupt and altogether changed' (Luther 1955–75: I.166). This position was explicitly contrasted with the prevailing scholastic view. The 'sophists in the Papacy', Calvin complained, 'feign that some part of the reason remains sound and entire' whereas in fact 'the whole soul is vitiated, from reason even to the affections' (Calvin 2003: XI.375).

As a consequence of this emphasis on the corruption of natural reason the major Reformers tended to deny that the Christian revelation was in any sense a completion or fulfilment of the philosophical quest of the classical philosophers (Harrison 2002). Based as they were on a corrupted human reason, such quests were almost entirely misdirected. It followed that neither the Aristotelian understanding of *scientia*, nor his classification of the sciences, could simply be accepted at face value. In short, the whole relationship between theology and philosophy (including natural philosophy) needed to be reassessed. To a degree, the position of the Reformers represents a return to the Pauline opposition

---

[17] 'And religion approaches nearer to God than the other moral virtues, in so far as its actions are directly and immediately ordered to the honour of God. Hence religion excels among the moral virtues' (*ST* IIa IIae, q. 81, a. 6).

between worldly wisdom and the true wisdom in which 'Aristotle' comes to personify the folly of earthly wisdom.

If the Reformers called into question the Thomist classification of knowledge and its implicit relationship between science, theology and wisdom, they were also sharply critical of the Aristotelian–Thomist understanding of the virtues. Aristotle's teaching on the virtues had come to underscore what in their view was the erroneous scholastic doctrine of merit, according to which one might actually attain genuine credit in God's eyes through the performance of good works. It was, after all, a basic premise of the *Nicomachean Ethics* that through the continued practice of virtue one acquires the virtues, and that the virtues make one good. As Luther himself expressed it: 'Aristotle taught that he who does much good will thereby become good' (Luther 1983: VI.187).[18] This, indeed, was the very notion of *habitus*. Elsewhere, Luther was to attribute such a view to Thomas as well:

> Here Thomas errs in common with his followers and with Aristotle who say, 'Practice makes perfect': just as a harp player becomes a good harp player through long practice, so these fools think that the virtues of love, chastity, and humility can be achieved through practice. It is not true. (Luther 1883–1948, in Althaus 1966: 156, n. 71)[19]

The use of Aristotle's conception of virtue in the context of the Christian notion of justification was singled out by Luther as a fundamental mistake. Such a view, in his estimation, ran counter to the Pauline position that human beings are not righteous in God's sight. Justification is not an internal change in the person, but rather a change of their situation.[20] This, the doctrine of justification by grace through faith, was opposed to the Catholic position, characterized by its opponents as a doctrine of justification through the performance of good works. In this erroneous doctrine Luther saw the palpable influence of Aristotle's ethical theory: 'Righteousness is not in us in a formal sense, as Aristotle maintains, but is outside us, solely in God's grace' (Luther 1955–75: XXVI.234).

As a consequence of these theologically motivated attacks, the relatively innocuous Aristotelian doctrine of virtues as habits, along with the conception of the unity of the virtues, suffered considerable collateral damage. The whole

---

[18] Cf. Aquinas: 'A human virtue is one "which renders a human act and man himself good" [*Ethic. ii, 6]' (*ST* IIa IIae, q. 58, a. 3; cf. *ST* Ia IIae, q. 55, aa. 3 & 4; *ST* IIa IIae, q. 81, a. 2).

[19] For Aquinas's explicit appropriation of the Aristotelian idea of habit, see Aquinas 1964: bk. 1, lec. 20, sct. 244). A similar Aristotelian view of merit was also promoted by some humanist scholars. Thus, Francesco Piccolomini: 'Since this is Aristotle's position, he is to some extent in agreement with our theologians.... Merits, as they pertain to us, proceed from our virtuous actions, for faith alone is not sufficient....' (Kraye 1997: I.74).

[20] For Luther on the Aristotelian notion of *habitus* see Ebeling 1970: 150–8. *Simul iustus et peccator* (simultaneously justified and a sinner) was Luther's famous maxim. Luther and Calvin both considered this to be the teaching of St Paul; see especially Luther's *Lectures on Galatians* (Luther 1955–75: XXVI.232 and *passim*).

notion of virtues as habits began to unravel, and along with it the idea that practical wisdom could provide a link between speculative, moral and theological virtues. *Scientia*, then, was no longer regarded as a mental capacity related to the moral and theological virtues, becoming instead an objectified and externalized body of doctrines or methodological strategies.[21] In this reconceived notion of *scientia* – most familiar to modern minds – the virtue of wisdom no longer played any significant role.

Protestant theologians were by no means the only critics of Aristotle. Advocates of the new sciences also attacked on a number of fronts, challenging the traditional classifications of knowledge, the aims of science, the methods of acquiring knowledge and, crucially, the prevailing conception of what it was to be a natural philosopher ('scientist'). The English philosopher Francis Bacon (1561–1626) provides an instructive example. On the issue of scientific knowledge, Bacon was to insist that previous thinkers had misunderstood the nature of both 'science' (natural philosophy) and the 'scientist' (philosopher). Most damaging of all, in his view, natural philosophy had been regarded primarily as a matter of contemplation and speculation, and had been severed from action and production. Science was not a matter of contemplation, Bacon insisted, but was an activity that should unite knowledge and charitable action, to the end of relieving the present sufferings of the human race, redressing the curse that Adam's sin had brought upon all of his descendants.[22]

Bacon's science does not call for the perfection of the human faculties, moral or intellectual. It is instead a more modest enterprise, premised on insight into human weaknesses and limitations. Hence, Bacon can be said to adopt the pessimistic anthropology of the Protestant Reformers. Indeed, I have argued elsewhere that the epistemology of experimental philosophy arises out of Protestant anthropology (Harrison 2002). It follows that the goals of natural philosophy cannot be achieved by the single mind in the act of contemplation. *Scientia* cannot be a virtue that achieves the perfection of the intellectual faculties. For Bacon, the accumulation of scientific knowledge did not call for genius or even a superior intellect. 'The course I propose for the discovery of science', he insisted, 'is such as leaves little to the acuteness and strength of wits, but places all wits and understandings nearly on a level' (Bacon 1857–74: IV.62). Here then, is the emergence of what the historian I. Bernard Cohen has

---

[21] Thus Charles Lohr: 'Writers of the Reformed Confession broke with this [Aristotelian] conception. In their approach science was understood not as a habit but as a body of knowledge' (1988: 632). This tendency, then, was more pronounced among Calvinists. The Lutheran Philip Melanchthon, by way of contrast, attempted to re-establish something like the Aristotelian conception with his insistence on the importance of 'method' and his understanding of method as habit (see Kusukawa 1997: 336–8). This development can partly be explained by the fact that while Luther's target was Aristotle, Melanchthon's was the 'unmethodical' theology of the Anabaptists.

[22] 'as if there were to be sought in knowledge a couch, whereupon to rest a searching and restless spirit; or terrace, for a wandering and variable mind to walk up and down with a fair prospect ... and not a rich store house, for the glory of the Creator and the relief of man's estate' (Bacon 1857–74: III.294).

referred to as the 'democratization of science', according to which, in principle, any individual can make a contribution to the accumulation of empirical knowledge (Cohen 1985: 146f.). This approach to science, it has been suggested, 'is the epistemological mirror of men's equality before God' (Pérez-Ramos 1996: 315). As such it might plausibly be linked to the Protestant Reformers' critique of the hierarchical medieval 'estates' that sharply distinguished clergy and laity (Luther 1970: 12; Calvin 1960: I.502; II.1473). At any rate, as a consequence of this democratization of natural philosophy the benefits of science were no longer seen to lie in the augmentation of the mental abilities of the individual: the aim of Baconian science was not to make an elite individual wiser, but to relieve the sufferings of the human race. To put it another way, for Bacon, Christian charity is not the virtue that works moral perfection in the individual, but rather a practical activity that confers benefits on the whole of society (Bacon 1857–74: IV.20).

It follows that natural philosophy is based upon the painstaking accumulation of knowledge that takes place over protracted periods of time. It is the work not of one, but of many minds working determinedly and concertedly. For this reason, it requires not so much the possession of intellectual virtues, but a shared commitment to a common method. It is a publicly available set of procedures that makes the accumulation of scientific knowledge possible – not the cultivation of the intellectual virtue of *scientia*. Science thus becomes not only a corporate activity (as opposed to an individual act of contemplation), but an objectively identifiable method that in principle can be appropriated by anyone, irrespective of what personal virtues they may possess.[23] Wisdom, in short, is no longer a prerequisite for the pursuit of science, and neither does scientific activity confer wisdom upon its practitioners.

If the influence of Bacon's inductive philosophy on the subsequent conduct of science has proven controversial, it is undeniable that his conception of the natural philosopher and of the social role of science has been enormously important (Pérez-Ramos 1996). Significant features of his programme were adopted by the Royal Society of London and were thus incorporated into the practices of English science.[24] It is true, of course, that throughout the seventeenth century vestiges of the older conceptions of *scientia* persisted.

---

[23] John Leary has thus written that Bacon's instauration called for 'men of science to submit to the regimen embodied in Bacon's methodological and organizational prescriptions' (1994: 218). Stephen Gaukroger has likewise suggested that Bacon's account of method can be seen 'either as elaborating stringent procedures that individual scientists should follow, or as setting out the rules governing a new elite community subject to stringent measures designed to organise the investigation of nature at a social level' (1998: 5f.).

[24] Thomas Sprat's apologetic *History of the Royal Society* (1667) thus accords Bacon a central place in the development of the science of the moderns. Fellows of the Society strived to remain true to the 'democratic' ideals espoused by Bacon: '*Philosophy* ought not only to be attended by a select company of *refin'd spirits*. As they desire that its productions should be *vulgar*, so they also declared that they may be promoted by *vulgar hands*. They exact no extraordinary preparation of *Learning*: to have sound *Senses* and *Truth* is with them a sufficient qualification. Here is enough businesses for *Minds* of all sizes' (Sprat 1667: 435).

Galileo, for instance, still subscribed to significant elements of the Aristotelian programme, and in a discussion of the nature of divine wisdom insisted that the human mind, in the pursuit of mathematically informed science, becomes like the divine mind (Galilei 2001: 117–19).[25] René Descartes, too, is somewhat closer to the medieval ideal of *scientia* as contemplation than his English coun- terparts – hence the title of his most famous work – *Meditations* – and his conviction that a universal science could be imagined by a single mind.[26] Nonetheless most theorists of the new sciences tended to stress the importance of new externalized disciplines or sets of practices, over the possession of inner virtues. We need only consider the titles of Descartes' methodological works – *Rules for the Direction of the Mind* and *Discourse on the Method of Rightly Conducting One's Reason* – to see the force of this. The legitimacy of a body of knowledge is now derived from the following of a strict protocol rather than from the personal piety of the investigator.[27] In this insistence on the public nature of scientific activity, and on procedures that in principle can be adopted by anybody – irrespective of their possession of either virtue or wisdom – we have the begin- nings of the idea that objectivity and disinterestedness are key features of science.

So much, then, for the transformations undergone by *scientia* and their implication for the new natural sciences. What of the fortunes of theology, its status as a science, and its relation to the other sciences? In certain respects it can be said that the conception of theology as science undergoes similar changes. First, the intellectual virtue of *scientia* is no longer a common mental habit shared by the theologian, the mathematician and the natural philosopher. (This was reflected in revisions of the university curriculum in which, pre- viously, the study of Arts had been regarded as a necessary preparation for the higher faculty of Theology.) At the same time, practical wisdom no longer presides over and unifies the theological, moral and intellectual virtues. Equally importantly, the notion that the knowledge of God, attained through the study of theology, gradually brings the knower into conformity with the divine likeness recedes into the background (at least in part, because of the Reformers' insistence that justification is a change of status of the individual rather than an ontological change). Theology, to overstate the case somewhat, ceases to be a transformative act of contemplation, and tends to become the study of publicly available sets of propositions.

---

[25] For Galileo's conception of science, see Plotinsky and Reed 2001; Dear 1998; McMullin 1978; Jardine 1988: 709.

[26] For similarities between Descartes' *Meditations* and the traditional meditational genre, see Jones 2001; Rorty 1986; Stohrer 1979; Thomson 1972; Beck 1965: 28–38; Vendler 1989. More sceptical about the link between Descartes' work and the traditional spiritual exercises is Rubidge (1990).

[27] These two works were written before the *Meditations*, however. It is likely that what Descartes is attempting with the *Meditations* is a justification of his own novel methods in terms of the traditional understanding of knowledge. On the theme of Descartes' attempts to give legit- imation to his natural philosophy, see Gaukroger 1995.

These changes in the nature of theology cannot be fully understood without considering a parallel transformation of the notion of religion (*religio*) that took place at the same time. *Religio*, which for Aquinas is primarily a moral virtue, takes on its more familiar modern guise, and comes to be understood as a set of beliefs and practices. As a consequence of this process of reification, theology becomes the formal treatment of the propositional aspects of the newly ideated 'religion'. To put it another way, theology becomes the intellectual component of a more general category 'religion'. The emergence of a generic 'religion' also made possible the appearance of the plural 'religions', again conceptualized in terms of their beliefs and practices. This was the precondition for the modern problem of religious pluralism – conceptualized not in terms of whether one's faith is correctly formed, or whether one's worship is sincere, but rather in terms of whether one subscribes to the correct doctrines.[28]

In order to grasp the significance of this new conception of religion, consider the declaration of the Renaissance Platonist Marsilio Ficino, for whom 'Christian religion' (no definite article) is evidenced when one lived a life oriented towards truth and goodness. 'All religion', he wrote, 'has something good in it; as long as it is directed towards God, the creator of all things, it is true Christian religion' (1574: I.6). This contrasts rather starkly with the modern conception of religion, in which religions are characterized and distinguished largely according to their propositional content. On this modern view, Christianity was *the* true religion, because the doctrines that it comprised were true. Moreover, these doctrines were supported in various ways by rational proofs – the so-called 'internal' and 'external' evidences. Hence the 'proofs' for the existence of God, and the evidence provided by miracles and prophecy, were such that in principle they provided acceptable evidences to an impartial judge. Again, as in the comparable case of *scientia*, the elements of objectivity and disinterestedness play a significant role, in this instance by adjudicating the claims of the competing 'religions', now propositionally conceived.

To sum up, modern 'science' and 'religion' both come into existence as a consequence of the objectification of what were once regarded as inner virtues. Not only do these transformations entail a reification of internal states, they also involve a denial of the medieval view that knowledge brings about some inner transformation or ontological change in the knower. The sixteenth and seventeenth centuries thus witness the beginning of an alienation of the idea of virtue from the practice of science, including the science of theology. The new natural science is associated with civic or public virtues and increasingly its practice is available to all who are prepared to submit to the external discipline of its specific methods and practices. In much the same way that the *moral* virtues of the individual became irrelevant in the Reformer's forensic understanding of justification, so the possession of specific *intellectual* virtues was to become irrelevant to the practice of science. What counted was the following of

---

[28] See e.g. Smith 1972; Despland 1979; Harrison 1990, 1995; Lash 1996; Feil 1986.

a scientific regimen, and the generic virtue of wisdom had little or no role to play in that process.

All of this makes possible a new kind of relationship between science and theology. In much the same way that the modern conception of 'religion' is necessarily accompanied by a new problem – that of relating the propositional claims of the various 'religions' – so the relationship between 'science' and 'religion' is conceptualized primarily in terms of a relationship between two sets of truth-claims or, alternatively, in terms of the authority and power of two competing social institutions. It is to this latter development that we now briefly turn.

4. Professionalizing the Sciences

For the final stages of the dissociation of wisdom and knowledge we need to shift our attention away from the inner dynamics of Western theories of knowledge, to a more sociological consideration of the emergence of modern institutions. I will offer some brief remarks about this process before concluding.

The objectification of the virtues of *scientia* and *religio*, and their transformation into external bodies of knowledge, is accompanied by the appearance of differentiated social systems – economy, polity and law (see e.g. Luhmann 1982, 1989; Beyer 1998; Roberts and Turner 2000: 10–12, 83–93). The shift from the hierarchically differentiated social systems of the medieval period to the functional differentiation of modernity is of vital importance for an understanding of modern religion and science and their relation. Consider here the fact that the medieval subordination of natural philosophy to theology reflected both the vertically ordered 'estates' of clergy and laity (the latter including the aristocracy) and the relationship in the universities between the 'lower' faculties of arts and the 'higher' faculties which included theology. Integral to the functional differentiation of these modern institutions was increasing professionalization and specialization. On the latter score it can be said that the success of the natural sciences is premised on the modesty of their ambitions and the narrow focus of their enquiries. The idea that a single mind might possess an overarching knowledge that encompassed not only all of the sciences but the moral realm as well, became a practical impossibility.

By the beginning of the nineteenth century, the sheer vastness of accumulated knowledge of nature and the specialization it required precipitated something of a crisis. The English philosopher and Divine William Whewell expressed concern that 'physical science itself is endlessly subdivided, and the subdivisions insulated'. 'The disintegration goes on', he lamented, 'like that of a great empire falling to pieces' (Whewell 1834: 59). As part of his mission to retain the unity of the natural sciences, Whewell coined the term 'scientist' to describe all those engaged in what he regarded as a common scientific mission (Ross 1962). No longer were practitioners of science regarded as 'natural philosophers', and with the demise of that designation, yet another link with the classical ideal of the philosopher as the wise sage was severed. The nineteenth-century invention of the term 'scientist' was accompanied by the rise of a new professional class and the demise of the amateur naturalist. At this time the first professional bodies for scientists came into existence – the British Association for the Advancement of Science, for example, was established in the early 1830s. The founding of such associations brought with it a new status for scientific practitioners, and accompanying this status, a new set of professional commitments. Whereas natural history, for example, had for the most part been dominated by the clergy (in England at least), the new scientific discipline of biology gradually gained its independence from clerical dominance, while at the same time legitimizing a new set of non-ecclesiastical authorities (Turner 1978; Brooke 1991: 5, 50; Livingstone 1997; Desmond 1984). These vocational shifts reinforced the narrow specialization of the sciences.[29] By the end of the century there was an almost universal, if tacit, understanding that the term 'science' excluded aesthetic, ethical and theological considerations. By 1922, in his essay on science as a vocation, Max Weber was thus able to speak of the narrow specializations of science, in which no place could be found for the broader questions of value and meaning (Weber 1989; Durbin 1999). Thus, while disagreements persist into the twenty-first century about precisely which activities might be included under the rubric 'science', there is a general consensus that certain things are to be excluded.[30]

Taken together, these developments spelt the final disjunction of wisdom and science. To a degree, however, it might be said that the cultural prestige of the natural sciences has meant that some prominent scientists may act as surrogates for the older type, the 'wise philosopher'. Consider, for example, the reverence accorded to the extra-curricular pronouncements of Albert Einstein, Stephen Hawking or even Richard Dawkins. It is the case, as A. W. Benn observed one hundred years ago, that 'a great part of the reverence once given to priests and to their stories of an unseen universe has been transferred to the astronomer, the geologist, the physician, and the engineer' (1906: I.198).

Conclusion

My main concern in this paper has been primarily descriptive – to trace historical developments in the enterprises of science and theology in relation to the

---

[29] A number of Victorian practitioners of science were initially reluctant to identify their activities as something distinct from philosophy, ethics and theology. Herbert Spencer, for example, considered the Victorian classifications of the sciences to be artificial, particularly in the separation of science and art, or science and common sense (Spencer 1854: 152–9; Yeo 1993: 49f.).

[30] Above all else, science was regarded as excluding religious considerations. Adrian Desmond writes that 'Something more surrounded the man of science's credentials – an agnostic moral order. "Pope Huxley" had fused the little sciences into a universal corpus – one Catholic Apostolic Church of True Knowledge. Science, with a capital "S" now, a monolithic entity matched by a name for its acolyte, the "Scientist"' (1997: II.248).

idea of wisdom; to try to provide insights into the unique developments of these conceptions in the West. These developments amount to this: *When science, theology and religion become objectified and disengaged from the inner moral states of the individual, they begin to assume their familiar modern guise while at the same time being alienated from a more traditional understanding of wisdom.* It remains to enquire what, if anything, is the relevance of all this for our current understanding of the nature of science and theology and their relation. I shall make three observations.

First, what this history suggests is that the contemporary relationship between science and theology is at least in part a function of the modern categories themselves. Whereas we tend to imagine the chief issues at stake in science–theology discussion to be substantive ones – to do with propositions about the world or human beings, for example – the very fact that we conceive of science and theology primarily in these propositional terms is itself a function of a particular historical turn. In much the same way that it can be argued the contemporary problem of the competing truth-claims of the world religions arises out of the modern concept 'religion', it can be said that to some degree the science–religion relation is a creature of the categories 'science' and 'religion' that emerged over the course of the sixteenth and seventeenth centuries. From the sociological perspective, the same point can be made in a slightly different way – that some clashes between science and religion might better be regarded as boundary disputes between professional groupings, and thus more related to questions of cultural power and prestige than of intellectual substance.

Second, it is worth asking what lessons can be learned from some of the medieval debates. Is theology a contemplative/speculative enterprise concerned primarily with knowledge, or is it a practical one concerned with action? Or is it some combination of both? Furthermore, should the claim still be made that theology is a science, and what criteria should be used that would enable us to identify an enterprise as science? To frame this same question in another way: What was lost to modernity as a consequence of the changes that we have been considering? Are there features of the earlier conception of theology as an agent of personal transformation that are worth preserving? Does the classical ideal of wisdom still have anything to recommend it, and is it still possible in some measure to recapture elements of it?

Finally, to provide a partial answer to this last question, it seems to me that there was something of value in the traditional conception of the philosopher not as an innovator in the sphere of knowledge, but as the trustee of an ancient legacy and the guardian of a deposit of wisdom. Integral to this vision was a modesty about what could really be known, combined with a respect for the past and a refreshing absence of any conception of progress. We would do well to recall that the religious traditions can themselves be regarded as repositories of a wisdom that ought not to be lightly abandoned in the face of apparently conflicting data from the modern sciences. This is particularly so, in my view, when we come to consider the contributions of the so-called human sciences.

More specifically: that such recent disciplines as socio-biology, evolutionary psychology or the social sciences in general could provide information about human nature that should take automatic precedence over the insights of theological anthropology seems to me to be misplaced. There are truths in the religious traditions that should not be lightly surrendered. To a degree, then, theologians might still be regarded as custodians of a wisdom that should be preserved. On this general point, and finally to conclude, I can do no better than repeat the words of John Donne, who wrote at a time when the new sciences were carrying all before them:

> And yet, here in this world, knowledge is but as the earth, and ignorance as the sea; there is more sea than earth, more ignorance than knowledge; and as, if the sea do gain in one place it loses in another, so it is with knowledge too; if new things be found out, as many, and as good, that were known before, are forgotten and lost. (Southgate 1989: 249)

References

Althaus, P.
1966   *The Theology of Martin Luther* (Philadelphia: Fortress).
Annas, J.
1993   *The Morality of Happiness* (Oxford: Oxford University Press).
Aquinas, Thomas. See Thomas Aquinas.
Aristotle
1984   *Complete Works of Aristotle* (2 vols, ed. J. Barnes; Princeton: Princeton University Press).
Augustine of Hippo
1991   *Confessions* (trans. H. Chadwick; Oxford: Oxford University Press).
1996   *The Trinity* (trans. Edmund Hill; New York: New City Press).
Bacon, F.
1857–74 *The Works of Francis Bacon* (14 vols, ed. James Spedding, Robert Ellis and Douglas Heath; London: Longman & Co.).
Barbour, I.
1990   *Religion in an Age of Science* (London: SCM Press).
Beck, L. J.
1965   *The Metaphysics of Descartes: A Study of the 'Meditations'* (Oxford: Oxford University Press).
Benn, A. W.
1906   *A History of English Rationalism in the Nineteenth Century* (2 vols; London: Longmans, Green).
Beyer, P.
1998   'The Modern Emergence of Religions and a Global Social System for Religion', *International Sociology* 13: 151–72.
Blumenberg, H.
1961   'Augustin's Anteil an der Geschichte des Begriffs der theoretischen Neugiergde', *Revue des Etudes Augustiniennes* 7: 35–70.

1962   '*Curiositas* and *veritas*: Zur Ideengeschichte von Augustin, Con-
         fessiones X 35', *Studia Patristica* 6 (Texte und Untersuchungen,
         81): 294–302.

Bonaventure
1882–1902
         *Commentaria in Quatuor Libros Sententiarum, Opera Omnia S. Bona-
         venturae* (Quaracchi: Ad Claras Aquas).

Brooke, J. H.
1991   *Science and Religion: Some Historical Perspectives* (Cambridge: Cam-
         bridge University Press).

Calvin, J.
1960   *Institutes of the Christian Religion* (2 vols, ed. J. McNeill, trans. F.
         Battles; Philadelphia: Westminster).
2003   *Calvin's Commentaries* (22 vols; Grand Rapids: Baker).

Cohen, I. B.
1985   *Revolution in Science* (Cambridge, MA: Harvard University Press).

Cross, R.
1999   *Duns Scotus* (Oxford: Oxford University Press).

Daston, L.
1995   'Curiosity in Early Modern Science', *Word & Image* 11: 391–404.

Dear, P.
1998   'Method and the Study of Nature', in D. Garber and M. Ayers
         (eds), *Cambridge History of Seventeenth-Century Philosophy*, vol. 1 (2
         vols; Cambridge: Cambridge University Press): 147–77.

Desmond, A.
1984   *Archetypes and Ancestors: Palaeontology in Victorian England: 1850–
         1875* (Chicago: University of Chicago Press).
1997   *Huxley* (2 vols; London: Michael Joseph).

Despland, M.
1979   *La religion en occident: évolution des idées et du vécu* (Montreal: Fides).

Duns Scotus, J.
1950–   *Opera Omnia* (eds C. Balíc *et al.*; Vatican City: Typis Polyglottis
         Vaticani).

Durbin, W.
1999   'What Shall We Make of Henry Margenau? A Religion and Sci-
         ence Pioneer of the Twentieth Century', *Zygon: Journal of Religion
         and Science* 34: 167–93.

Ebeling, G.
1970   *Luther: An Introduction to his Thought* (London: Fontana).

Feil, E.
1986   *Religio: Die Geschichte eines neuzeitlichen Grundbegriffs vom Früh-
         christentum bis zur Reformation* (Göttingen: Vandenhoeck &
         Ruprecht).

Ficino, M.
1574   *Opera*, 2 vols (Basel).

Freddoso, A.
1999   'Ockham on Faith and Reason', in Paul Spade (ed.), *Cambridge Companion to Ockham* (Cambridge: Cambridge University Press): 326–49.

Galilei, Galileo
2001   *Dialogue Concerning the Two Chief World Systems* (trans. Stillman Drake; New York: Modern Library).

Gaukroger, S.
1995   *Descartes: An Intellectual Biography* (Oxford: Oxford University Press).

Gaukroger, S. (ed.)
1998   *The Soft Underbelly of Reason: The Passions in the Seventeenth Century* (London: Routledge).

Harris, C.
1927   *Duns Scotus* (2 vols; Oxford: Oxford University Press).

Harrison, P.
1990   *'Religion' and the Religions in the English Enlightenment* (Cambridge: Cambridge University Press).
1995   'British Views on Religion and Religions in the Age of William and Mary', *Method and Theory in the Study of Religion* 7: 273–81.
1998   *The Bible, Protestantism and the Rise of Natural Science* (Cambridge: Cambridge University Press).
2001   'Curiosity, Forbidden Knowledge, and the Reformation of Natural Philosophy in Early-Modern England', *Isis* 92: 265–90.
2002   'Original Sin and the Problem of Knowledge in Early Modern Europe', *Journal of the History of Ideas* 63: 239–59.
2003   'Science', *Encyclopedia of Protestantism* (4 vols, ed. Hans J. Hillerbrand; New York: Routledge).

Inciarte, F.
1996   'Scotus' Gebrauch des Begriffs der Praktischen Wahrheit im Philosophiegeschichtlichen Kontext', in L. Honnefelder, R. Wood and M. Dreyer (eds), *John Duns Scotus: Metaphysics and Ethics* (Leiden: Brill): 523–33.

Ingham, M.
1996   'Practical Wisdom: Scotus's Presentation of Prudence', in L. Honnefelder, R. Wood and M. Dreyer (eds), *John Duns Scotus: Metaphysics and Ethics* (Leiden: Brill): 551–71.

Jardine, N.
1988   'Epistemology of the Sciences', in C. Schmitt and Q. Skinner (eds), *Cambridge History of Renaissance Philosophy* (Cambridge: Cambridge University Press): 685–712.

Jones, M.
2001   'Descartes's Geometry as Spiritual Exercise', *Critical Inquiry* 28: 40–72.

Kraye, J. (ed.)
1997　　*Cambridge Translations of Renaissance Philosophical Texts* (2 vols; Cambridge: Cambridge University Press).

Kusukawa, S.
1997　　'*Vinculum concordiae*: Lutheran Method by Philip Melanchthon', in D. Di Liscia, E. Kessler and C. Methuen (eds), *Method and Order in Renaissance Philosophy of Nature* (Aldershot: Ashgate): 336–8.

Lash, N.
1996　　*The Beginning and End of Religion* (Cambridge: Cambridge University Press).

Leary, J.
1994　　*Francis Bacon and the Politics of Science* (Ames: Iowa State University Press).

Livingstone, D.
1997　　'Science and Religion: Toward a New Cartography', *Christian Scholar's Review* 26: 270–92.

Lohr, C.
1988　　'Metaphysics', in C. Schmitt and Q. Skinner (eds), *Cambridge History of Renaissance Philosophy* (Cambridge: Cambridge University Press): 537–638.

Luhmann, N.
1982　　*The Differentiation of Society* (trans. S. Holmes and C. Larmore; New York: Columbia University Press).
1989　　'Die Ausdifferenzierung der Religion', in N. Luhmann, *Gesellschaftsstruktur und Semantik: Studien zur Wissenssoziologie der modernen Gesellschaft*, vol. 3 (Frankfurt am Main: Suhrkamp): 259–357.

Luther, M.
1955–75 *Luther's Works* (55 vols, eds Jaroslav Pelikan and Helmut Lehmann; Philadelphia: Concordia).
1970　　*To the Christian Nobility of the German Nation* in *Three Treatises* (Philadelphia: Fortress).
1983　　*Sermons of Martin Luther* (8 vols, ed. and trans. John N. Lenker *et al.*; Grand Rapids: Baker).

McMullin, E.
1978　　'The Conception of Science in Galileo's Work', in Robert Butts and Joseph Pitt (eds), *New Perspectives on Galileo* (Dordrecht: Kluwer): 209–57.

Migne, J.-P. (ed.)
1844–1905
　　　　Patrologiae cursus completus (Series Latina, 217 vols; Paris: Garnier).

Pérez-Ramos, A.
1996　　'Bacon's Legacy', in Markku Peltonen (ed.), *Cambridge Companion to Bacon* (Cambridge: Cambridge University Press): 311–34.

Plato
    1963   *Collected Dialogues of Plato* (eds Edith Hamilton and Huntington Cairns; Princeton: Princeton University Press).

Plotinsky, A. and D. Reed
    2001   'Discourse, Mathematics, Demonstration, and Science in Galileo's Discourses Concerning Two New Sciences', *Configurations* 9: 37–64.

Roberts, A. and J. Donaldson (eds)
    1989   *The Ante-Nicene Fathers* (10 vols; Edinburgh: T&T Clark).

Roberts, J. H. and J. Turner
    2000   *The Sacred and the Secular University* (Princeton: Princeton University Press).

Rorty, A. (ed.)
    1986   *Essays on Descartes' Meditations* (Berkeley: University of California Press).

Ross, S.
    1962   ' "Scientist": The Story of a Word', *Annals of Science* 18: 65–86.

Rubidge, B.
    1990   'Descartes's *Meditations* and Devotional Meditations', *Journal of the History of Ideas* 51: 27–49.

Schaff, P. and H. Wace (eds)
    1952–64 *Nicene and Post-Nicene Fathers*, Series II (14 vols; Grand Rapids: Eerdmans).

Serene, E.
    1988   'Demonstrative Science', in N. Kretzmann, A. Kenny and J. Pinborg (eds), *Cambridge History of Later Medieval Philosophy* (Cambridge: Cambridge University Press): 496–518.

Smith, W. C.
    1972   *The Meaning and End of Religion* (London: Macmillan).

Southgate, B. C.
    1989   ' "Forgotten and Lost": Some Reactions to Autonomous Science in the Seventeenth Century', *Journal of the History of Ideas* 50: 249–68.

Spencer, H.
    1854   'The Genesis of Science', *British Quarterly Review* 20: 108–62.

Sprat, T.
    1667   *History of the Royal Society* (London).

Stohrer, W.
    1979   'Descartes and Ignatius Loyola: La Flèche and Manresa Revisited', *Journal of the History of Philosophy* 17: 11–27.

Thomas Aquinas
    1924   *Summa Contra Gentiles* (trans. English Dominican Fathers; New York: Benziger).
    1932   *On the Power of God* (trans. English Dominican Fathers; London: Burns, Oates & Washbourne).
    1951   *On the Virtues in General* (trans. John Reid; Providence: Providence College Press).

1952   *Disputed Questions on Truth* (trans. Robert Mulligan; Chicago: Henry Regnery).

1961   *Commentary on the Metaphysics of Aristotle* (trans. John Rowan; Chicago: Henry Regnery).

1964   *Commentary on the Nicomachean Ethics* (trans. C. Ritzinger; Chicago: Henry Regnery).

1964–76 *Summa Theologiae* (60 vols, Blackfriars Edition, ed Thomas Gilby; London: Eyre & Spottiswoode).

1986   *The Division and Methods of the Sciences* (4th edn, trans. Armand Maurer; Toronto: Pontifical Institute of Mediaeval Studies).

Thomson, A.

1972   'Ignace de Loyola et Descartes: L'influence des exercices spirituels sur les oeuvres philosophiques de Descartes', *Archives de philosophie* 35: 61–85.

Turner, F.

1978   'The Victorian Conflict between Science and Religion: A Professional Dimension', *Isis* 49: 356–76.

Vendler, Z.

1989   'Descartes' Exercises', *Canadian Journal of Philosophy* 19: 193–224.

Weber, M.

1989   'Science as a Vocation', in Peter Lassman and Irving Velody (eds), *Max Weber's 'Science as a Vocation'* (London: Allen & Unwin).

Whewell, W.

1834   'Mrs Sommerville on the Connexion of the Physical Sciences', *Quarterly Review* 51: 54–68.

Yeo, R.

1993   *Defining Science: William Whewell, Natural Knowledge, and Public Debate in Early Victorian Britain* (Cambridge: Cambridge University Press).

Wisdom through Communion and Personhood

From Patristic Theology to Contemporary Science

Alexei V. Nesteruk

Introduction

It is now customary to use the term 'wisdom' in all sorts of contexts without a clear observance of its etymological meaning and its ontological reference to being. The notion of wisdom is employed when one wants to say that one must be wise either in the sense of attainment of some knowledge or in terms of being ethical while making some social decisions or developing technical applications for the good or evil of people. A characteristic feature of this kind of wisdom is that it operates in the context of a pre-given order of things, so that, strictly speaking, wisdom thus understood is quite often associated with choice between some pre-given situations which leads to allegedly positive outcomes for that particular community which is eager to be wise. This approach makes all discussions about wisdom part of ethics by phrasing ethical problems in a *sophianic* language. It is then clear that the invocation of wisdom carried out in the context of the pre-given has relevance to the human condition in the world only in terms of 'better' or 'worse', but not in terms of the possibility of this condition as such. Wisdom is often invoked in an existential context, but without any ontological dimensions as related to the very fact of being. It is often implied that scientific advance takes place in a stream of wisdom: science makes human life better and longer, it gives knowledge and conquers ignorance. But this scientific wisdom does not address the issue of existence: with all respect to its success in answering the question 'What is the universe?', it does not answer the question 'Why is the universe?' As we have said above, scientific wisdom operates within the limits of the pre-given which is accessible to the discursive mind. In a way scientific wisdom is tacitly embedded in a wisdom of another kind, that is, the wisdom of being, the wisdom which is affirmed through the very fact of our existence and life in the universe; and it is the understanding of this ultimate existential wisdom that became a major preoccupation of Christian theology since its early patristic period. The message of Christian theology was not the possibility of better life, but the fullness of life as such through articulating the difference between being and non-being. And this is the reason why the patristic contribution to formulating and understanding wisdom of existence is very relevant to the contemporary dialogue between science and theology; for contemporary science, in its exploration and transformation of the world, experiences some serious difficulties in controlling its own advance in terms of preserving the genuine human condition, linked to the fullness of being in a Christian sense.

Patristic theology as formulated by the Fathers of the Church aimed to address the immediate needs of humanity; in so doing it was essentially an existential theology and this is the reason why the invocation of patristic ideas can be so fruitful for restoring living spirituality in modern academic theology which attempts to engage in dialogue with science. By employing patristic ideas in a contemporary context we advocate the relevance of these ideas in the postmodern world. This involves the risk of being criticized for using some archaic ideas of the past in the contemporary setting in which the efficacy of these ideas can be doubtful. However, by insisting that patristic insights are indeed necessary in discussions concerned with the concept of wisdom in the science–religion dialogue, we exercise a purely theological conviction that Orthodox theology is meaningless and inconceivable without reference to the tradition of the Church, and that the presence of the tradition in the Church is the condition for the Church to claim that it has access to wisdom and truth. Contemporary theology needs a new synthesis, similar to that which was achieved by the Greek Fathers who expressed the wisdom of the gospel message in Hellenistic terms while preserving its fundamentally existential character. For these reasons the whole discussion in this paper can only be conceived in the context of the Neo-Patristic Synthesis which was advocated since the 1930s by one of the leading Orthodox theologians of the twentieth century, Georges Florovsky. His slogan was 'back to the Fathers' in order to acquire the 'patristic mind' as 'an *existential attitude* and as a *spiritual orientation*' (Florovsky 1975: 21). This new theological synthesis does not simply imply that the teaching of the Fathers must be quoted and used as a tribute to some antique thought in the modern context. It means rather that contemporary theologians, who attempt to make their thoughts existentially important, must try to acquire that lost intentionality of human subjectivity, which is driven not by the self-interests and ambitions of the all-encompassing human *ratio*, but by the Spirit of God who is acting upon human history. In a way, to have the 'patristic mind' means to enter communion not with the Fathers' texts, but with the Fathers as persons. And this communion is not an abstract theologizing but the living experience of God through the mind of the Fathers. The wisdom of the Fathers thus is not a compendium of knowledge, but an existential endurance of their affirmation that the world around us exists, and the truth of its existence originates in God.

In spite of all scientific achievements, the mystery of existence as such cannot be addressed by science. For, in a paradoxical way, the truth and wisdom of existence, being manifest in fragmented spatio-temporal forms of the created world, is absent from scientific discourse. In the same way that God is revealed to the world through the works of his creation, being absent from this creation as person (so that we know about God's presence in absence), we are left in science with an *apophatic* mystery of wisdom: wisdom is present in science because science in its very definition manifests created wisdom; however, science does not understand why there is the world which can be studied by scientists, i.e. why there is wisdom in science and where it comes from. One can claim that it is through science that we are wise. But, paradoxically, we are wise in actual absence of wisdom. Science is wise and unwise: it is wise when it explores new phenomena, clarifies our vision of the world around us, helps us to survive hardship of growing demands, cures diseases, and so on; science is unwise because it does not deal with its own foundations, it does not understand clearly its own limits and does not anticipate its ultimate goal, i.e. its *telos*. It is in this sense that one can claim that scientific vision is paradoxically blind: it advances but does not control the consistency of this advance with the initial goal of science to serve the human condition. There is wisdom in science, but there is not the fullness of wisdom in science. Science co-operates in approaching this wisdom so that the whole essence of the dialogue between science and theology can then be seen as an attempt to address the paradox of wisdom present in absence.

Theology plays an indispensable role in clarifying this paradox (of wisdom present in absence) and thus giving meaning to science as related to wisdom. But theology, since patristic times, approaches wisdom only in the context of communion. For the early Church the truth and wisdom of existence have never been separate from communion with the person of God, so that any theological affirmation of wisdom in the world was linked to the exploration of the ways of this communion. In other words, theology attempted to articulate this wisdom as the link between the world and God who created it, and in this sense the wisdom in patristic theology differs considerably from the created wisdom of discursive thinking, which operates in the rubrics of the created pre-given, but does not attempt to clarify the wisdom of existence as such. This is the reason why it will be of interest to remind the reader about the forgotten wisdom of the Fathers which can be helpful in understanding why modern science, in its pretence to the fullness of wisdom, in fact needs to be complemented by *theologia*, understood in a patristic sense as the living experience of God, as participation in God through personal communion within the ecclesial context.

Wisdom, Communion and Personhood in Patristic Thought

In the early patristic writings one can find an incredibly innovative trend of thought which linked human existence with communion with God through the Eucharist. The Eucharist was understood not as a religious rite of an ethical nature performed in order to attain good in contradistinction to evil but, in fact, as the principle of our very existence, understood as life and immortality. Since in our everyday life human beings are subject to decay and death, life in the Church implies a shift from our rootedness in biological nature toward what is called the hypostasis of ecclesial existence, which can only be attained through life in worship and the Church's Eucharist. To attain the ecclesial hypostasis meant also lifting an individual up to their true catholic integrity in the personhood of God. The wisdom of existence was associated thus with Christ who is the centre of the Eucharist, and who is the principle of life. Patristic writers used the language of incorruptibility and immortality in order to affirm existence in its ultimate sense. The wisdom of this earthly passage of existence is to achieve some glimpse of eternity, to taste it through the bread of the Eucharist in whose *Anaphora*[1] all of time is suspended and the gates of the Kingdom are open through the invocation of the Spirit. And the type of our possibility to attempt this true existence is Christ himself. According to St Irenaeus of Lyons:

> For it was for this end that the Word of God was made man, and He who was the Son of God became the Son of man, that man, having been taken into the Word, and receiving the adoption, might become the Son of God. For by no other means could we have attained incorruptibility and immortality, unless we have been *united* to incorruptibility and immortality.[2]

Irenaeus makes a clear connection between his vision of life, as has just been formulated, and the Eucharist. Proclaiming the truth of Christ as the truth of incorruptible and everlasting life, he concludes that true life is achievable only through the eucharistic fellowship and union of the flesh and spirit:

> for as bread, which is produced from the earth, when it receives the invocation of God, is no longer common bread, but the *Eucharist*, consisting of two realities, earthly and heavenly; so also our bodies, when they receive the *Eucharist*, are no longer corruptible, having the hope of resurrection to eternity.[3]

It is characteristic of Irenaeus to say that the Eucharist as a liturgical sacrament of the Christian Church changes man in a way such that he attains another 'spiritual' (more precisely ecclesial) dimension of his existence, as the life in the 'world to come'. It means that the Eucharist as a principle of truth

---

[1] This is a special moment at the celebration of the Divine Liturgy when all times, past, present and future, are *condensed* in the point of their ultimate unification in eternity of truth in the prayer of the *Anaphora* (The Liturgy of St John Chrysostom): 'Bearing in remembrance, therefore, this commandment of salvation, and all those things which came to pass for us; the Cross, the Grave, the Resurrection on the third day, the Ascension into Heaven, the Sitting on the right hand, the Second and glorious Coming again' (Hapgood 1996: 104).

[2] Irenaeus of Lyons, *Against the Heresies* III.19.1, see also IV.38.4. English translation: Irenaeus of Lyons 1962: 448 and 522.

[3] Irenaeus of Lyons, *Against the Heresies* IV.18.5. English translation: Irenaeus of Lyons 1962: 486.

and ontological affirmation of the Church's existence is possible only as an eschatological move toward fulfilment not of a particular, individual mode of sanctification but rather as participation in building the Body of Christ, i.e. the Church.[4] This participation, seen from the eschatological perspective, manifests the ontological affirmation of the Church's reality, not only on the visible historical scene, but also as life in the Kingdom of God; for it is the Kingdom which is experienced by us liturgically in its eschatological future.

One sees again that the Eucharist is not a means for cleansing oneself from sin and acquiring goodness, it is not an ethical or psychological precept of well-being (which was the case of the pagan mystery-cults before Christ) but rather 'the *creation* of the people of God as Body of Christ, the manifestation of the Church as new life in the New Aeon' (Schmemann 1996: 107–8). True creation comes into existence by being driven towards its non-worldly source through communion; it is in this sense that existence is not possible without God and the wisdom about this existence can only be grasped through ecclesial communion with God. Christian liturgy as the gathering of people for worship and for the Eucharist becomes thus the principle of truth, which one can call *ecclesiological* truth. Eucharist thus becomes the principle of truth which affirms Church itself.[5] This means that there is no Church outside the liturgy and there is no liturgy outside the Church.

For St Maximus the Confessor life (as being, existence) is truly possible only through the Church whose *logos* is unity in Christ. He says that it is the purpose of Christ and of his Church to fulfil the principle of unity of the faithful with God, in order for them to live truly and avoid the risk of disintegration and then oblivion in non-being: 'the creations and products of the one God be in no way strangers and enemies to one another by having no reason or centre for which they might show each other any friendly or peaceful sentiment or identity, and not run the risk of having their *being* separated from God to dissolve into *non-being*'.[6]

It is the Church that is preserving the *being* of the faithful (as united in Christ) from its natural predisposition to disintegration into *non-being*. The truth of life and being is thus inseparable from the life of the Church and her worship.

It is then not difficult to realize that an approach to wisdom in a mundane sense differs considerably from a theological understanding of wisdom as linked

---

[4] This constitutes the shift from hypostasis of biological existence to hypostasis of ecclesial existence which forms man as person, as man whose archetype is Christ. See Zizioulas 1997: 49–65. It is also important to stress that the ontological significance of individual sanctification cannot be fulfilled outside the eucharistic experience as affirmation of the Church by the eucharistic community.

[5] See: 'Our opinion is in accordance with the Eucharist and the Eucharist in turn establishes our opinion.' Irenaeus of Lyons, *Against the Heresies* IV.18.5. English translation: Irenaeus of Lyons 1962: 486.

[6] Maximus the Confessor, *Mystagogy* 1. English translation: Maximus the Confessor 1985: 187.

to the existential ontology of the human condition, which in its essence is relational upon God, and existence through relation is attainable only on the grounds of communion which is not a part of the natural history of humanity, but rather an intentional break from this history by means of invocation of the Spirit who acts upon history. One can describe the distinction just made in terms of the difference between created wisdom and divine wisdom. For patristic writers, such as Clement of Alexandria, for example, this distinction was paralleled with the distinction between philosophy and theology or between reason and faith. One can describe wisdom in terms of knowledge. In this case the wisdom of the Church, that is divine wisdom, is saving knowledge to which all mundane activities such as science and philosophy contribute and with which they co-operate. But by co-operating in attainment of truth the wisdom of the sciences and philosophy never exhaust this truth because they are contingent upon this truth existentially: they contain a glimpse of the divine wisdom through the sheer fact that science and philosophy exist; they exist as mental creations of human beings who participate in divine wisdom because they are alive. The sciences and philosophies aspire to this wisdom, but in themselves can never attain it within their own boundaries, that is, without the presence of faith and communion with God, which itself sanctifies all sorts of created wisdom. Clement defines wisdom in a characteristic way as being eternal uncreated Wisdom, which the human mind attempts to comprehend in creaturely conditions; wisdom thus becomes accessible to mind in the rubrics of the empirical spatio-temporal world, demonstrating itself (i.e. wisdom) as an open-ended ideal in human desire for its attainment. Clement writes:

> And we define Wisdom to be certain knowledge, being a sure and irrefragable apprehension of things divine and human, comprehending the present, past, and future, which the Lord hath taught us, both by His advent and by the prophets ... And so it is wholly true according to [God's] intention, as being known through means of the Son. And in one aspect it is eternal, and in another it becomes useful in time. Partly it is one and the same, partly many and indifferent – partly without any movement of passion, partly with passionate desire – partly perfect, partly incomplete. This wisdom, then – rectitude of soul and of reason, and purity of life – is the object of desire of philosophy, which is kindly and lovingly disposed towards wisdom, and does everything to attain it.[7]

One can anticipate in Clement a certain desire to assign to Wisdom, as eternal wisdom, some hypostatic properties by linking it to Christ. Then to acquire wisdom means to participate in the hypostatic Wisdom, which is Christ. Philosophy and the sciences as co-operating in truth can lead to wisdom, if they are related to faith in Christ, that is, if they are embedded in the framework of communion with God: 'If then, we assert that Christ Himself is Wisdom ... then it follows that the gnosis, which is the knowledge and apprehension of things present, future and past ... as being imparted by the

---

[7] Clement of Alexandria, *Stromateis* VI.7. English translation: Clement of Alexandria 1962: 492–3.

Son of God, is wisdom' (ibid.). One can suggest that wisdom as the saving knowledge is that transformation of the created, temporal wisdom which happens when knowledge becomes Christian gnosis, that is, knowledge of worldly things is brought to communion with God. It is in this, so to speak, epistemological sense that wisdom manifests itself as the link which relates the world to God and vice versa. The contemplation of this wisdom is paramount thus to comprehension of the world as created by God; that is, the whole creation is seen thus as a medium through which and in which wisdom is revealed. It is in this context that Origen asserts that wisdom 'fashions beforehand and contains within herself the species and causes of the entire creation'.[8] But wisdom is understood to be the Word of God because 'wisdom opens to all other beings, that is, to the whole creation, the meaning of the mysteries and symbols which are contained within the wisdom of God' (Origen 1973: 16). It is through wisdom and in wisdom that the meaning of existence can be comprehended: thus wisdom enters an ontological level of theologizing, for existence as such (i.e. as a meaningful and articulated state of affairs) receives its origin in the wisdom of God. One can also see some confirmation for our previous claim that theological wisdom is dealing with an existential issue: 'Why is the world?' and 'Why are human beings?' But this also implies that the wisdom which deals with these issues has an ontological dimension as the link between the world (and man in it), and the transcendent God who, while being separated in his essence from the world by a transcendent gulf (Gr.: *diastema*), is still hypostatically present in the world (see Nesteruk 2004).

Augustine of Hippo articulated wisdom as the link-piece between creation and God by making a distinction between the uncreated and created wisdom as it appears to the human spirit which is involved in knowledge of earthly things as well as in contemplation of eternal truths. 'Yet action, by which we use temporal things well, differs from contemplation of eternal things; and the latter is reckoned to wisdom, the former to knowledge.'[9] Augustine insists that in spite of the fact that both, the word of wisdom and knowledge, are given by the same Spirit (1 Cor. 12.8), they are distinct.[10] And wisdom, in this context as also being created, is dependent upon something else that originates beyond creation. Here he makes an analogy with the light that gives origin to illumination, which is caught by the human grasp. But human grasp, being the manifestation of the created wisdom, itself depends on the *uncreated light* through which the *natural light* of human mind, as made in the divine image, is seen: 'But we ought rather to believe that the intellectual mind is so formed in its nature as to see those things which by the disposition of the Creator are subjoined to things intelligible in a natural order, by a sort of *incorporeal light* of

---

[8] Origen, *De principiis*, bk. 1, ch. 2.3. English translation: Origen 1973: 16.
[9] Augustine of Hippo, *On the Trinity* XII.14.22. English translation: Augustine of Hippo 1975: 37.
[10] Augustine of Hippo, *On the Trinity* XII.15.25. English translation: Augustine of Hippo 1975: 40.

a unique kind.'[11] What is important here is that, even if the human mind is capable of articulating things in the universe because of the inherent co-ordination between the world and mind originating from the image of God, it does not immediately imply that this mind is wise by itself through the natural capacity which is granted to it at the moment of its creation: 'just as there is a difference between light which illuminates and that which is illuminated, so also there is an equivalent difference between the *wisdom which creates* and that which is created ...'[12] The human mind can become wise if it makes an ecstatic transcendence in faith when the natural light present in this mind will be brought to communion with the supreme Light in which the supreme wisdom of the very existence will be revealed. And it is only through communion as participation that the supreme Wisdom can be revealed and all forms of created wisdom can be sanctified. But this also implies that it is through man's communion with God that the link between God and the world, that is, the ultimate sense of existence, is hypostasized and revealed to humanity as wisdom. This conclusion points sufficiently enough to the demarcation between what can be called wisdom of knowledge and wisdom of communion; it is only through the latter that the former can be assessed and sanctified. The attainment of existential wisdom thus requires one to complement all sorts of scientific wisdom by means of invoking communion with God and his Wisdom; but this implies in turn that all attempts at such an attainment will lead to the necessity of ecclesial experience as that medium in which communion becomes effective through the action of the Holy Spirit.

The importance of the participation of the Holy Spirit in attainment of existential wisdom through spiritual contemplation, or, in different words, through communion of the natural light of human mind with the supreme Light, was articulated by St Maximus the Confessor:

> Just as it is impossible for the eye to perceive sensible objects without the light of the sun so the human intellect cannot engage in spiritual contemplation without the light of the Spirit ... The faculties which search out divine realities were implanted by the Creator in the essence of human nature at its very entrance into being; but divine realities themselves are revealed to man through grace by the power of the Holy Spirit descending upon him.[13]

Since communion with the divine wisdom or, in different parlance, with the supreme Light can only be achieved through the invocation of the Spirit, and since the action of the Spirit upon history takes place in the eucharistic context of the Church, the ecclesial dimension in the desire to attain the divine wisdom becomes indispensable. But this makes inevitable the conclusion that any sort

[11] Augustine of Hippo, *On the Trinity* XII.15.24. English translation: Augustine of Hippo 1975: 39. Emphasis added.

[12] Augustine of Hippo, *Confessions* 12.15. English translation: Augustine of Hippo 1991: 255. Emphasis added.

[13] Maximus the Confessor, *Various Texts on Theology, the Divine Economy, and Virtue and Vice* 4.17, 18. English translation: Palmer, Sherrard and Ware 1984: 239.

of the so-called scientific wisdom is fundamentally incomplete if it is not related to eucharistic experience. Science can be considered as para-eucharistic work (Nesteruk 2003), but what it lacks is communion with the eschatological Kingdom which alone can bring a scientist to transfiguration and *theosis* as the acquisition of the ultimate wisdom.

What makes all enquiries about wisdom in rational thinking (in science and philosophy) different from a genuine religious consciousness is that science and philosophy attempt to answer the question 'What is truth?' whereas a Christian believer is always looking for truth as 'Who is truth?', remembering the words of the Sinaite revelation 'I am Who I am.' As communion with God is personal, the search for the wisdom of God cannot be impersonal. As the Holy Spirit is the person who pours his grace on the Church by granting it access to truth, the wisdom of God, which is attainable through the Spirit, is not impersonal, but, on the contrary, hypostatic, as the mode of personal communion of the intrinsically catholic humanity of Christ with the head of its body, that is, Christ-Logos himself. The bridge between the world and God can thus be expressed as the hypostatic inherence of the world in the Logos of God who, according to St Maximus the Confessor, himself represents the hypostatic Wisdom of God. It is in the Logos as Wisdom that the whole world inheres through the *logoi* of created things as underlying and forming principles – ideas corresponding to every created thing brought into existence in its proper time and destined to be reunited in God in the end of time. Wisdom of God is the bridge between the world and the Hypostasis of the Logos – Christ, who holds all the *logoi* of the worldly things together:

> For the *wisdom* and sagacity of God the Father is the Lord Jesus Christ, who holds together the universals of beings by the power of *wisdom*, and embraces their complementary parts by the sagacity of understanding, since by nature he is the fashioner and provider of all, and through himself draws into one what is divided, and abolishes war between beings, and binds everything into peaceful friendship and undivided harmony, 'both what is in heaven and what is on earth' (Col. 1.20), as the divine Apostle says.[14]

The contemplation of the divine Wisdom as the link between God and the World constitutes a whole theology of mediation between divisions in creation and between creation and God in Maximus.[15] This theology of mediation is rather mystical and ascetic and it aims to transform human intentionality in order to direct it to the search for True and uncreated Light of the Divine Wisdom. Uncreated Wisdom can only be attained on the way of one's hypostatic transcendence beyond the created, the way which has been exercised by advanced ascetics and mystics who acquired the grace of the Holy Spirit, for just as without the sunlight one cannot see empirical things, so the human *spiritual*

---

[14] Maximus the Confessor, *Ambigua* 41. English translation: Louth 1996: 161–2; Greek text: *PG* 91.1313B.

[15] See details in Thunberg 1995 and von Balthasar 2003.

intellect (*nous*) cannot engage in spiritual knowledge, which transcends all thought, without the light of the Holy Spirit.

We see thus that the question about existence and its underlying wisdom in patristic thought leads to a fundamental antinomy between all formal and rational quests for wisdom in the sciences and philosophy on the one hand, and the attainment of the divine wisdom through hypostatic communion with God in the ecclesial setting, where the Holy Spirit, being eucharistically invoked, grants to the people of Christ access to the supreme Light, on the other hand. The question of wisdom in patristic theology is intrinsically existential and therefore unavoidably personal. It is in the same sense that the Eucharist is treated as the bread of life for persons, but not for abstract objects; the wisdom of personal existence as unique relationship with one's own Creator is the gift of communion with that personal God whom we call the Father, the Son and the Holy Spirit. As wisdom manifests itself through the relationship between God and man, that is, as the link-piece between God and the world which is comprehended in the hypostasis of humanity, this wisdom, being involved in the circle of relationships, manifests itself in the duality of its personal origin in God and the impersonal empirical actuality of the world. Wisdom is paradoxically hypostatically present in the universe created by God, but it is present through its actual absence from various non-hypostatic (impersonal) works of creation. The paradox which emerges here is similar to the paradox of human subjectivity in the universe in which humanity, while being treated as the works of creation, is paradoxically absent as creating consciousness of the universe, as the personal voice of the universe, through which the universe receives its sense and meaning. The procession from scientific wisdom to wisdom as existence-communion corresponds to the search for the lost personhood in the foundation of the scientific. This search, expressed in the language of phenomenological philosophy, demands the deconstruction of the natural attitude of the human mind, which attempts to identify wisdom from within the pre-given, and the transformation of this attitude into the *presence* of the One who, in his response to the seeking hypostatic humanity can say 'I am Who I am.'

The wisdom of the Fathers, rediscovered and placed in the context of the science–religion dialogue, thus corresponds first of all to the reinstatement of the lost personhood present behind scientific assertions about the world in the form of its (i.e. personhood's) paradoxical absence from the content of scientific theories. For the quest for wisdom of existence-communion is essentially the search for personhood as the link between the world (articulated by humanity) and its ultimate source – the person of God. Communion and personhood are intrinsically interwoven as both expressing the presence of God in creation in his absence.

Scientific Wisdom and Lost Personhood: Paradox of Human Subjectivity in the Universe

The fact that science in isolation from the wide experience of the divine cannot cope with the paradox of personhood and wisdom of creation can be illustrated by an example in which the above-mentioned paradox reveals itself as a paradox of human subjectivity in the world. This paradox can easily be approached from a scientific side if one tries to demonstrate the whole grandeur of the world in quantitative terms, for example in terms of a typical size, putting in the same diagram micro-objects (atoms, molecules, DNA, etc.) together with mega-objects like planets, stars, galaxies, clusters of galaxies and even the whole universe. Then human beings find themselves in a somewhat strange situation because the planet earth inhabited by human life occupies only a tiny portion of space equal to 10^{-57} of the volume of the visible universe. In a similar way if one follows the evolutionary point of view, according to which the universe had a beginning in the past, approximately 10–15 billion years ago, and then developed so that the humanoid type of life appeared on the planet Earth approximately 1 million years ago, it is not difficult to realize that the phenomenon of humanity came into existence at a very late stage in the history of the universe, occupying only one ten-thousandth of its overall duration. Then it is not difficult to realize that if the human presence in the universe is judged from the point of view of its spatial and temporal dimensions, human beings, considered as physico-biological organisms, represent an insignificant part of the universe.

The paradox, which is present in such a description of the place of humanity in the universe, arises when one realizes that the very representation of the universe as a whole, including all different levels of its physical structure, is the product of human intellectual activity. All constituents of the universe, its 'objects', are constituted by human transcendental subjectivity in a single chain of the whole. The paradox is obvious: the finite, even insignificant corporeal human agencies in the vast universe articulate the entire universe from a point-like position in space and time. Human beings make the totality of the universe be an intentional correlate of their subjectivity, which exhibits fundamentally non-local properties of human being-in-the-world, manifesting a mode of being which transcends the finitude of space and time, as well as all particular objects and laws.

This paradox, which entered our discourse on the grounds of cosmology and physics, represents a well-known problem in philosophy. Edmund Husserl described this paradox in his last book, *The Crisis of European Sciences and Transcendental Phenomenology* (1970: 179), as the paradox of human subjectivity being a subject for the world and at the same time being an object in the world. Maurice Merleau-Ponty (1982: 72) summarized the same paradox in simple words: 'On the one hand man is a part of the world; on the other, he is the constituting consciousness of the world.'

The paradox makes it explicit that any speculation about nature as such must be supplemented by anthropology (understood widely, not only in a scientific sense) and vice versa, so that one could say that 'man and the universe are like two parts of the same book which can be understood only by means of one another' (Dondeyne 1958: 10), or that 'a philosophy of nature and a philosophy of man are mutually complementary; ... neither can be completed unless it shows itself as the counterpart of the other' (Laguna 1966: 81–2). One can go further by invoking the metaphor of the container and of the contained applied to human beings in the universe. On the one hand by its physical and biological dimension (nature) humanity is contained in the universe, on the other hand the universe itself, being an articulated image of the being-with-man, is contained by human beings in their immanent intentional subjectivity. One must not be misled, however, by the seeming symmetry between man and nature in the last metaphor. For ultimately nature and human beings as part of its formation, as well as the paradox about their relationship, are articulated by human beings, so that the content of the paradox represents an intentional curiosity of human subjectivity, which is puzzled by its non-trivial position in the universe, being *de facto* split between its natural attitude, when it interprets humanity as a thing among other things, and its philosophical attitude, when it realizes that human incarnate subjectivity in the world appears to itself as an 'object' of its own intentions, containing in itself the whole universe as the integrity of its conscious acts. Finally, one can argue that the paradox of human subjectivity in the world points to a fundamental existential mystery of human incarnate (embodied) subjectivity.[16]

Let us now point towards some implications of this paradox, which are important in the articulation of the centrality of the problem of human subject for the dialogue between science and theology, as well as to a fundamental limitedness and insufficiency of scientific wisdom. One can state as a fact that physics and cosmology cannot recognize the philosophical and theological convictions about the indispensable role of human subjectivity in the world because physics is quite hostile to philosophy in general while using philosophy for rescuing itself from the difficulties which it feels as its own. Even more, one can say that physics intentionally avoids speculations about human subjectivity which is silently present behind all physical concepts and developments. The human subject, that is, human personhood, is missing from the field of physics. This situation can be described as the sheer dominance of *scientific naturalistic rationalism*, which, as assessed by phenomenological thought, contributes towards the existential crisis of the sciences in the sense of the loss of understanding of their own foundations.

The neglect of, or the lack of desire to take into account, those aspects of the human condition in the universe which are inherent in all structures of human

---

[16] The mystery of the incarnate existence, according to some existentialist philosophers of the twentieth century, constitutes the central theme of metaphysics. For example, according to Gabriel Marcel (1965: 16), 'Incarnation – the central "given" of metaphysics. Incarnation is the situation of a *being who appears to himself to be*, as it were, bound to a body.' Emphasis added.

discursive consciousness that speculates about the universe, points to a regrettable fact that the whole human phenomenon is subjected to 'naturalization', that is, reduced to the deficient physico-mathematical functioning of its corporeal component in which the foundation of personhood and freedom are lost. One can strengthen this last thought by pointing out that the whole complexity and multivariance of the human phenomenon is reduced *de facto* to one universal, abstract, impersonal, anonymous and interchangeable consciousness which is responsible for the affirmation of the mathematized nature. This consciousness appears as a sort of universal logical structure common to all men, but, as believed in science, itself representing only a sector of cosmic determinism, an integral part of the impersonal equation, that is, the universe. But this shows the complete incapacity of rationalistic science to address the problem of how the physico-biological functioning of human bodies is linked to their consciousness, which articulates the world and has access to that universal and anonymous consciousness tacitly present behind all scientific affirmations. In other words the issue of incarnate hypostatic existence (embodiment) is neglected. Once again all individual beings in the commonality of their scientific consciousness are reduced to a disembodied and depersonified subject. This makes it nearly impossible to understand the possibility of *community as communion* in a deep existential sense of love, passion, empathy, and so on.

It is then not difficult to see that in such a vision the entire ontology of humanity is distorted, for such aspects of the human condition as its historicity, incarnate intersubjectivity as personal communion, as well as the very fundamentals of personhood, are removed as an essential element of human existence. As a result of human reality being mathematized, humanity inevitably finds itself in a state of having been emptied of its intrinsic reference to the transcendent and personal God who is worthy of worship. The whole issue of God is also reduced in a mathematical fashion to Deity, which is the bearer of the common and universal intelligence in the world.[17]

Thus the major difficulty which underlies modern scientific discourse is that the human subjectivity inherent in scientific theories of the world is paradoxically absent from all these theories. Science operates with concepts and ideas whose ultimate origin in some sense-forming level of reality (linked to the human condition) is hidden and obscure. A. Gurwitsch eloquently elucidated this last point:

> All questions concerning human reason ... are eliminated from the sciences, not only from the natural sciences which anyhow confine themselves to the corporeal aspect of reality, but from the human sciences as well ... However, if the human mind and human rationality are either overlooked or explained away in a naturalistic fashion, the sciences themselves become unintelligible. Since they are products and creations of the human mind, the foundations upon which they rest, the sense of their procedures and accomplishments, and the limitations of their legitimacy

---

[17] See an extensive discussion of this point in Husserl 1970 and Sherrard 1992.

cannot be brought to light except by referring the very products to the generating and producing mental activities. If this most essential context is overlooked ... the sciences appear as most ingenious technical devices which one may learn to use ... but whose interior mechanism and functioning remain utterly obscure. (Gurwitsch 1966: 399–400)

But this happens not by accident, nor by the naivety of the proponents and enthusiasts of the picture of the world, detached from this human condition. It happens because human subjectivity as such, with its overwhelming tendency to project its own content on the 'screen' of universal discursive thinking, believing thus that those projections form the ultimate 'objective' foundational bricks of what this consciousness is inclined to call 'reality', leaves behind the 'screen' the whole grandeur of the human condition in the universe with its mysteries, emotions, beliefs and feelings which cannot be verbalized in scientific and discursive language. All those who are involved in mediation between science and theology have to address a serious philosophical and theological problem of human personhood which is, paradoxically, manifest in its absence.

But one then asks: how is it possible to engage the dialogue of science which cannot account for its own roots and its historical and existential context, with theology which is through and through historical and existential? If science places itself dogmatically in the framework of naturalistic rationalism, so that the existential dimension of being does not enter scientific discourse (which is built anyway in rubrics of the natural attitude), any correlation of this science with theology becomes very problematic, because such a 'naturalistic' con-sciousness approaches the truths of a theological order in a natural attitude, so that the existential and ontological meaning of theology is discarded, that is, it cannot be seen and conceived at all. If nevertheless a naturalistic mind persists in its speculations about the relationship between science and theology, the whole enterprise, unfortunately, acquires the features of no more than a mental exercise whose sense and value are completely unclear. The presence of the paradox of human subjectivity in the universe, or, in different words, the paradox of personhood present in its absence, in the problematic of science and theology points towards an essential insufficiency of scientific wisdom to comprehend its own origin and its dependence upon that divine hypostatic wisdom which can only be revealed to human beings as persons through communion with a personal God.

The presence of an implicit theological dimension in the paradox of human subjectivity makes it no surprise that, in fact, this paradox was addressed by patristic theologians. In theological terms the paradox attempts to express the essence of humanity as made in the image of God. It is enough to mention St Maximus the Confessor, who formulated the content of the 'paradox' in his theology of man as microcosm and mediator. For example, when he discusses the function of man as mediator between sensible and intelligible realms in creation, he anticipates this paradox using words similar to the above-mentioned metaphor of man as being contained and being a container: 'As a compound of soul and body he [man] is limited essentially by intelligible and sensible realities, while at the same time he himself defines [articulates] these realities through his capacity to apprehend intellectually and perceive with his senses.'[18]

For Maximus, however, the dialectics present in this affirmation did not constitute a problem, for, according to his theological position, the fundamental non-locality, which is present in human insight about the universe, originates from the human ability to comprehend the intelligible realm which contains ideas about the universe as a whole. This ability of human beings to correlate the empirical universe as containing human living organisms with the universe as a global idea, which is articulated by human subjectivity, was described by Maximus using the terms *microcosm* and *mediator*, so that the unity of the empirical and noetic in the universe is guaranteed through the unity of the sensible and intelligible in human hypostatic constitution, the unity which reveals the meaning of the *logos* of human being (as essentially being the *diaphora* (difference) between body and soul), which is similar to the *logos* of creation of the universe (as being the *diaphora* between the sensible and intelligible).[19] It can then be conjectured that the resolution of the paradox of human subjectivity in the world, as we formulated it above, could come from the theology of the similarity between the *logoi* of human beings and the *logoi* of the universe as originating in their common source – the Logos of God. What makes human beings, however, asymmetric with respect to other things in the universe is that their *logoi* are hypostatic, that is, while being inherent in the Logos, human beings are open to communion with the hypostatic Logos. It is only through this communion that the wisdom regarding the role of humanity in the universe and the mystery of the co-ordination of human subjectivity with the whole universe can be articulated as the wisdom of being a person who is able to receive God's revelation about the wisdom of all existence as a personal gift of communication. Thus the wisdom of existence can be disclosed only to persons, but not to the depersonalized anonymous consciousness of the collective. It is in this sense that science can be very useful in an *apophatic* sense by articulating in its impersonal wisdom exactly what is not that hypostatic wisdom of God, which is disclosed in the fullness of personhood. This means that if one attempts to proceed from the scientific wisdom of the pre-given to the ultimate wisdom of existence one must realize oneself as a person in a deep ontological sense as an ultimate reference with respect to being. It is in the same sense that personhood is paradoxically present behind the works of science in its actual absence, that the hypostatic wisdom of God is paradoxically present in science in its absence. For science to identify this wisdom would be equivalent to asking the questions 'Why is there the universe?' and 'Why is the knowledge of the universe through science possible?' But both these questions point to the

---

[18] Maximus the Confessor, *Ambigua* 10.26. English translation: Palmer, Sherrard and Ware 1984: 277; Greek text: *PG* 91.1153B.

[19] See Maximus the Confessor, *Mystagogy* 7. English translation: Maximus the Confessor 1985: 196. More details can be found in Nesteruk 2003: ch. 7.

only genuine source of their own origin – that is, to the human person, who was made with a gift to imitate the divine personhood in its created existence sustained through communion with the person of God, the author of creation and creativity who is paradoxically absent from his works.

Conclusion

The significance of the philosophical and theological introspection upon science, and of the dialogue between science and theology, originates in a deep human desire to look beyond the theoretical and technological achievements of science, beyond the immediacy of the given. Humanity as personhood is not content with the presence of beings in the world as they are given to it empirically. Man attempts to understand the underlying meaning of things not only through what can be called their 'nature', but also through the purposes and ends of these beings as they stand with respect to place and goals of humanity in creation. This understanding is not what can be expressed physically and biologically; it is sustained by humanity's ideals and religious aspirations, which portray man as the crown of creation made in the image of God. And this is the reason why, in a God-like fashion, humanity wants to recognize all sorts of beings (either simple physical objects or living organisms) not according to their nature (which is the objective of scientific research), that is, according to their compelling givenness, but as results of humanity's free will.[20] But human freedom is linked to communion with God, so that by subjugating that wisdom, which is gained on the grounds of the scientific, to the desire for wisdom of existence originating in communion with God, humanity exhibits its hypostatic essence, that is, its personhood, through the tragic paradox of the presence of the wisdom of communion in its actual absence in the empirical and theoretical. Humanity as personhood prefers to express its own presence by appealing to the wisdom of God in the conditions of its own incapacity to overcome the absence of personhood in science. Humanity makes this effort as an alternative to being contained by nature, or being comprehended by some object-oriented thinking. It does not want to be manipulated through circumscribability and individualization, which are inherent in spatio-temporal forms of creation. It is in this sense that humanity as personhood longs for wisdom which is *in* this world – through man – but not

---

[20] The analogy comes from St Maximus the Confessor's discussion on whether God knows created things according to their nature. His answer is negative: God knows things according to his will: '... when Christians were asked by some outsiders puffed up with their learning, how they can claim God knows existent things ... and that he knows intellectual beings intellectually and sensible things sensibly, they replied that he neither knows sensible things sensibly nor intellectual things intellectually. For it is out of the question that the one who is beyond existent things should know things in the manner proper to beings. But we say that God knows existent things as the products of his own acts of *will* ...'. Maximus the Confessor, *Ambigua* 7. English translation: Maximus the Confessor 2003: 61–2; Greek text: *PG* 91.1085B. Emphasis added.

of this world. This longing points toward the *telos* of all creaturehood, in which the paradox of wisdom present in its absence, as explicated in the science–religion discussion, will have to be finally resolved. What is left for humanity here and now is to experience wisdom eucharistically by establishing communion with the age to come in a sense of realized eschatology. By so doing, all mundane sorts of wisdom, as they are made available from scientific research, acquire the status of para-eucharistic achievements.

References

Augustine of Hippo
  1975   *The Essential Augustine* (ed. V. J. Bourke; Indianapolis, IN: Hackett, 2nd edn).
  1991   *Confessions* (trans. H. Chadwick; Oxford and New York: Oxford University Press).
Balthasar, H. U. von
  2003   *Cosmic Liturgy: The Universe According to Maximus the Confessor* (San Francisco: Ignatius Press).
Clement of Alexandria
  1962   *Stromateis*, in A. Roberts and J. Donaldson (eds), *The Ante-Nicene Fathers*, vol. 2 (Grand Rapids, MI: W. B. Eerdman).
Dondeyne, A.
  1958   *Contemporary European Thought and Christian Faith* (Pittsburgh: Duquesne University Press).
Florovsky, G. V.
  1975   'Patristic Theology and the Ethos of the Orthodox Church', in *Aspects of Church History* (Collected Works of Georges Florovsky, 4; Belmont, MA: Nordland): 11–30.
Gurwitsch, A.
  1966   *Studies in Phenomenology and Psychology* (Evanston, IL: Northwestern University Press).
Hapgood, I. F. (ed.)
  1996   *Service Book* (Englewood, NJ: Antiochian Orthodox Christian Archdiocese).
Husserl, E.
  1970   *The Crisis of European Sciences and Transcendental Phenomenology* (Evanston, IL: Northwestern University Press).
Irenaeus of Lyons
  1962   *Against Heresies*, in A. Roberts and J. Donaldson (eds.), *The Ante-Nicene Fathers*, vol. 1 (Grand Rapids, MI: W. B. Eerdman).
Laguna, G.
  1966   *On Existence and the Human World* (New Haven and London: Yale University Press).
Louth, A.
  1996   *Maximus the Confessor* (London and New York: Routledge).

Marcel, G.
  1965   *Being and Having* (London: Collins).
Maximus the Confessor
  1985   *Maximus the Confessor: Selected Writings* (trans. and ed. G. C. Berthold; New York: Paulist Press).
  2003   *On the Cosmic Mystery of Jesus Christ: Selected Writings from St. Maximus the Confessor* (trans. and eds P. M. Blowers and R. L. Wilken; Crestwood, NY: St Vladimir's Seminary Press).
Merleau-Ponty, M.
  1982   *Sense and Non-Sense* (Evanston, IL: Northwestern University Press).
Migne, J.-P. (ed.)
  1857–83 Patrologiae cursus completus … Series graeca (166 vols; Paris: Petit-Montrouge).
Nesteruk, A. V.
  2003   *Light from the East: Theology, Science and the Eastern Orthodox Tradition* (Minneapolis, MN: Fortress Press).
  2004   'The Universe as Hypostatic Inherence in the Logos of God (Panentheism in the Eastern Orthodox Perspective)', in P. Clayton and A. Peacocke (eds), *In Whom We Live and Move and Have Our Being: Panentheistic Reflections on God's Presence in a Scientific World* (Grand Rapids, MI: William B. Eerdmans): 169–83.
Origen
  1973   *On First Principles* (trans. G. W. Butterworth; Gloucester, MA: Peter Smith).
Palmer, G. E. H., P. Sherrard and K. Ware (trans. and eds)
  1984   *The Philokalia: The Complete Text Compiled by St Nikodimos of the Holy Mountain and St Makarios of Corinth*, vol. 2 (London: Faber & Faber).
Schmemann, A.
  1996   *Introduction to Liturgical Theology* (Crestwood, NY: St Vladimir's Seminary Press).
Sherrard, P.
  1992   *Human Image, World Image: The Death and Resurrection of Sacred Cosmology* (Ipswich: Golgonooza).
Thunberg, L.
  1995   *Microcosm and Mediator: The Theological Anthropology of Maximus the Confessor* (Chicago, IL: Open Court).
Zizioulas, J. D.
  1997   *Being As Communion: Studies in Personhood and the Church* (Crestwood, NY: St Vladimir's Seminary Press).

Walking on Hermeneutic Territory

The Horizons of Sense for a Pilgrim

Lucio Florio

1. The Historicity of the Human Being

A human being is permanent in nature but never absolutely fulfilled. He keeps defining his personal originality *in* and *through* his story. This historicity is *collective* and *individual*. The latter, the individual or personal temporality, allows talk of the *biographical structure* of each human being.[1] The individual's development in history is produced in a unique way not only because of his individual originality, but also because of the successive vital choices that the human subject keeps making all through life.

The metaphor of the way and travelling

The expression 'way' primarily means a space which is destined for human transit. There is also a metaphorical use of the word in an anthropological order. Thus, we speak about 'being on the way' or 'journeying' to refer to decisions taken in time. From this perspective, man has been considered as a walker, a traveller, a pilgrim, in a physical and spiritual territory.[2]

---

[1] We can talk of the 'argumental character' of human life as Julián Marías does (1994: 22).

[2] In medieval language the Latin expression *viator* – pilgrim, walker – meant this aspect of the human condition. Thus, Josef Pieper explains: 'We call worldly life *pilgrimage*, pointing out in ordinary vocabulary what the theological term *status viatoris* – pilgrim situation – tries to express . . . This expression tends to clarify that as long as man exists in his worldly life, he is characterized by an ontological condition that consists in being on the way. The human life, which is threading through history, has the configuration of "a becoming", the "not yet", a "hope". On the roads of our life we have an infinite number of possibilities: we may wander and take the wrong way; we may stop and, perhaps, in a certain sense even retreat; but, above all, we have the chance of going further along the true path. We may be anything but we cannot avoid being a walker, being "on the way" . . . This feature of human existence that consists in a "becoming" has been described innumerable times in modern anthropology, above all in existentialism, from Pascal ("we are not but we hope to be") to Gabriel Marcel, Ernst Bloch and Jean Paul Sartre' (Pieper 1970: 132–4).

Moreover, from studies of comparative religion, history of literature and art,[3] it has been concluded that this image applied to human life constitutes part of a symbolic archetype.[4]

The metaphor of journeying offers various advantages for the integration of knowledge. Among other things, it situates human knowledge historically: it is *temporal*, for the subject and for cultures and humanity as a whole. But it is also *provisional*: it is not subsumed completely by any conquest or theory. Similarly, this metaphor gives reasons to integrate *extra-rational factors*, such as the imagination, into the cognitive process. What has been the impact of science fiction literature, such as that of Jules Verne or Ray Bradbury, in exciting interest and promoting research on the solar system and space in general?[5] Every dimension of human knowledge includes temporality and imagination without which there would not be knowledge itself. This is emphasized by contemporary hermeneutic philosophy (Heidegger, Gadamer, Ricoeur and others).[6]

The metaphor of the 'journey' has to be applied by analogy

This is so, given that each story is original. There are children who live only a few days and old people whose lives last for almost a hundred years. There are those who will never know hunger and others who will walk hand in hand with famine. There are those who will access higher studies with complex specialist writings and those who will only know oral language. There are men and women whose habitual landscape will be the natural world and others whose daily background will be grey walls and artificial city lights. In brief, there are no two exactly identical ways.

[3] 'The ideas of way, travel and return have formed the Western awareness whether Greek or biblical. Abraham and Ulysses, Aeneas and Tobias return to their homeland, march towards the foundation of a new city or to the discovery of a promised land. They would stop being if they stopped marching. To be a man is to become one, managing to get to the homeland. To exist is to march towards the finish, the goal, after having discovered the way. From the Platonism of Plotinus and Saint Augustine to the militant Marxism of Bloch, these two words: "way – homeland", make the human adventure make sense' (González De Cardedal 1995: 485–6).

[4] As Alonso Schökel uses it in the exegesis of the Psalms: 'I call this symbol (the way) archetypical because it departs from a radical experience of space and in a latter moment it generates symbols'; it is characterized as being 'basic and universal', not conditioned by culture (Alonso Schökel 1984: n. 6). The subject of way and road is recurrent in biblical thinking (cf. 'way' in AAVV 1975: 72–4). The metaphor of the journey is used in Christian thinking, e.g. the Christian undergoes a 'long journey with small boats' (Gregory of Nazianzus, *Theological Poems* 1).

[5] Cf. the recent statements of the author of 'Martian Chronicles' about the need to conquer Mars and space in general, basing it in the vastness of the cosmos and man's loneliness in it (Bradbury 2004).

[6] Cf. Ricoeur 1982–5.

2. The Person as the Ultimate Knower

Modern Western philosophy based its thinking on the knowing subject (Descartes: *ego cogitans*; Kant: the transcendental subject). Scientific thinking and hermeneutical philosophy have more recently contributed to the dissolution of the idea of an isolated man, a *tabula rasa*, a 'blank sheet', which can receive knowledge with an absolute naivety.

On the one hand, science has shown us that we are part of an evolutionary process and that we carry in our bodies and genes the accumulation of such a process. Somehow we *are* this process and we watch the universe by means of the features given by our genetic structure. There is a 'transcendental' structure of perception which is in our inner self, and that implies a very slow and complex evolution of matter and living corporality. In other words, we sense the cosmos because we have it in our structure.[7]

On the other hand, the sciences of language and hermeneutic philosophy have shown us that we always learn from a given language. Our current debate would not be the same if we lived in the tenth century and expressed ourselves in Latin, even less if we were in the same century but in the land of the Inca, in modern Peru. Obviously, language is also a result of intellectual activity and it is modified by the acquisition of new knowledge and new techniques.[8] Nowadays we are less naive as regards human knowledge.

3. The Horizon

Literal sense: geographical and anthropological

'Horizon' has primarily a *geographical* meaning: it is the line that limits the visible surface of the Earth from an observer's position. It can also be used with a different scope; thus, in the psychological or logical sphere it may be the more or less broad field where thinking takes place.

Philosophical sense

In philosophical discussion, the term 'horizon' offers different meanings.[9] The basic meaning of this word may be linked to Kant, who used it to mean the 'limit of knowledge'.[10] Nevertheless, phenomenology has given it a greater force: for example, Husserl points out that 'every personal experience has an horizon'.[11]

---

[7] Artigas 2003.

[8] 'Each language expresses the world in its own way. Each language build worlds and counter worlds in its own way' (Steiner 1993: 75–6).

[9] Cf. Ferrater Mora 1969: 873.

[10] Cf. Ferrater Mora 1969: 872.

[11] *Cartesianische Meditationen*, 19, Husserliana, I. 81, both cited in Ferrater Mora 1969; the quotation from Ferrater Mora 1969: 872.

Ortega y Gasset develops the concept of horizon making reference to a 'vital horizon'[12] and a 'historic horizon'.[13] When interpreting the circumstances in which we have to live, and by interpreting ourselves insofar as we pretend to be within such circumstances, 'we define the horizon within which we have to live'. He adds that *'such a group of securities as we manage to produce, to construct an understanding of our circumstances* ... is the world, the vital horizon'. The vital horizon is closely linked to the historic horizon: people are formed within 'horizons'. Xavier Zubiri points out another reflection about the horizon: the familiar 'dealing with things' forms the horizon of human vision.

The philosopher of hermeneutics Hans Georg Gadamer has used this idea abundantly. His concept of horizon is as follows:

> The horizon is the range of vision that includes everything that can be seen from a particular vantage point. Applying this to the thinking mind, we speak of narrowness of horizon, of the possible expansion of horizon, of the opening up of new horizons etc. The word has been used in philosophy since Nietzsche and Husserl to characterise the way in which thought is tied to its finite determination, and the nature of the law of expansion of the range of vision. A person who has no horizon is a man who does not see far enough and hence overvalues what is nearest to him. Contrariwise, to have an horizon means not to be limited to what is nearest, but to be able to see beyond it. A person who has an horizon knows the relative significance of everything within his horizon, as near or far, great or small.[14]

The horizon is something not closed but expanding:

> Just as the individual is never simply an individual, because he is always involved with others, so too the closed horizon that is supposed to enclose a culture is a abstraction. The historical movement of human life consists in the fact that it is never utterly bound to any one standpoint, and hence can never have a truly closed horizon. The horizon is, rather, something into which we move and that moves with us. Horizons change for a person who is moving. Thus the horizon of the past, out of which all human life lives and which exists in the form of tradition, is always in motion.[15]

4. Humans Culturally Situated

A human being is an incomplete and structurally half-capable being. He must necessarily build culture to survive: he is naturally cultural. Culture is a hermeneutical and relational horizon. On the one hand, culture offers the person a particular interpretation of reality nourished by the complex assembly of worldviews given by traditions, beliefs, art, philosophy, and so on. Through culture, the subject understands and guides himself. At the same time, culture

---

[12] *En torno a Galileo, Obras Completas*, V.32 (quoted from Ferrater Mora 1969: 873).
[13] *Obras completas*, III.289–95 (quoted from Ferrater Mora 1969: 873).
[14] Gadamer 1988: 269.
[15] Gadamer 1988: 271. Cf. the exposition on horizon by Gadamer in Gómez Heras 1985: 49–59.

gives a link with reality: the person settles down in his/her connection with the world drawn from this immense pre-comprehensive cultural net, at a particular place and time.

Hermeneutic horizons of culture

Culture is composed of diverse dimensions acting as horizons of interpretation for the individual person.

Common experience: popular wisdom

The common experience of the people is treasured as popular wisdom. Sayings, proverbs, popular symbols, knit a very complex net of understanding of the world, of the divine and the human, which is synthesized and transmitted in a simple way and which acts as a referent of sense for the living situated person.[16]

Aesthetic experience

By means of art, man generates a new space in the cosmos; somehow, he creates a new territory of figures which is transformed into a perceptive and hermeneutic space of the universe and of the human, a new audible, tactile and visible universe which enables an original perception of the world within which the human being lives, journeys and draws nourishment. It is a kind of 'map of the world'.[17] This new stage set by artistic activity produces a modification not only in geography but also in the perceiving subject. On the one hand, the exterior territory changes: the existence of paintings, sculptures, buildings, musical compositions, novels, implies a phenomenal and ontological novelty. On the other hand, this *iconic* novelty awakens a multiplicity of sensations and unique understandings. The 'sensing' subjects enter a new world that somehow *transforms them.*[18] Thus, art transforms not only the physical but also human territory. It makes no difference whether Hamlet existed or not: in the human universe there is at work a view of revenge and destiny that constitutes a hermeneutic space, which one can enter and then exit somehow transformed.

Philosophical knowledge

A particular way of conscious interpretation of the universe is philosophy. As a cultural fact, philosophical thinking functions as a reference space for big questions about reality. The traveller meets a set of interwoven discussions that acts as a frame in which to raise and attempt to answer questions about the

---

[16] As an example of interconnection between popular wisdom and religious revelation, cf. Alonso Schökel 1984.

[17] Balzer 1975: 200.

[18] 'After visiting a museum, you leave with a different vital feeling than that with which you went in: if you have really experienced art, the world would have become lighter and more luminous' (Gadamer 1977: 73).

mystery of being. The mere presence of figures such as Plato, Aristotle, Descartes, Aquinas, Kant and Hegel operates as a strong horizon of confrontation with reality: to ask yourself about nature or knowledge without them is different from asking the same questions with them. Contact with the universal philosophical tradition provokes an awareness of the interconnection of problems and solutions which have been accepted or rejected by others, a series of practical consequences which have taken shape in the actual history of peoples.

Scientific knowledge

More recently in human history, the sciences have taken on an increasing role becoming the hermeneutic horizon that most powerfully influences the understanding and transformation of the world. By means of a combination of experience and the mathematization of reality, the natural sciences offer the individual a perspective on the microscopic and macroscopic dimensions of the universe far superior to that which can be sensed by an isolated individual. A twenty-first-century person knows there are bacteria and viruses, molecules and atoms, infinitesimal realities at normal levels of sight; and also knows that there are stars thousands of millions of light years distant and, consequently, knows of time and space. This offers a prodigious expansion of observation of the landscape which a person crosses.

Religious experience

Religions offer a horizon with the tonality of the Absolute: there is someone or something that transcends the relative and ephemeral dimensions of the rest of the landscape which man crosses. This may be called 'god' or 'gods' and its fundamental feature is to appear as absolute. Historical religions have been built on this belief. In general terms, religions admit some kind of revelation or intercourse with divine beings. These beings may or may not have a personal character, but they all confer on the human horizon a definite, 'strong', clear dimension. This is the 'Horizon' (with a capital letter) under which the horizons of other cultural fields link up. In other words, there is something definite in the landscape, something that gives it its ultimate tonality and consistency. Without it, the rest of the partial horizons lose their meaningfulness. In fact, religious experience tends to produce a perspective centred in the absolute otherness of *someone* or *someones* or *something* that provides a definite meaning to the subject and his or her background. Religion acts as an ultimate structure of configuration of the perception of the journeying subject: there is nothing beyond; eventually, whatever there may be lies under the religious horizon.

Theology: an experience reasoned from the revealed absolute

Theology is the conjunction of the experience of revealed religion and the historical use of human rationality.[19] Briefly, theology is the intelligence of faith, such as I present it based on my experience of the religious tradition itself – '*fides quaerens intellectum*' (Anselm).

From the point of view of the present paper, theology must be considered as an objective frame of symbolic and speculative discourses that acts as a referent, either rational or trans-rational, for the believer.[20] As a cultural fact, theology has had a high orientating efficacy: it has enlightened the formulation of faith, of the substrates of moral life both individual and collective, of religious art, of concrete ways of living spirituality, and so on. Europe, for example, would be unthinkable without the influence of figures such as Saint Augustine, Saint Athanasius, Saint Maximus the Confessor, and others. That is to say, not only has religion a historical efficiency but theology too has historical and cultural effects.

Christian theology in particular has used philosophy as a primary intellectual tool. Disciplines such as philology, literary criticism, and so forth, were also used, but until well into the modern age were secondary to philosophy. From the nineteenth century onwards an overwhelming incorporation of scientific disciplines – human and natural sciences – took place.[21] Naturally, this integration coincided with the development of the sciences during the last two centuries. Nowadays a theology that excludes philology, history, textual criticism, and similar studies is unthinkable.[22] Diverse theological streams use other disciplines such as sociology, psychology and different versions of hermeneutics. For instance, in Latin America, particularly since the 1970s, social sciences have been used in theological reflection.[23]

5. Excluding Horizons?

The question of whether theology is a science was stated in the thirteenth century, using the concept of Aristotelian *episteme*[24] as a model. The revolution in modern times in the concept of 'science' continues in the present epistemological debate in which philosophy and theology have not only lost the main, guiding role that they used to have but also have to legitimate themselves

---

[19] Kern 1990: 483–4.

[20] Cf. Forte 1990.

[21] Florio 2002.

[22] In Roman Catholic thought it is enough to quote two official documents: Pontificia Comisión Bíblica 1996 (original 1993); Comisión Teológica Internacional 2000 (original text in *Enchiridion Vaticanum*).

[23] Boff 1998.

[24] Cf. Saint Thomas Aquinas, *ST* Ia, q. 1, aa. 2–6. As a historical view, cf. Wohlmuth 1995, especially ch. 3: 'Theologie als Wissenschaft', pp. 63–99. For a reflection from a dialogue with the modern concept of science: Peacocke 1993.

in a context which *a priori* excludes them as partners in dialogue.[25] However, nowadays a new space has opened for philosophy and religion probably because of disenchantment with reason as it was conceived by modernity and recognition of the limitation of the sciences in understanding the universe and handling the forces it reveals. To some extent, the need for reflective instances different from merely experimental ones in thinking about reality is being admitted in the scientific community.

The informative and visual tide that each individual receives is such that it should be taken into account that the concrete subject has a permanent perceptive fragmentation. If it is true that the actual person is one who understands, we have to admit that the process of synthesis is carried out at the same time in the light of an objective epistemological debate in every individual, as each one essays successive attempts at developing a worldview starting from the multiplicity of phenomena and experiences of which they are subjects.

The religious horizon is the most mysterious one because it is manifested as hidden among other phenomenal frames. This horizon is distant and close at the same time: distant because it cannot be reached by factual experience or by merely rational understanding; close, because it is regarded as a 'frame of frames', i.e. as a necessary condition for the existence of the landscape, as the intimate consistency of the contours that face one's senses and intelligence.

According to those religions that sustain a personal idea of the divinity, the Horizon takes the shape of the personal. In this way, a 'someone', an entity which can be addressed as 'you', embraces the whole. The global landscape acquires the characteristic of the personal. This does not mean that rational and empirical explanations of the cosmos fade, but that the last referent of the whole is not a theory, or a mathematical formula, not even an immobile motor or a faceless architect, but, on the contrary, a personal subject with physiognomy and expression. Moreover, for revealed religions, the Horizon takes the initiative and comes to meet the person. In fact, for these religions the divine personal enters worldly topography and the human stage.[26] Something absolute and personal appears in the landscape: it is a Someone who takes part and talks. In this way, the apparently 'objective' and anonymous reality acquires not only the dimension of something 'made' personally but also something which becomes a vehicle and location through which the divine 'You' manifests Himself and acts.

A last detail about the theological Horizon is given by the Christian religion: this Horizon is three-personal and – by the way it is present in the cosmos and

---

[25] In his voluminous work *La investigación científica*, the physicist and epistemologist Mario Bunge states: 'Science is a style of thinking and acting: precisely, the most recent, the most universal and fruitful one of all the styles' (p. 3). 'An aspect of objectivity that common sense and science share is *naturalism*, i.e. the reluctance to admit entities which are not natural (e.g. an abstract thought) and ways or sources of knowledge which are not natural (e.g. metaphysical intuition)' (p. 4). These remarks clearly show the autonomy of science but likewise look down on other ways of knowledge. Bunge 2000.

[26] Cf. Florio 1999.

history – it takes the figurative shape of the same cosmic and human horizon. In the first place, it is trinitarian. This means that the Someone who is personal and absolute is in fact threefold, three 'whos': Father, Son and Holy Spirit. The Horizon splits into threé. This division of the last frame of perception and understanding does not imply an attenuation of the personal horizon, as if it were diluted in a plurality – as happens in polytheism. On the contrary, this distinction implies a stressing of the personal colouring since it is about a mystery of communion in the same Absolute Horizon. The horizon at the end of the landscape and of human life, is a 'familiar' Horizon.

On the other hand, by means of the Incarnation and the effusion of the Spirit, the Horizon gets closer, almost blending with the cosmic and anthropological horizon. Integrated in the human landscape, acquiring the biology and physics of the human being, it unfolds its presence under the phenomenology of man. Some people think that at some point of the human journey there was an irruption of the Horizon in the middle of the way. Some found it, listened to it, touched it, laughed and ate with it, abandoned it, murdered it, experienced it as newly alive. This episode, unique and non-repeatable, object of historical questionings but above all a trans-generational experience of faith, sustains the journey of innumerable multitudes. The certainty that in a given moment the Absolute Horizon ate and drank on the human way, opening a new space of understanding for humanity, nourished and nourishes the journey of many individuals.

The personal as horizon

Is there a personal entity behind the set of images that appear in the traveller's consciousness? We may wonder if the hermeneutic horizons that accompany man give him a personal dimension. Sciences do not offer a personal frame. The same consciousness of methodological limitation has caused the restriction of every 'personalizing' intention of reality:[27] there is no Watchmaker or Architect beyond the universe. The philosophy of the last centuries, except for certain streams (deisms, personalisms, transcendental existentialisms) was generally not able to visualize a personal face at the end of the analyses. On the other hand, not all religions offer an absolute with a personal character. In some cases, the personality of the divinities is too different from that of humans.

The question that we may now ask is: Do we need this personal horizon? Or rather, is the existence of a Destiny or simply an impersonal Logos enough, as was suggested by high cultural expressions such as the Greek tragedies?[28] The modern age in the West knew similar ways of wisdom in the observance of impersonal forces: the Hegelian absolute Spirit, Kantian practical reason, the

---

[27] Think about the difficulty that anthropology has in determining the historical origin of the person: cf. Arzuaga 2003.

[28] Cf. Moeller 1989.

Freudian unconsciousness, Marxist social dialectic, Comtian science, Spencerian evolutional becoming, the plain freedom of French Illuminism, the capital of economic liberalism. In every case, the same salvific effect was sought: serenity in thinking and action as a consequence of docility in the face of *something* – not *someone*.

Philosophical personalisms rise up in the face of this possibility, above all in the religions of the Person. In all these cases, serenity on the way lies in the certainty that there is a 'Who' in the origin, in the destination and on the same journey. One is not alone. In contrast to other 'soteriologies', these religions believe salvation is found in a 'meeting-with-someone' and not in an 'obedience-to-something'.

The question about the *real or not-real existence* of the personal subject on which personalisms are based is another topic upon which there are serious disagreements. At the beginning of modernity, everything seems suspicious of this subject: projection (Feuerbach), illusion (Freud), alienation (Marx), fiction (Hume,[29] Borges). There is no longer the idea of the divine, but rather the idea of a personal divinity, since absolute impersonality may be understood within a universe that seems to be almost infinite. The *disjunction* is whether there is a *person or not*.

For this reason, solitude, or rather loneliness,[30] is a key word: you are either accompanied or a lone pilgrim in an impressive cosmos with thousands of millions of years of history and almost infinite distances crowded by stars.

6. The Comprehensive Horizon

Is there one horizon that encompasses the rest? Naturally, this is a question about the Absolute.

The personal absolute

It must be noted that the Absolute Horizon is not necessarily personal. Not all religions refer to personal divinities as Judaism and Christianity do. I wish to highlight the idea that the Absolute Horizon can respond as a 'who' or simply stand out as a mysterious but anonymous support for the human way. The fact that an absolute You accompanies transcendentally the history of the cosmos and humanity is highly relevant. For the moment, it is a Horizon that takes part and engages with, acts freely and intelligently in, the cosmic and human scene.

An original feature of Christianity: trinitarian monotheism

Christianity supplied the concept of a trinitarian Absolute together with the idea of the incarnation or humanization of God. The novelty of the message of

---

[29] Cf. Hume 2003: 209.
[30] González de Cardedal 1995: 149.

Jesus Christ about the divine ontology is that God is three someones – Father, Son and Holy Spirit – without any one being unique. This is about an absolute, sole reality but with three personal poles: a triple fragmentation within a unique transcendent reference. In other words, the definite horizon is conceived as one and, simultaneously, threefold. The late text of Matthew 28.20 presents a resuscitated Jesus Christ who exhorts his disciples to announce the gospel and to 'baptize in the name of the Father, the Son and the Holy Spirit'. The fact is that the primitive Christian community believed that God is one and plural at the same time. This is a central certainty and forms part of the liturgy of primitive Christianity. Moreover, it marks a difference from Jewish mono-personalist monotheism. Nevertheless, trinitarian belief did not find its conceptual frame quickly, thus causing a complex theoretical controversy during the following centuries.

The history of Christian theology teaches that this theological perception – a threefold absolute – was not always a clear one, at least in practical faith and thinking. A theologian from the last century, Karl Rahner, pointed out that in the theology and spirituality of his time a 'forgetfulness' of Trinity had taken place.[31] This situation has been reversed and, in the Christian churches, there has been a new discovery during recent decades of the identity in communion of the unique Absolute.[32]

An absolute in communion

The idea of a tri-personal God caused the elaboration of a category that Aristotle did not know: the substantial relation. Primitive Christianity thought that the deepest reality is this substantially relational reality that is God Himself.[33] Father, Son and Holy Spirit are 'to be for the other' absolutes in the single nature or divine substance.

A way to express this is through the concept of 'communion'. God is a mystery of communion in His deepest reality.[34] Father, Son and Holy Spirit are a unique divine reality, intercommunicating between themselves without reservation. The technical expression *perichoresis* or 'circumincession' was also elaborated.[35] It means that each of the divine persons is in the others without confounding or annulling themselves. Further, each of them is more itself because of its donation to the others. This word expresses a peculiar way of

---

[31] Rahner 1977.

[32] Cf. Florio 1996. Cf. furthermore García Andrade 2000 and González 2000.

[33] 'By means of analogy, the *communio*-Trinitarian unity appears as a *Christian way of understanding reality*. In fact, the elaboration of the Trinitarian doctrine implies the overcoming of an idea of reality characterized by the pre-eminence of the substance and essence that gives way to the primacy of the person and the relationship. The ultimate reality is no longer the substance that lies in itself, but the person who is only conceivable fully in the give and take relation' (Kasper 1986: 351–2).

[34] 'Communion is the deepest and the most founding reality' (Boff 1990: 18).

[35] Dewailly 1970; Prestige 1928.

communion characterized by a donation without reservation and, simultaneously, without confusion.

Projections on the human way

This image of the 'Absolute-communion' has had a great influence on the perception not only of God Himself but also of the whole of reality. It has implied an illumination of the rest of the hermeneutic horizons wherein human being is interpreted. Obviously, this is not about detecting threefold structures in nature and in human life. This has already been done, although without any serious value for knowledge. What lies deep beneath this theological tradition is the following double idea: (a) There is something in common between the triune God and the world, especially the human part, in such a way that we can understand something about the absolute taking our experiential universe as a point of departure; (b) This idea can help us to interpret nature and humanity at a deep level, taking into account that we understand them from their source. Thus, a 'hermeneutic circularity' is produced: the created realities help us understand God, and from this comprehension we come back to seize more deeply natural and human things.[36] In other words, the partial horizons enable us to see the absolute horizon more clearly. The latter, presented as communion, makes it possible to interpret more clearly the horizons that accompany the historical person.

The human traveller, accompanied by various horizons of perception and sense, can be interpreted under the trinitarian pre-comprehension. Nature does not find its ultimate horizon in the numerically impersonal or in physical or chemical forces, nor even in a powerful explosion that may have set everything in motion, but in a mystery of love that expands in a prodigious universe. This process may leave traces of its movement, and even biological life unfolds some aspect of the mysterious eternal *Koinonia*.[37]

The human realm is a privileged place of trinitarian interpretation. The particular human being, especially in the interrelation of human love, family and society, can be read in the light of the Trinity. Considering that God is a mystery of loving relationship, the arenas of loving integration are privileged places for a trinitarian hermeneutics.

This is how we speak about the 'trinitarian family' while parting from it: we interpret the central experiences of the human family – affiliations, paternity, engagement – as an echo of divine communion. For instance, the generation of a human being may be a matter of study for a biologist, the daily experience of an

---

[36] Kasper 1986: 309–11.

[37] 'Today's Christian theology of creation will use, in distinction from Newton, the possibilities of the doctrine of the Trinity in order to describe the relationship of God's transcendence and immanence in creation and in the history of salvation. Perhaps a renewed doctrine of the Trinity would combine the Logos doctrine of the ancient church with contemporary information theory and recognize the activity of the divine spirit in the self transcendence of life and its evolution' (Pannenberg 1993: 65–6).

obstetrician, the frame of understanding of a psychologist or teacher, and even a subject of interest to the philosopher.[38] Likewise, an artist could reflect how wonderful childbirth and maternal tenderness could be. These are all valuable and complementary interpretative horizons. Theology offers a more fundamental perspective: the absolute is trinitarian and familiar. Thus, every birth and every familial community have some correspondence to what God lives intimately, generating the Son, breathing out the Holy Spirit, communing eternally between the three persons.[39]

Social reality has also been conceived by theological thinking from its trinitarian root. Just as the ultimate horizon is a mystery of equality in diversity, society must be seen as an area of different balances. Inequalities do nothing but eclipse the vocation of being a trinitarian image of a person in the social dimension. Furthermore, massification and any type of collectivism threaten this mission since they are ways of depersonalization: in the Trinity, the persons are themselves in plenitude, within a bond of reciprocal communion. This is why the Trinity has been called a 'utopia' or 'social programme'. The trinitarian horizon guides us to an interpretation of the socio-political world that integrates differences in unity. In this sense, it offers an interpretative frame, which is suggestively clear.[40]

7. Conclusion

Let my paper finish with a psalm. It is a poetic prayer in which someone, several centuries before Jesus Christ, expresses awe – a feeling which is common to religion, art, science and philosophy – before the visible and, especially, human being itself.

> O LORD, our Lord, how majestic is your name in all the earth!
> You have set your glory above the heavens.
> From the lips of children and infants you have ordained praise
> because of your enemies, to silence the foe and the avenger.
> When I consider your heavens, the work of your fingers,
> the moon and the stars, which you have set in place,
> what is man that you are mindful of him,
> the son of man that you care for him?
> You made him a little lower than the heavenly beings
> and crowned him with glory and honour.
> You made him ruler over the works of your hands;
> you put everything under his feet:

---

[38] Cf. Piossek Prebisch 1995. Cf. also von Balthasar 1977: 29–30: The child experiences in the face of the mother that the being is beautiful, good and true; at the same time, he feels reality as unity between him and his mother – there is neither cut nor division. The transcendentals or features of the being are, thus, perceived from the very first instants of life.

[39] Just to mention a few authors, cf. Castilla y Cortázar 1996; Del Cura Elena 1991; O'Donnel 1988.

[40] Cf. Nicholls 1981; Gutiérrez 1986; Silanes 1991; Cambón 2000.

> all flocks and herds, and the beasts of the field,
> the birds of the air, and the fish of the sea,
> all that swim the paths of the seas.
> O LORD, our Lord, how majestic is your name in all the earth![41]

Each man and woman that inhabits this universe and moves through its geography in his/her brief personal history is able to experience awe towards reality. Does everyone do it? Did the men and women from Gran Dolina in Atapuerca (Spain) stand in awe of reality 800,000 years ago? Undoubtedly, this type of feeling was present in the masses of anonymous pre-Columbian aborigines – Mayas, Incas, Aztecs, Guaranis – who articulated a religious and artistic answer to the mystery of life. Obviously, awe lies under the experience of the transit from the Myths to the Logos, as happened with the Presocratics. Likewise, Aristotle knew how to express it clearly when he pointed out that awe is the mother of philosophy. Are we to ignore the innumerable artists – painters, sculptors, musicians, poets, dramatists – who have tried to shape some of the beauty latent in the world which they experienced as mystery and plenitude? Even if we move ahead in the apparently cold universe of the scientists who are protected by a legitimate shield of methodological neutrality, we will surely find in a great number of them a feeling of surprise at the prodigious creativity of physical and living beings.

Awe at the originality of humanity and its place in the cosmos can be overshadowed when contemplating its dark side. In fact, war, environmental destruction, oppression of peoples or races, are part of the human phenomenon. Nevertheless, we have to admit that the global panorama of the figure of the human being on earth through time comprises fabulous achievements together with extraordinarily cruel interventions. As a consequence of all these, the human being appears as something different from the rest, not totally explicable just because of evolutionary fate.

Not everyone admits the third idea that springs out of the psalm. However, so long as the horizons of sense with which man tries to interpret the cosmos and himself are broadened and deepened, the density of the question about the Absolute Horizon seems to be increased. This question the psalmist links to the human enigma through a simple question:

> what is man that you are mindful of him,
> the son of man that you care for him?

References

AAVV
    1975   *Concordancia de la Biblia. Nuevo Testamento* (Bilbao: Desclée de Brouwer y Mensajero).

---

[41] Psalm 8 (NIV).

Alonso Schökel, L.
1984   'Una oferta de sensatez. Ensayo sobre la literatura sapiencial', in L.
        A. Schöckel and J. Vilchez (eds), *Sapienciales*, vol. 1: *Proverbios*
        (Madrid: Cristiandad): 17–38.
1986   *Treinta salmos. Poesía y oración* (Madrid).
Artigas, M.
2003   'El diálogo entre ciencia y religión en la actualidad', in E. Urrutia
        Albisua and J. J. Blasquez Ortega (eds), *Ciencia y Religión hoy.*
        Diálogos en torno a la naturaleza (Puebla: OPAEP): 33–57.
Arzuaga, J. L.
2003   *El collar del Neanderthal. En busca de los primeros pensadores* (Barce-
        lona: Debolsillo, 2nd edn).
Balthasar, H. U. von
1977   'El camino de acceso a la realidad de Dios', *Mysterium Salutis* II
        (Madrid: Cristiandad, 2nd edn): 29–30.
Balzer, C.
1975   *Arte, fantasía y mundo* (Buenos Aires: Plus Ultra).
Boff, C.
1998   *Teoria do método teológico* (Petrópolis: Vozes).
Boff, L.
1990   *La Santísima Trinidad es la mejor comunidad* (Madrid: Paulinas).
Bradbury, R.
2004   'Por qué los hombres deben ir a Marte' (Why men must go to
        Mars), *La Nación*, Buenos Aires, 25 January.
Bunge, M.
2000   *La investigación científica* (Mexico: Siglo Veintiuno Editores).
Cambón, E.
2000   *La Trinidad, modelo social* (Madrid: Ciudad Nueva).
Castilla y Cortázar, B.
1996   'La Trinidad como familia. Analogía humana de las procesiones
        divinas', *Annales Theologici* 10: 381–416.
Comisión Teológica Internacional
2000   *Memoria y reconciliación: la Iglesia y las culpas del pasado* (Buenos
        Aires: Paulinas).
Del Cura Elena, S.
1991   'Dios Padre/Madre', in AAVV, *Dios es Padre* (Salamanca: Secre-
        tariado Trinitario).
Dewailly, L. M.
1970   'Communio-communicatio', *Revue des Sciences Philosophiques et
        théologiques*: 46–63.
Ferrater Mora, J.,
1969   *Diccionario de Filosofía*, vol. 1 (Buenos Aires: Sudamericana).
Florio, L.
1996   'Un final de milenio trinitario', *Estudios Trinitarios* 30.3: 421–36.
1999   'El drama y su uso teológico. La novedad metodológica de la

Teodramática de Hans Urs von Balthasar', *Communio* (Argentina) (1999/1): 65–72.

2002 'Teología y disciplinas', *Proyecto* (Argentina) 41: 31–40.

Forte, B.

1990 *La Teología como compañía, memoria y profecía* (Salamanca: Sígueme).

Gadamer, H. G.

1977 *La actualidad de lo bello* (Barcelona: Paidós).

1988 *Truth and Method* (New York: Crossroad).

García Andrade, C.

2000 *La Trinidad: 'software' de Dios* (Reinstalando a Dios en la cultura occidental); (Madrid: Ciudad Nueva).

Gómez Heras, J. M.

1985 *Historia y Razón* (Madrid: Alambra).

González De Cardedal, O.

1995 *Raíz de la esperanza* (Salamanca: Sígueme).

González, M.

2000 *La Trinidad: un nuevo nombre para Dios* (Buenos Aires: Paulinas).

Gutiérrez, G.

1986 *La verdad los hará libres. Confrontaciones* (Lima: Inst. Bartolomé de las Casas).

Hume, D.

2003 *Investigación sobre el conocimiento humano* (Madrid: Alianza editorial).

Kasper, W.

1986 *El Dios de Jesucristo* (Salamanca: Sígueme).

Kern, W.

1990 'Teología', in P. Eicher (ed.), *Diccionario de conceptos teológicos*, vol. 2 (Barcelona: Herder).

Marías, J.

1994 *Mapa del mundo personal* (Madrid: Alianza Editorial, 2nd edn).

Moeller, C.

1989 *Sabiduría griega y paradoja cristiana* (Madrid: Encuentro).

Nicholls, D.

1981 'Images of God and the State: Political Analogy and Religious Discourse', *Theological Studies* 42: 195–215.

O'Donnel, J.

1988 'The Trinity as Divine Community: A Critical Reflection Upon Recent Theological Developments', *Gregorianum* 69: 5–34.

Pannenberg, W.

1993 *Toward a Theology of Nature: Essays on Science and Faith* (Lousiville: Westminster/John Knox Press).

Peacocke, A.

1993 *Theology for a Scientific Age: Being and Becoming – Natural, Divine, and Human* (Minneapolis: Fortress Press).

Pieper, J.
1970　　*Muerte e inmortalidad* (Barcelona: Herder).

Piossek Prebisch, L.
1995　　'Notas acerca de la mujer y la filosofía', *Communio* (Argentina) (1995/1): 45–51.

Pontificia Comisión Bíblica
1996　　*La interpretación de la Biblia en la Iglesia* (Madrid: PPC).

Prestige, L.
1928　　' "Perichoreo" and "Perichoresis" in the Fathers', *Journal of Theological Studies*: 242–52.

Rahner, K.
1977　　'El Dios Trino como principio y fundamento trascendente de la historia de la salvación', in *Mysterium Salutis*, vol. 2 (Madrid: Cristiandad, 2nd edn): 269–77.

Ricoeur, P.
1982–5　*Temps et récit* (3 vols; Paris: Seuil).

Silanes, N.
1991　　*La Santísima Trinidad, programa social del Cristianismo* (Salamanca: Secretariado Trinitario).

Steiner, G.
1993　　*Presencias reales* (Buenos Aires: Espasa-Calpe).

Wohlmuth, J. (ed.)
1995　　*Katholische Theologie heute. Eine Einführung* (Würzburg: Echter Verlag).

Where Streams Meet?

Ecology, Wisdom and Beauty in Bulgakov, von Balthasar and Aquinas

Celia Deane-Drummond

An area of perhaps surprising neglect in science and religion debates is the relationship between religious concern and environmental science, including the science of climate change. The topic is avoided, perhaps, because of its political implications and its association with campaign groups and organizations filtered through media debates. But what could be more relevant to a consideration of cultural dynamics than reflection on the applied sciences that bear on the global commons? What is more pressing in a global cultural context than both scientific and religious reflection on not simply the survival of non-human species, but threats to human survival as well? While such a discussion inevitably includes ethics, it also impinges on religious beliefs. For issues that arise from such reflection strike at the core of human existence on this planet, human identity and meaning and the survival of life, alongside how to interpret an understanding of God.

There is also a tendency in science and religion debates to avoid those sciences that seem to be less clear-cut in terms of predictability. Climate change is one such area, but in view of its cultural, social and political importance, it is a critical area for engagement with religious concern. While it is becoming fashionable, at least in some theological circles, to speak about theology from particular situated contexts, the difficulties with such an approach is that global issues are not always addressed, and the possibility of a genuine conversation with traditions other than one's own becomes problematic. The present discussion is limited by being confined to the Christian tradition, but aims to look wider than one particular strand in this tradition, while recognizing that the issues presented in environmental science are global and multicultural and would therefore deserve wider analysis with other religious traditions in order to do justice to such complex issues.

I will begin this discussion with a brief introduction to the science of climate change. Space does not permit a full discussion of these issues; the intention is rather to set the scene for subsequent theological analysis. The intention of this outline is to give some indication of the scientific debates, while not presuming that theological reflection can directly contribute to such debates. The questions that arise from this discussion are threefold. First, what are the implications for theological reflection in the light of predictions anticipated by climate change? In other words, what kind of envisioning might be needed in order to deal theologically with such complex global problems? Are notions of divine providence intellectually sustainable in such a scenario? Second, what positively can theological analysis bring to the discussion? Third, what might theological ethics contribute to setting priories for action?

Rather than offer a general account of Christian theological reflection in response to the science of climate change, I am homing in on a critical discussion of the wisdom tradition of the Eastern Orthodox writer Sergii Bulgakov, comparing this with an analysis of beauty in the thought of the Roman Catholic theologian Hans Urs von Balthasar, and moving towards a more practical consideration of the virtues in the thought of Thomas Aquinas.[1] I will argue that wisdom in such writers is a powerful reminder of the way theology can contribute to a hermeneutics of environmental science. In addition, I will suggest that further reflection on the notion of beauty provides, like wisdom, a way of mediating between scientific and theological language.[2] In the light of ecological concerns, both Eastern and Western streams of wisdom can meet and complement each other. I will argue that it is in the meeting of these strands that the theological approach to the somewhat gloomy results predicted through climate change science can become enlivened and enriched, and that it becomes possible to reawaken a sense of caring for the global commons that is difficult when faced with rational scientific discourse alone. Such discussion inevitably includes some theoretical and somewhat abstract theological analysis; the challenge is to move from such analysis to liturgical and ethical practice, to permeate such theological reflection into what might be termed the performative dimension.

Climate Change

The projected rate of climate change this century is far greater than anything experienced by the earth in the last 10,000 years, mostly caused by human activity through the burning of fossil fuels (Houghton 2004). There have always been sceptics who challenge the detailed predictions anticipated through climate change models. Some will also argue that the climate is simply too complex to model with any accuracy. Mostly the challenges relate, nonetheless,

---

[1] In drawing on the work of these writers I am not thereby claiming that these authors represent the Eastern and Western traditions in their entirety, but rather serve as illustrative examples of complementary thinking that can arise from a cross-cultural discussion.

[2] In offering a discussion of beauty as well as wisdom I would like to acknowledge conversations with Peter Barrett, who stimulated me to think further about the importance of beauty as well as wisdom, especially in the context of cross-cultural debates (see Barrett 2004).

to the *extent* of change anticipated, rather than whether there is any change taking place at all. While media exaggerations of global disaster need to be resisted, the accumulated scientific evidence seems to weigh far more in favour of increasing unpredictability. The intergovernmental panel on climate change accumulated detailed empirical evidence from a network of hundreds of distinguished scientists working all over the world, who came to consensual agreements about climate change.[3] This panel was also ready to admit where there were gaps in information, and the extent to which predictions are reliable.[4] The overall consensus is, in spite of the uncertainties, that most of the observed global warming over the last fifty years is due to changes in greenhouse gas concentrations. Hence, it would not make any sense to ignore such warnings, for even if the sceptics are right, changes will inevitably take place, but it will just take slightly longer compared with the most pessimistic forecasts. It is also possible to measure more accurately the probability of expected changes taking place, and the level of uncertainty in such predictions. Hence it becomes possible to ascertain the level of confidence one can have in the claims that are made as a result of climate change models.

The impacts of climate change on the ecology of both human and non-human communities are through effects such as rising sea level and the increase in number and frequency of climate extremes; floods and droughts are becoming more common due to a more intense hydrological cycle (IPCC 2001). The changes that are considered to be very likely, that is have a 90–99 per cent probability, if trends continue, include higher maximum temperatures and more hot days over nearly all land areas, higher minimum temperatures, fewer cold days and frost days over nearly all land areas, reduced diurnal temperature range over most land areas, increase in heat index over most land areas, and more intense precipitation events over many areas. Those nations that are the most subject to loss are commonly the poorer parts of the world, especially those in the subtropical regions, where there is far more limited capacity to deal with the problems. Geological data suggests that the eustatic sea level, which corresponds to volume, has changed at an average rate of 0.1–0.2 mm/year over the last 3,000 years, one tenth of that occurring in the twentieth century (IPCC 2001: 175). Low-lying lands, such as Bangladesh, or island communities, are the most vulnerable to sea level rises, which could lead to swamping of entire communities (Houghton 2004: 150–2). Such devastating loss will lead to a huge number of environmental refugees, estimated to be 150 million by 2050 if

---

[3] See, for example, www.ipcc.ch.

[4] The remaining uncertainties include, for example, (a) An honest admission of some remaining discrepancies between temperature change seen in observations and models. However, the models have improved over time. (b) Uncertainties in estimates of internal climate change variability from both models and observations. These uncertainties do not, however, negate the claim that climate change has taken place. (c) Uncertainty in the extent of impact of solar and volcanic forcing, since these measurements have only been accurate for two decades. (d) Uncertainties in the extent of anthropogenic forcing other than greenhouse gas, e.g. effects of aerosols and changes in land use. (IPCC 2001: 199–201)

present rates of change continue (Myers and Kent 1995). The resulting social problems inevitably raise the issue of environmental justice, namely the proportionally greater impact of climate change on the poorer communities of the world, which are, in relative terms, contributing significantly less to the anthropogenic effects on climate change.

The estimated reduction in carbon dioxide emissions required to stabilize climate exceeds that of the Kyoto protocols. So far the concentration of carbon dioxide as predicted by emissions has not normally taken into account the effect of climate change itself on the carbon cycle, so that at higher temperatures there is an increase in respiration from living organisms in soil, as well as dieback of forests. Hence the problem is likely to be even worse than that predicted on the basis of emissions originating from human activities (Houghton and Jenkins 2004: 5). In the UK a reduction in carbon dioxide emission by 60 per cent from current levels might seem an idealistic task. However, the actual cost of making such a change would amount to 0.02 per cent of GDP, or six months economic growth over a half century to 2050 (UK Government Policy and Innovation Unit 2002: 7.115; IPCC 2001: 291–354).

There are, of course, many other signs of environmental degradation including unsustainable population growth, deterioration of land quality, river and sea pollution, and loss in biodiversity, much of which is indirectly related to the former. The rate of extinction of species caused by human activity is a thousand times that due to natural extinctions. What is lacking is the necessary will and motivation to make changes, to move away from a sense of inertia. In addition, environmental science requires a multidisciplinary approach that is counter to the trends in modern science towards specialization and fragmentation.

Trinitarian Wisdom in Sergii Bulgakov

Christian theology, especially through the wisdom tradition, can serve as a means through which to think holistically, a hermeneutic for reflection on complex scientific knowledge, such as of climate change, and also a means of recapturing the importance of both creation and the earth for Christian theology.[5] The more specific question to be addressed here is: What are the special features of Bulgakov's theology that are important to revisit in the light of contemporary ecological concerns? In particular, how might it be possible to appropriate elements of Orthodox thinking so as to find ways through the theological and ethical dilemmas presented by current research on climate change? Climate change research anticipates a breakdown of order, an unpredictable future, a pushing beyond the limits of what is sustainable in terms of human and non-human ecology. What does divine providence mean in such circumstances? Wisdom, I suggest, appears at the boundary of order and chaos,

---

[5] I have given an outline elsewhere of the importance of wisdom for theology, and its contribution to dialogues with science (Deane-Drummond 2000).

it figures as a limit concept where both scientific and theological models come up against their own limitations. While ecology is now more likely to speak of disturbance, rather than order and harmony, disturbance from the perspective of climate change is more likely to have very negative connotations, since the conditions anticipated become inhospitable for life. Such studies could easily lead to a sense of despair. Wisdom, on the other hand, seeks to incorporate the truth embedded in such claims in terms of empirical knowledge, while pointing beyond them to transcendental images that serve to reawaken a love and passion for the earth.

Bulgakov (1871–1944) was a controversial figure, whose theology attempted to stretch beyond the limits of what many regard as acceptable within the Orthodox tradition, yet he was also someone who was dedicated to finding ways to foster ecumenism across different Christian traditions (Galaher 2002: 24–55).[6] Bulgakov's early work on the *Philosophy of Economy* (1912) emphasized Sophia as the unity and the coherence of the cultural process in all fields, including economics, politics, science and the arts. In *The Unfading Light* (1917) his theology of creation is not simply about divine condescension, but also the upward aspiration of all creatures towards God. This is important, for it puts correct emphasis on human responsibility. Bulgakov's sophiology mediates between the possible extremes of an abstract pantheism, which is a deified world lacking humanity, and abstract trinitarianism, which amounts to a super-essential Trinity disconnected from the world. He tries to achieve this through his notion of Sophia, as divine and creaturely, yet not existing as a separate hypostasis.[7]

In reinstating theology in sophiological terms Bulgakov wanted to go beyond the more traditional Orthodox notions that Sophia (or divine Wisdom) simply means that God created the world wisely, or that Sophia is equivalent to the second person of the Trinity, the Logos. It is therefore necessary to outline the shape of his sophiology in trinitarian terms in order to spell out in more depth the rich meaning that he attributes to Sophia in a theological sense. This is, of course, abstract theological speculation, but I suggest that it gives much more theological depth to simply stating that God is Wisdom. Authors such as Nicholas Lash have commented on the tendency for a lack of depth of theological reflection in science-and-religion discourse (Lash 1996). Hence I suggest that there is a need to present constructive approaches to theology as an aspect of the dialogue, rather than simply a passive adjustment of theology in the light of science.

---

[6] He sought to mediate between the rejection of modernity as the Antichrist by conservative traditionalists and its acceptance as a coming of age of humanity by liberals (Valliere 2000: 262). This is more helpful than the position adopted by other contemporary Orthodox theologians, such as Philip Sherrard, who equates science with modernity, this being itself causative of ecological devastation (Sherrard 1992).

[7] Paul Valliere believes that Bulgakov portrays Sophia as a fourth hypostasis in the Trinity in *The Unfading Light*, but this is a position that Bulgakov vigorously denies in his book *The Wisdom of God* published subsequently in 1937 (Bulgakov 1993) (Valliere 2000: 271).

Bulgakov gives primacy to the Father in the initial creation of the world through Sophia, but the Son and Holy Spirit are also involved, since Sophia is a common characteristic of all persons of the Trinity (Bulgakov 1993: 104–5). Viewing Sophia in trinitarian terms is important, for it is a reminder of the interrelationships that are at the heart of the Godhead. While some theologians have taken such interrelationships to be an endorsement of God as Trinity in ecological terms, I suggest that in reflecting on issues such as climate change it is necessary to go even beyond an endorsement of the importance of inter-relationships (Moltmann 1985; Deane-Drummond 1997). Climate change presents us with highly complex global interrelationships linking living beings with the earth, on a scale previously unimaginable through ecological studies alone. For Bulgakov the revelation through Wisdom of the second and third persons of the Trinity in the creation of the world is also a form of *concealment*, or kenosis, under the guise of the hypostasis of the Father (Bulgakov 1993: 69). In the initial creation of the world, the hovering shadow of Wisdom in the Logos is the locus of ideal forms or prototypes, while Wisdom in the Holy Spirit acts through giving capacity for existence as such. Bulgakov argues that Sophia is non-hypostatic, while capable of being hypostatized in any given hypostasis of Father, Son or Holy Spirit. Divine Sophia, like divine Glory, is embedded in the divine *ousia*, or Being.[8]

The Father is the initial Subject of Sophia, and in this sense 'She represents the disclosure of his transcendence, of the silence and mystery of the Godhead; she is the Father manifesting himself through the Son and the Holy Spirit' (Bulgakov 1993: 51). The reference to Sophia in terms of *silence* and *mystery* is important, for it presents Sophia in contemplative, mystical mode and reminds the reader of the holiness of God as paradigmatic for thinking theologically. Of course, there are other modes of thinking about Sophia that are more practical, but I suggest that the contemplative mode is the initial basis on which right action can be fostered. This step is important when facing complex issues, such as climate change, which threaten to disorientate and lead to fatalism and despair.

What is the precise relationship between Sophia and Logos in the second person? The Logos is the hypostasis of the Word, but the content of divine thought disclosed in the hypostasis of the Word is 'in the form of Sophia, or the divine Wisdom. It is this content, in particular, which touches and embraces everything' (Bulgakov 1993: 69). It is for this reason that Bulgakov can describe Sophia as the Image of the Logos, which itself is the Image of the Father. It is in this sense that Bulgakov writes of 'all the manifold forms of being, as many as, having their own specific character, are thereby included in

---

[8] This, itself, is controversial from an Orthodox perspective, since Orthodox theologians prefer to speak of the energies of God being visible, while the essence of God is necessarily *always* hidden from view (Lossky 1957: 78–9). Bulgakov does seem to try to take this teaching into account in his admission that God as Absolute is unknown and unknowable, hence expressive of theological antinomy. He suggests that 'The Absolute is God, but God is not the Absolute insofar as the world relates to him' (Bulgakov 1993: 76).

the content of divine Sophia' (Bulgakov 1993: 43). Here he reflects the traditional teaching of John of Damascus, Maximus the Confessor, Athanasius,
Augustine and Gregory the Theologian (Nazianzus), where God contains the
divine prototypes or *paradeigmata* as reflected in the destinies or *proorismoi* of all
creatures (Bulgakov 1993: 64–5). This aspect is important, for it provides a way
of giving special value to all the variegated creatures of the earth, not just
human beings, as all are caught up and in some sense expressive of divine
Wisdom. In this sense one might argue that destroying such creatures or
putting impediments to their flourishing are not simply an attack on the
creatures themselves, as gifts from God, but also an attack on the Creator.

   Bulgakov gives the Logos a special status in that 'The hypostasis of the Logos
is the only one which completely determines by himself the content of Sophia,
the ideal all, the all-embracing "organism" of ideas, and the ideal unity of them
all' (Bulgakov 1993: 47).[9] At the same time the importance of the concrete
appearance of the Logos in the Son should not be overlooked. For it is a
reminder once more of the love of God for creation, rooted and grounded in
self-giving as both Christ incarnate and Christ crucified and risen (Deane-
Drummond 2004a). Bulgakov has achieved a clever synthesis, for Sophia is in
herself lacking a hypostasis, so could be thought of as analogous to the energies
of God, such as Justice, or Life, while at the same time Sophia is both expressed
in the hypostases of the Trinity and integral to God's *ousia*.[10] In addition,
Bulgakov is at pains to insist, at least in his later work, that Sophia remains
non-hypostatic, even though the Father, Logos and Spirit are the Subjects of
Sophia.

   What might be the role of the Holy Spirit through Sophia? Bulgakov puts
emphasis on the role of Spirit as Sophia in engendering *form*, rather than *content*,
the provision of Logos as Sophia. He also speaks of the activity of the Holy
Spirit in portraying the transparency of the relationship of love between Father
and Son, linking the work of the Spirit specifically with beauty. Yet the Holy
Spirit is not just form, but also the one who 'transforms the world of ideas into
a living and real essence, into a self sufficient creation of God' (Bulgakov 1993:
48). This echoes something of the association of the Holy Spirit with the giver
of life, hence, affirmative of all the processes that go to make life possible
(Edwards 2004). While Bulgakov acknowledges an evolutionary history of the
world, so that he can say that it is characterized by 'becoming, emergence,
development, fulfilment', at the same time he believes that this process is the
expression of divine prototypes, of divine Sophia in the creaturely, still in a

---

[9] In this he seems to be taking into account the primacy given by the Orthodox tradition to the
    connection between Sophia and the Logos, while resisting restricting Sophia to the Logos.

[10] Lossky (1957) argues that Bulgakov puts the personhood of God before God's nature in an
    exaggerated reaction to Western theology. What seems to be at issue here is the way Bulgakov
    has used what has normally been considered an aspect of the Logos, namely Wisdom, to
    interpret God's *ousia*. Yet to suggest that this puts personhood before God's nature only
    applies if a reinterpretation of the nature of God is impermissible, and if there is no con-
    nection between them.

present state of potentiality, or *dynamis*, awaiting its full actualization through Sophia (Bulgakov 1993: 75).

Sophia's dynamism is important, for it counters the tendency for more static thinking that can be attributed to aspects of the classical tradition. The notion of Sophia challenges more traditional concepts of divine providence, which imply static conservation in the creaturely sphere, while it affirms that God as Sophia is a permanent characteristic of God, reaching to the heart of Godself as expressed in the three persons of the Trinity. This implies that the destruction of species and the disordering of patterns of climate change are an offensive to God as Sophia, in that life on earth represents in some sense God's expression of creaturely Sophia. However, there can be no fixed guarantee that such destruction will not occur, which puts much greater responsibility on humanity to imitate that wisdom found in God.

Humanity's role is to represent all of creation, and thereby not only show divinity in humanity, but also humanity in God (Bulgakov 1993: 117). Humanity as representative of all creation is a microcosm of the macrocosm of the created order. Yet, by the same token, humanity is also caught up into God. How far is such a view convincing in the modern era? Certainly, there are aspects of modernity that need to be challenged by theology, in terms of its arrogant claim for knowledge, while lacking wisdom. Yet one might argue that in as much as all humanity bears within it not just the genetic material of 'lower' organisms, but also the atoms that go to make up stardust, humanity could be viewed as in some sense representative of the cosmos. The analogy should not be overdrawn, nor should it be seen as literal in scope – hence humanity bears a huge burden of responsibility for the earth, but it is not alone either. I suggest that the analogy makes most sense in a liturgical context, where the Divine Liturgy is celebrated, and in one sense marks out the connectivity and hospitality that humanity bears for all creatures, and for the cosmos as a whole.

Overall Bulgakov has a positive view about humanity, for, 'even at their fall human beings cannot destroy the image of God within them; it is only obscured' (Bulgakov 1993: 81). Is the notion of creaturely Sophia, which he distinguishes from divine Sophia, sufficient in order to take into account both the 'natural' suffering of creation and the direct and indirect human responsibility for environmental devastation as evidenced through climate change? He seems to recognize this, at least partially, through his concept of a 'shadow' side of creaturely Sophia.[11] However, he does suggest that after the Fall humanity falls *under* the power of nature because humanity has the mistaken belief that higher spiritual knowledge can be attained through the elements of this world

---

[11] Bulgakov speaks of evil as a 'shadow' and 'illusion', which tends to weaken its force, for evil is associated with misdirected freedom, which 'sooner or later must wither before the radiance of Wisdom' (Bulgakov 1993: 147).

alone.[12] Such a belief, he suggests, means that nature now is vulnerable to non-being and chaos, thus expressing the dark face of fallen Sophia (Graves 1972: 28).

Bulgakov points to the connection between Sophia and glory, which he seems to believe are near equivalent terms in the Trinity, so that: 'We must in speaking of Wisdom imply glory also: for Wisdom is the matter of glory, and glory the form of Wisdom' (Bulgakov 1993: 50). The Roman Catholic theologian Hans Urs von Balthasar has also developed a theological aesthetics, linking aesthetics with Glory, but his position is much more at pains to point to the disjunction between the world and God, so that Aidan Nichols, commenting on von Balthasar, notes that: 'If the God of glory wished to show his beauty to the world in his incarnate image, he must at once take up forms within the world and shatter them, so as to express the Glory beyond beauty' (Nichols 1998: xix). Von Balthasar moves from recognizing the contrast between God and the world, influenced by Karl Barth, towards acknowledging an *analogy* between God and the world.

There are some similarities in their approach, nonetheless. Both authors argue for a mystical, contemplative, kenotic (self-emptying) approach to the Godhead. Both remind their readers of the importance of divine Glory and Wisdom, and both seek to be positive about insights arising from secular culture. Von Balthasar's notion of analogous relationships avoids some of the difficulties associated with divine and creaturely Sophia in Bulgakov.

Bulgakov and von Balthasar on Theological Aesthetics

Bulgakov, like von Balthasar, argued for theological aesthetics, rather than aesthetic theology, which dissociates beauty from the other transcendentals of goodness and truth. The threat of climate change and other environmental degradations could be seen not simply as loss of wisdom, defined as a principle of order, but also a loss of beauty. Yet beauty in theological terms goes further than simple aesthetics.

Gregory of Nyssa writing in the fourth century, and Symeon the New Theologian, writing at the turn of the tenth century, were happy to see in the beauty of creation a form of 'symphony' of praise to God as creator, pointing also to divine Wisdom (Keselopoulus 2001: 19–20). In one of St Symeon's hymns we find the doxological dimension linking the wisdom of God with the beauty of the created world (Keselopoulus 2001: 20 n. 21). Bulgakov takes up this tradition, and as already hinted earlier, first and foremost he connects beauty with the work of the Holy Spirit, which is also connected with Joy, understood as 'the natural grace of creation' (Bulgakov, 'Uteshitel', 233–4, in Valliere 2000: 351).

---

[12] See below. A fuller discussion of the debates in science and religion on the nature of the Fall is outside the scope of this chapter.

Similarly, he views the power of the Holy Spirit as perfecting and completing, so that beauty in the natural world also corresponds with glory in God. Thus, 'The Holy Spirit, who imparts to ideal forms their reality, represents the power of Beauty or divine Glory. The Father confers glory on creation after the likeness of divine Glory. This leads to divine affirmation of "very good"' (Bulgakov 1993: 71). Yet such beauty is not simply confined to the work of the Spirit on its own, but is an integral part of the workings of the whole of the Trinity through the interrelationships between them. He also speaks of the beauty of the Holy Spirit in the work of the second person of the Trinity, the Word of *Truth* (Bulgakov 1993: 48, 49). Moreover, it seems that Bulgakov wants to give primacy to the Father as the originator of Beauty, in much the same way that he speaks of the Father as the origin of Wisdom: 'Wisdom belongs to the Father as First Principle, "the transcendental principle".... He is the source of all beauty, which must exist before beauty can come to be' (Bulgakov 1993: 39).

In consideration of the effects of the Fall, Bulgakov seems to take the view that the beauty of nature is 'arrested' by the darkness existing in creaturely Sophia after the Fall of humanity. The beauty of nature has no moral attributes; it is neither good nor evil in the sense of moral decision-making. However, following the Fall, humanity begins to direct undue attention to Beauty in the created world, so that it becomes the object of human possession and thereby an occasion for sin. In this sense it is impossible for the Holy Spirit to enkindle the universal spiritual transfiguration of creation until the Parousia, but in the meantime the Holy Spirit acts as the 'natural grace of creation', working towards the sophianizing of the created world, when creaturely Sophia will be united with divine Sophia, and God will be all in all (Graves 1972: 233–4).

Hans Urs von Balthasar, while devoting many volumes to outlining a theological aesthetics, unlike Bulgakov, pays surprisingly little attention to beauty in the created order. This may be one reason why Oliver Davies has criticized him for failing to apply his theological aesthetics to social and political issues, for a consideration of ecology might have forced such a concern (Davies 2004: 141). However, Davies suggests that the reason that he has failed in this capacity is because his theology is too contemplative. It seems to me that contemplation is not in and of itself a bar to social and political action, rather it is the *content* of that contemplation that is important, and how far this then is used in order to impinge on issues concerning the created order. I would go further than this and suggest that contemplation is actually *necessary* in order to arrive at the kind of practical wisdom that follows from living in a contemplative and liturgical way, drawing on the transcendentals of beauty, goodness and truth, as well as Sophia. Nicholas Lash also suggests that reclaiming the doctrine of God is highly relevant to thinking about our contemporary culture and its predicaments (Lash 2004).

Von Balthasar's understanding of beauty includes some elements similar to Bulgakov, in that he associates beauty with the work of the Holy Spirit. Like Bulgakov he argues for positioning beauty alongside truth and goodness, but he is more insistent that beauty is necessary for salvation (Balthasar 1982: 18). In addition, he suggests that the self-contemplation of Sophia is the means through which beauty can be seen, casting an aesthetic light backwards and forwards over salvation history. Hence, while beauty accompanies Sophia in Bulgakov's theology, it is the other way round in von Balthasar; and while Bulgakov uses the language of divine Wisdom, von Balthasar prefers the language of divine Glory. In von Balthasar a theological aesthetics takes the place of sophiology in that it provides both a theory of vision about the form of God's self-revelation, and a theory of rapture about the incarnation of God's glory and elevation of humanity to participate in that glory. While he is more intent to speak about aesthetics in the human sphere, he does seem to recognize the cosmic scope of Christ's involvement with the world, viewing the world eschatologically as in some sense 'a body' of God, but understood as expressed through the traditional notion of hypostasis, rather than pantheism (Balthasar 1982: 679).

He also, in common with Orthodox tradition, asserts that 'the whole plenitude of forms that the imagination of the divine nature has brought forth belongs analytically to the nature of man' (Balthasar 1982: 679). However, unlike Bulgakov, who seems to be more optimistic about the possibility of discovering wisdom/beauty in the world, von Balthasar overcomes this difficulty by suggesting that there are layers of manifestation of beauty in the world, so that there is always a 'non-manifested depth' to beauty, leading to 'its enrapturing and overwhelming character' (Balthasar 1982: 445).

Is his aesthetics too prone to the positive affirmation of beauty in the classical tradition, and less conscious of art in the contemporary world, as that which can also be expressive of ugliness and disorder (Davies 2004: 139–40)? I suggest his notion of beauty is precisely rescued from any preciousness by his concentration on divine Beauty in Christ, though he could have made more connections with contemporary art in such a context. Yet is not the power of such modern attempts precisely in the paradox that they raise in terms of what we think of, normally, as beautiful? His attempt to posit Christ's beauty in stark contrast to that of the world is, in such a context, overdrawn. However, the shattering of ordered processes of climate change provides an ever widening scope for Christological reflection on not just structural sin, but its global consequences.

While he does not give much prominence to the theme of wisdom, he does acknowledge in his commentary on St Bonaventure that there is a danger of seeing absolute beauty in finite things, which is only possible in Christ, also named as an expression of eternal Wisdom so that 'As the incarnate art of God (*ars divina*), he is the appearing of absolute beauty, and this appearing is free from all outward show, for it is in itself the substantial truth' (von Balthasar 1984: 347).

Hence, the hiddeness found in the beauty of the natural world is revealed finally in Christ, who also is expressive of absolute truth and beauty. While, like Bulgakov, he associates Christ with incarnate Wisdom and beauty on earth, he is far more concerned to put emphasis on beauty as the *goal* of all creation, and Christ as the exemplar of that goal. Christ becomes an icon of beauty that serves to present a challenge to other forms of beauty. This challenging role of beauty in Christ as one who overturns other images of beauty has its parallels in New Testament expositions of the wisdom of the cross, though Bulgakov does not make use of such paradoxical claims. Von Balthasar is also insistent that affirmations of the wonderfulness of creation, such as that found in the Fransciscan tradition, can only be mediated through the illumination of Christ as radiating light, *splendor pulcherrimus* (Balthasar 1984: 347). Hence, creation epitomizes a trace and copy of that trinitarian beauty found even at Christ's crucifixion, where beauty was concealed by becoming inward, rather than outward (Balthasar 1984: 354).

Balthasar describes beauty in classical terms as having 'form' and 'splendour', but also linked with notions of integrity and perfection. Given the priority that he gives to the Son as the archetype of all beauty, the role of the Holy Spirit in von Balthasar is more limited, drawing as he does on the Western understanding of the Holy Spirit as the bond of love between Father and Son, so that he can suggest that 'in this incomprehensible unity he is the locus of the beauty of God' (Balthasar 1982: 494). While he is content to speak of a cosmic Christology, unlike Bulgakov he does not develop a cosmic Pneumatology (Sherry 1992: 103–6). However, his suggestion that the Holy Spirit retains the bond of love between Father and Son even on Holy Saturday is suggestive of a radical role of the Spirit when all might have seemed to be lost. While his more limited interpretation of the place of the Holy Spirit suffers certain disadvantages compared with the cosmic vision of the Orthodox tradition represented in Bulgakov, it offers a way of considering more closely the significance of the passion of Christ and love remaining even in the shadow of death. While Bulgakov's understanding of the Holy Spirit lends itself to an affirmation of all of creation, through the role of the Spirit in the natural order, von Balthasar's Christological focus demonstrates the power of the Spirit of love and beauty even in death, and hence faces rather more squarely the question of suffering and evil in the world.[13]

A Recovery of Temperance and Prudence

The science of climate change inevitably provides a challenge to human behaviour, to the requirement to think through in a clearer way the place of humans on the earth. I have argued so far that our understanding of who God is must also be set in the context of the ecological and global community in which we are situated. While ever since Darwin we have become acutely aware of the continuity between ourselves and other living creatures of planet earth, climate change calls to mind in a sharper way a requirement for responsible human

---

[13] A full exploration of the implications for theodicy, enlarged so as to include evolutionary suffering, is outside the scope of this chapter.

behaviour. For Christian believers a theological vision of wisdom and beauty as expressed in the human and non-human world, portrayed by authors such as Bulgakov and von Balthasar, is necessarily a prelude to practical action. Such a shared responsibility is also inevitably cross-cultural. Simone Weil was aware of the need to detach ourselves from egocentric desires; I suggest that such detachment is facilitated through contemplation of God in sophiological and aesthetic categories. She was also aware of the connection between wisdom in God, human love fostered by beauty and right relationships fostered by intelligence (Weil 1971: 295). She linked beauty specifically with 'the radiance of truth', in a manner analogous to both von Balthasar and Bulgakov. This means that 'The world's beauty gives us an intimation of its claim to a place in our hearts' (Weil 1968: 178).

How might we move from an appreciation of beauty understood in theological terms and as appreciated in the natural world, to finding ways of expressing that beauty in the human sphere? Aquinas's reflection on beauty is important, as it provides a way of linking beauty with the virtues, in particular, the virtue of temperance. For Aquinas, good is what all things desire, but beauty is more specifically linked with knowledge according to 'right proportion' (Aquinas 1963: Ia, q. 5, a. 4; Aquinas 1967a: Ia IIae, q. 27, a. 1). Thus beauty as *right proportion* is rooted in the reasoning mind and can be perceived by contemplation, including the contemplation of wisdom (Aquinas 1966: IIa IIae, q. 180, a. 2). Beauty, in Aquinas, includes the qualities of *integrity* or completeness, *right proportion* or harmony and 'brightness' (Aquinas 1976: Ia, q. 39, a. 8). Aquinas associated beauty with honour and right conduct more generally (Aquinas 1967b: IIa IIae, q. 145, a. 2). Aquinas admits beauty in God, and affords the Son all the properties of beauty, though he does not develop fully a relationship between beauty and the Holy Spirit (Aquinas 1963: Ia, q. 39, a. 8; Sherry 1992: 102). Drawing on Dionysius, he suggests that the virtue most associated with beauty is *temperance*, since this serves to restrain desires that obscure the light of reason (Aquinas 1967b: IIa IIae, q. 141, a. 3).

Popular understanding of temperance might imply some sense of restriction, or just not acting in excess. While there is an element of this in any interpretation of temperance, the classical meaning pointed to a real awareness and sense of the ordered unity of the human person, but it is in a way that is selfless, rather than selfish. It is therefore more active and less passive than the popular notions of temperance imply. Intemperance is the misdirection of the desires for self-preservation in actions that are selfish, and ultimately self-destructive. Such a virtue obviously has relevance for environmental ethics, for it allows a closer re-examination of the way to behave according to the needs of all in the global commons. Temperance is also associated with humility and chastity, where pride is a false sense of one's own self-importance, and unchastity means a disordered sense of sensual enjoyment. Unchastity has relevance in consideration of the range of goods that are parodied as needs, rather than wants, in Western consumer society, ultimately leading to excessive waste with associated environmentally destructive consequences.

Temperance is, then, a complex term embracing other virtues and includes chastity, continence, humility, gentleness, mildness, *studiositas*, while forms of intemperance are unchastity, incontinence, pride, uninhibited wrath and *curiositas*. Ultimately temperance renders the human person beautiful, arising from an ordered state of being, and is associated with true virility, hence it affirms biological nature and the gift of life, rather than denies it. The opposite, intemperance: 'not only destroys beauty, it also makes man cowardly; intemperance more than any other thing renders man unable and unwilling to "take heart" against the wounding power of evil in the world' (Pieper 1966: 203).

The link between beauty and temperance is, to some extent, also reflected in the Orthodox tradition, but more in terms of practice, rather than finding expression in theological terms. Hence, 'in ascetic use and in the ascetic life of the monk the world is restored to its original beauty' (Keselopoulos 2001: 129). Such reflection is more self-consciously linking temperance with concern for the environment, while for Aquinas beauty and temperance had more to do with the inner person. Both aspects can be complementary to each other, and an enlargement of the scope of temperance to include the natural world seems entirely appropriate.

Prudence, or practical wisdom, is named in the classical tradition as the first of the four cardinal virtues, the others being justice, temperance and fortitude (Deane-Drummond 2004b). Prudence is the 'cause, root, mother measure, precept guide and prototype of all ethical virtues, it acts in all of them, perfecting them to their true nature, all participate in it, and by virtue of this participation they are virtues' (Pieper 1966: 16). Deliberation and judgement are characteristic of the cognitive stage of prudence, while decision, volition and action demonstrate its practical nature. For Thomas prudence is 'wisdom in human affairs', rather than absolute wisdom, hence *phronesis* is also called *practical wisdom* (Aquinas 1974: IIa IIae, q. 47, a. 2). Prudence includes taking counsel, judging correctly and then moving to act in a certain way. Prudence does not define what the good is, rather it *facilitates what makes for right choices* by so acting in different virtues in accordance with the ultimate orientation towards the good (Aquinas 1974: IIa IIae, q. 47, a. 4; q. 47, a. 5). Prudence allows for some ambiguity in difficult decisions, which is particularly relevant when considering questions about environmental ethics, so 'the certitude of prudence is not such so as to remove entirely all uneasiness of mind' (Aquinas 1974: IIa IIae, q. 47, a. 9). Aquinas lists the various components of prudence as memory, insight or intelligence, teachableness, acumen (*solertia*), reasoned judgement, foresight, circumspection and caution (Aquinas 1974: IIa IIae, q. 49).

Beyond this Aquinas distinguishes between individual prudence, aimed at the good of the individual, domestic prudence for family life, and political prudence, aimed at the common good (Aquinas 1974: IIa IIae, q. 47, a. 1). Relating the three aspects of prudence, individual, domestic and political, is particularly significant in ethical action called for in the context of complex issues arising from climate change that includes decision-making at all levels.

What kind of qualities do we need in order to come to appropriate decisions, given the complexities involved? I suggest that in complex cases the simple precautionary principle is not enough, for it is directed simply by the worst possible imagined scenario. Rather, we need to include different facets of prudence. One facet is the ability to deliberate. Moreover, deliberation relies not just on the expertise of a few, but on common deliberation of citizens drawing on their own experience. The capacities to make decisions in emergency situations, to take advice from others, to have foresight in a way that accurately anticipates the future as far as it is feasible to do so; all these qualities of prudence are, I suggest, vital in environmental decision-making. Moreover, Aquinas's rejection of over-attachment to material goods provides a corrective to policy-making that benefits the few at the expense of the greater good.

Conclusions

Global environmental concerns, such as loss of biodiversity and climate change, point to threats that challenge traditional Christian understanding of God's providence, alongside questions about human identity and responsibility. Under current conditions not only are non-human species threatened with extinction, but also large-scale human communities are destined to become environmental refugees in an already overcrowded planet. In situations of crisis we need to ask ourselves what particular cultural resources within the Christian tradition are relevant in order to develop appropriate ways to think about the earth. I have argued that there are two theological themes worth considering which recognize the importance of science, but seek to place scientific discourse in a wider cultural context.

The first theme is wisdom, recognizing wisdom in the first place as a way of linking our understanding of who God is in trinitarian relationship with the world as created through the Wisdom of God. The twentieth-century Orthodox writer Sergii Bulgakov offers an important starting-point for such reflection. For he perceives Wisdom as integral to who God is, expressed in various ways through the Logos as Word, through origin in the Father, and through the Holy Spirit as one who brings the world into completion and perfection. His vision of God in sophiological terms is one that inspires those who have faith to see the wisdom of God in the world as created, to view the cosmological dimension to existence as bound up with the human story of salvation history.

Alongside this tradition, we find one that is more attuned to aesthetics, to seeing not simply wisdom working in the world, but the world's completion in terms of beauty. For the twentieth-century Roman Catholic writer Hans Urs von Balthasar, the description of God in terms of Glory more readily distinguishes God from creation. His language of beauty is more closely tied up with seeing Christ as the icon of that beauty. He also views human cultural activity in aesthetic terms, but does not really give sufficient attention to the beauty of the world, except in as much as it bears on the cosmic Christ. However, von Balthasar's attention to beauty is important, as it is a reminder that beauty is much more than the pleasure associated with artistic expression, or significant discoveries in science. Rather, the beauty of Christ is also one that is disguised, an inner transcendental. This also ties up with a theme that Bulgakov failed to develop adequately, namely the wisdom of the cross. This Christological theme is worth pondering in the light of the loss of beauty, the loss of ordering in climate, in biodiversity and in other environmental disruptions that threaten both human and non-human existence. It should also be noted that this disruption is very different from the flux that is characteristic of ecological systems generally, for it leads to fragmentation, rather than transformation of systems.

The discussion has also pointed to a number of fruitful avenues for environmental ethics. Beauty is associated with temperance, or clear acknowledgement of one's actual needs. It challenges a consumerist attitude that is bent upon more and more goods, with its negative environmental consequences. Asceticism within the Orthodox tradition is one that sees the goods of the natural order as blessings, rather than goods to be acquired at the expense of other creatures. The tradition of prudence in Aquinas spells out further the meaning of practical wisdom, which unlike art on its own, associated with beauty, includes both judgement and action. Prudential reasoning, while in more popular language might suggest a holding-back, is also positive about acting, but it is action in accordance with the circumstances of the time, alongside an acknowledgement of memory, taking counsel, and foresight, of being able to envision what it might be like to make different decisions. In this way prudence is not simply a theological version of the more secular precautionary principle, but enlarges its scope. One might even see such action as being what Symeon the New Theologian described as being co-creators with God, for human activity needs to be one that has equal regard for the welfare of the earth.[14] In addition, the Orthodox tradition would claim that a non-consumerist use of the world is a precondition for seeing its truth and beauty, hence there is a dialectical relationship between ethical practice and theological reflection (Keselopoulos 2001: 123). The relationship between a spirituality and theology of wisdom/beauty and ethics is summarized clearly in this commentary on St Symeon:

> The right relationship between man and the rest of creation requires the personal discovery of the inner principle of each thing, and at the same time leads to a eucharistic use of it. Such a relationship, however, means that man has in practice abandoned the tendency to subordinate everything, and respects what surrounds him, because he is convinced that things in creation are not impersonal objects of use, but works and creations, the result of action and creation by a personal God. (Keselopoulos 2001: 107)

---

[14] Symeon viewed the disharmony in the world as a refusal to cultivate gifts that God has given to each person, resulting in him becoming a 'useless instrument' (Keselopoulos 2001: 113–14).

References

Aquinas, Thomas. See Thomas Aquinas.

Balthasar, H. U. von
  1982   *The Glory of the Lord: A Theological Aesthetics*, vol. 1: *Seeing the Form* (trans. Erasmo Leiva-Merikakis and ed. Joseph Fessio; London: T&T Clark).
  1984   *The Glory of the Lord: A Theological Aesthetics*, vol. 2: *Studies in Theological Style: Clerical Styles* (trans. Andrew Louth, Francis Mc Donough and Brian McNeil, ed. John Riches; London: T&T Clark).

Barrett, P.
  2004   'The Quest for a Uniting Vision in South Africa: A Question of Beauty?', *Journal of Theology for South Africa* 119 (July): 15–31.

Bulgakov, S.
  1912   *Filosofiya khozyaistva* (*Philosophy of Economy*) (Moscow) (translated into English by Catherine Evtuhov; New Haven: Yale University Press, 2000).
  1917   *Svet nevechernii* (*The Unfading Light*) (Moscow) (extract translated into English by R. Williams in R.Williams, *Sergii Bulgakov: Towards a Russian Political Philosophy* (Edinburgh: T&T Clark, 1999)): 133–61.
  1993   *Sophia: The Wisdom of God: An Outline of Sophiology* (Hudson, USA: Lindisfarne Press); a revised edition of *The Wisdom of God: A Brief Summary of Sophiology*, trans. Patrick Thompson, O. Fielding Clarke and Xenia Braikevitc; New York: Paisley Press, 1937).

Davies, O.
  2004   'The Theological Aesthetics', in Edward T. Oakes and David Moss (eds), *The Cambridge Companion to Hans Urs von Balthasar* (Cambridge: Cambridge University Press).

Deane-Drummond, C.
  1997   *Ecology in Jürgen Moltmann's Theology* (Lampeter: Edwin Mellen Press).
  2000   *Creation Through Wisdom: Theology and the New Biology* (Edinburgh/London: T&T Clark/Continuum).
  2004a   'The Logos as Wisdom: A Starting Point for a Sophianic Theology of Creation', in Philip Clayton and Arthur Peacocke (eds), *In Whom We Live and Move and Have Our Being: Panentheistic Reflections on God's Presence in a Scientific World* (Grand Rapids: Eerdmans).
  2004b   *The Ethics of Nature* (Oxford: Blackwell).

Edwards, D.
  2004   *Breath of Life: A Theology of the Creator Spirit* (Maryknoll: Orbis Press).

Galaher, A.
  2002   'Bulgakov's Ecumenical Thought', *Sobornost* 24(1): 24–55.
Graves, C.
  1972   *The Holy Spirit in the Theology of Sergius Bulgakov* (Geneva: World
             Council of Churches).
Houghton, J.
  2004   *Global Warming: The Complete Briefing* (Cambridge: Cambridge
             University Press, 3rd edn).
Houghton, J. and G. Jenkins
  2004   'The Stabilisation of Climate: Some Scientific Aspects', *World
             Economic Forum* (Davos, Exeter: Hadley Centre for Climate Pro-
             tection and Research).
IPCC
  2001   *IPCC, Climate Change 2001: Synthesis Report of the Third Assessment
             of the Intergovernmental Panel on Climate Change* (Cambridge: Cam-
             bridge University Press).
Keselopoulus, A. G.
  2001   *Man and the Environment: A Study of St Symeon the New Theologian*
             (trans. Elizabeth Theokritoff; Crestwood: St Vladimir's Seminary
             Press).
Lash, N.
  1996   *The Beginning and End of Religion* (Cambridge: Cambridge Uni-
             versity Press).
  2004   *Holiness, Speech and Silence: Reflections on the Question of God*
             (Aldershot: Ashgate).
Lossky, V.
  1957   *The Mystical Theology of the Eastern Church* (trans. The Fellowship of
             St Alban and St Sergius; London: J. Clarke).
Moltmann, J.
  1985   *God in Creation: An Ecological Theology of God* (trans. Margaret
             Kohl; London: SCM Press).
Myers, N. and J. Kent
  1995   *Environmental Exodus: An Emergent Crisis in the Global Arena*
             (Washington, DC: Climate Institute).
Nichols, A.
  1998   *The Word Has Been Abroad: A Guide Through Balthasar's Aesthetics*
             (Edinburgh: T&T Clark).
Pieper, J.
  1966   *The Four Cardinal Virtues* (Notre Dame: University of Notre Dame
             Press).
Sherrard, P.
  1992   *Human Image: World Image* (Ipswich: Golgonooza Press).
Sherry, P.
  1992   *Spirit and Beauty: An Introduction to Theological Aesthetics* (Oxford:
             Clarendon Press).

Thomas Aquinas
   1963   *Summa Theologiae*, vol. 2: *Existence and Nature of God* (trans.
             Timothy McDermott; London: Blackfriars).
   1966   *Summa Theologiae*, vol. 46: *Action and Contemplation* (trans. Jordan
             Aumann; London: Blackfriars).
   1967a   *Summa Theologiae*, vol. 19: *The Emotions* (trans. Eric D'Arcy; Lon-
             don: Blackfriars).
   1967b   *Summa Theologiae*, vol. 43: *Temperance* (trans. T. Gilby; London:
             Blackfriars).
   1974   *Summa Theologiae*, vol. 36: *Prudence* (trans. T. Gilby; London:
             Blackfriars).
   1976   *Summa Theologiae*, vol. 7: *Father, Son and Holy Spirit* (trans. T. C.
             O'Brien; London: Blackfriars).
UK Government Policy and Innovation Unit (PIU)
   2002   *Energy Review 2002* (London: HMSO).
Valliere, P.
   2000   *Modern Russian Theology, Bukharev, Soloviev, Bulgakov: Orthodox
             Theology in a New Key* (Edinburgh: T&T Clark).
Weil, S.
   1968   *On Science, Necessity and the Love of God* (trans. Richard Rees; Lon-
             don: Oxford University Press).
   1971   *The Need for Roots* (trans. Arthur Wills; New York: Harper &
             Row).

Biotechnology and Ethics

A Locus for the Reintegration of Science and Wisdom?

Michael Fuller

This paper uses the ideas of Francis Fukuyama as a jumping-off point to explore two issues. The first is the interrelationship of wisdom, culture and history; the second, the possibility that advances in biotechnology in recent years suggest a forum in which the sciences and wisdom can unite in a fruitful way, through their mutual involvement in bioethical issues.

As the twentieth century drew to a close, Fukuyama famously proposed the idea that we have reached 'the end of History' – a provocative expression, surely designed to elicit a response. By these words, Fukuyama means the following. First, he assumes that modern societies are tending universally towards espousing what he terms 'liberal democracy' as the 'best' form of government. Second, he assumes that such 'liberal democracy' constitutes the 'end point of man's ideological evolution' (Fukuyama 1992: xi) – in other words, that it constitutes the inexorable end-point in the centuries-old struggle to find the best way to organize human societies. On the basis of these assumptions, Fukuyama maintains that, with the final establishment of 'liberal democracy' throughout the world, we will have reached the 'end of History'. By this, Fukuyama means 'not the occurrence of events ... but History: that is, history understood as a single, coherent, evolutionary process, when taking into account the experience of all peoples in all times' (Fukuyama 1992: xii). The 'end of History' thus means the end of wars and revolutions, because '[a]greeing on ends, men would have no large causes for which to fight' (Fukuyama 1992: 311). Fukuyama associates such an understanding of capital-H History to Hegel and his intellectual successors.

Fukuyama also writes of 'the last man [sic]', by which he means those living in such post-Historical times. Fukuyama takes the optimistic view that the conditions brought about by liberal democracies are such that '[t]he life of the last man is one of physical security and material plenty' (Fukuyama 1992: 312).

More recently, Fukuyama has revised this thesis, since the revolutions currently taking place in biotechnology signal an arena in which History (as he understands it) seems not to have ended. However, Fukuyama believes that biotechnology presents a 'significant threat' to humankind, to wit 'the possibility that it will alter human nature and thereby move us into a "posthuman" stage of history' (Fukuyama 2002: 7). This is a future which will see our biological species continuing to exist, but doing so in a context which serves to strip it of many features which we think of as essential to being human. This leads Fukuyama to stress the importance of concepts like human rights, human nature and human dignity, at the philosophical level; and to modify his advocacy of non-interference by the state, at the practical level. He urges the enaction of legislation to circumscribe the possibilities which may and may not be pursued in biotechnological research, writing: 'In the face of the challenge from a technology like this ... there can be only one response: countries must regulate the development and use of technology politically' (Fukuyama 2002: 182).

Fukuyama's concept of the end of history is an idea with strong theological resonances. This has been picked up by at least one commentator, who has urged that it represents 'a secular version of "realized eschatology"', which 'undercuts the Christian eschatological hope for the final consummation of God's purpose' (Scherer 1990: 402). However, it is noteworthy that theologians generally do not appear to have responded much to Fukuyama's ideas, either in terms of his 'secular eschatology' or in terms of his thinking on ethical issues of the kind that have, traditionally, been of particular concern to Christians (such as those relating to human uniqueness). This is surprising; and it is hoped that the present paper may stimulate more widespread responses within the theological community to this popular contemporary commentator.

Wisdom

This paper will urge that the kind of ethical intervention Fukuyama enjoins requires the exercise of wisdom. Let us now take a sideways step, and examine the concept of wisdom. What is it? What characterizes it? How can it be transmitted? These are all questions which might be approached in many ways. Some understandings of wisdom which were suggested at the 2004 ESSSAT conference are:[1]

> Wisdom is the integration of everything with everything else: it is something we can seek, but at which we can never finally arrive.

> Wisdom is a medieval concept, which has no real meaning in a modern context.

---

[1] The following definitions were given at the concluding plenary of the 2004 ESSSAT conference by, respectively, Celia Deane-Drummond, Peter Harrison, Walther Zimmerli and Mariano Artigas.

Wisdom is concerned with the management of our ignorance. It is a way in which we grapple with things about which we cannot fully know, but with which we must come to terms.

Wisdom functions in such a way as to introduce order into our lives. It includes qualities such as humility, patience, understanding and forgiveness, and it may be accounted a gift of the Holy Spirit.

Such disparate accounts of this word should make us chary of any attempt to define it more narrowly; but for the sake of the argument which follows, I shall develop the admirably concise definition of wisdom given in one modern dictionary, as 'the ability to make right use of knowledge' (Chambers 1983). Celia Deane-Drummond expands this slightly when she states that wisdom is 'an interpretation of knowledge that is not separated from the ethical claims of truth and goodness' (Deane-Drummond 2000: 153). From these definitions we may immediately note that a distinction is being made between wisdom and knowledge: wisdom is not simply about knowing things. It is, we might perhaps more accurately say, a disposition, a way of being, of thinking, and of doing.

Where can wisdom be found? There are books within the Judaeo-Christian corpus of scripture that are referred to as 'wisdom literature', and there is a strand of thinking within the historical Christian tradition that may be similarly labelled. Deane-Drummond observes that 'The advice given by wisdom writers is based squarely on human experience' (Deane-Drummond 2000: 17). However, she notes that this tradition also makes a distinction between 'wisdom as gift and wisdom as learned' (Deane-Drummond 2000: 27). The extent to which wisdom can be acquired through searching is thereby circumscribed. Some aspects of wisdom can only be acquired through its being given by God to the wise person (as is illustrated by the story of Solomon: cf. 1 Kings 3.5–14).

Now, what markers are there that might lead us to say of an individual that he or she is wise? One such marker, clearly, is experience – or more accurately, we might say with Jürgen Moltmann that wisdom comes not simply from experience but from the way we deal with our experiences (Moltmann 2003: 147). It is this which has led to the classic association of wisdom and age: older people, it might reasonably be assumed, have experienced more of life's vicissitudes and are therefore better able to judge wisely in novel situations. And if wisdom is not about knowing things, a second marker we can identify in our thinking about wisdom is surely a person's awareness of their ignorance – of the limits to their knowledge, and their experience. For many people, the paradigmatic 'wise' person of Western intellectual history is Socrates; yet he constantly professed his ignorance, and in response to the questions of others was more likely to question them about their presuppositions than to offer them any direct answers (cf. Plato 1982: 82). A third marker for wisdom might be the reputation accorded to someone within their community. Wisdom, thus understood, is something conferred on an individual by general consent of their peers. There are perhaps echoes here of Deane-Drummond's notion of wisdom as gift: she of course means a divine gift, but it may also be that a society can be considered to gift wisdom to an individual within it.

Wisdom and Culture

How can wisdom be transmitted? How do people acquire wisdom, insofar as wisdom is some combination of experience, awareness of ignorance, and a gift which is granted, rather than achieved? From an experiential point of view, one means of acquiring wisdom is through exploring as widely as is possible all that life has to offer. Such exploration might be direct, but it can also be carried out vicariously, through a person's experience of the work of others. This is where culture comes into play. Culture may be considered to be the deposit through history of all those ideas and artefacts which a society has felt worthy of pre-servation; and a major reason for that preservation will be the ability of those ideas and artefacts to convey vicariously the kinds of experiences that can lead to wisdom. I do not know what it was like to live through the Russian revolution, but I can read books of this period and thereby experience at second hand, through the genius of an Akhmatova, a Bulgakov or a Pasternak, something of what it must have been like to have done so. Interestingly, Fukuyama seems to acknowledge this possibility when he writes: 'human beings are by nature cultural animals, which means that they can learn from experience and pass on that learning to their descendants through nongenetic means' (Fukuyama 2002: 13). It is surely possible that the wisdom which has been acquired by indivi-duals alongside their experiential learning may similarly be passed on to others by this means.

What happens to culture at Fukuyama's end of History? Can culture be sustained in the kind of scenario he envisages? If people truly live 'beyond History', then culture properly understood becomes the preserve of a quirky minority, who are prepared, as it were, to imaginatively re-enter History in order to understand where culture is coming from. It is noteworthy that 'popular culture' often appears to be a-historical. Its artefacts and ideas are of the moment: appreciation of them does not depend on any understanding of their historical antecedents, and they are not (consciously, at any rate) staking any claim for their relevance in the future (although the best of them do endure, to become 'classics' in their turn). Culture in its broader understanding must, of necessity, have a historical component. We must be wary, therefore, lest the end of History turns out to mean also the end of culture, as it has traditionally been understood; because this in turn would mean the end of one of the principal means by which people have acquired wisdom.

Wisdom and Ethics

There is, clearly, an intimate connection between wisdom and ethics, as the very definition of wisdom as the *right* use of knowledge implies. Knowledge alone cannot ascertain the moral rightness of a decision. Moreover, if wisdom is the right use of *knowledge*, then it must relate also to science, since the sciences are generally considered to be a means of generating knowledge (however provisional). Moltmann has recently written: 'The emancipation of the sciences from moral philosophy and theology was in reality their emancipation from wisdom' (Moltmann 2003: 27). If we concur with this judgement, we will conclude that wisdom is not to be found purely in the pursuit of science.

Science and Ethics

It is generally recognized that science needs to be conducted in an ethical fashion, and that this may involve the imposition of boundaries around what a society will permit its scientists to do. In the UK a fruitful mechanism for arriving at such boundaries has been developed through the setting up of government committees. Typically, such a committee is constituted of experts and 'lay' people. It consults widely among interested groups and individuals regarding the controversial topic it is charged with investigating, and it then writes a report which may contain recommendations for legislation. For example, the Human Fertilisation and Embryology Act, establishing the Human Fertilisation and Embryology Authority (HFEA), which regulates the procedures surrounding IVF and embryo experimentation in the UK, came into existence in this way, following the report of the Warnock Committee (see Warnock 1985). This practice appears to be increasingly the norm in Europe, where 'Setting up an advisory body is now a standard precursor to legislation' (Pattinson 2003: 9).

It is worth noting that the Warnock report attracted heated debate (for a critique of the report itself, see Hare 1987, and for a scrutiny of the resulting governmental White Paper (which led to the Human Fertilisation and Embryology Act, and to the establishing of the HFEA) see Brazier 1990.) However, the value of the HFEA now appears to be widely acknowledged, on the grounds that 'Parliament and Ministers, having set the framework, can rely on the Authority for the day-to-day management of the many legal and ethical issues that have emerged from the field.... The public, in its concern that science does not outpace ethics, is assured that brakes are in place and are functioning well.... And the clinics themselves enjoy the support and legitimacy of a robust, ethical system that not only controls but also protects' (Deech 2003: 37).

Science, Wisdom and Religion

Does bioethical activity in the context of a body such as the HFEA provide a locus for the reintegration of science and wisdom? If societies are to follow the path advocated by Fukuyama and legislate on ethical matters raised by modern biotechnology, then a model such as that which the UK has adopted might indeed be seen as an appropriate way of harnessing both individual and collective wisdom in the process of framing and enacting such legislation, and bioethics does indeed become a locus for the encounter – and, it is to be hoped, reintegration – of science and wisdom.

A theologian might wish to ask at this point: Where does religion come into all this? It is often reckoned that ethics is a subject intimately bound up with religion (cf. Gould 2001: 55–8). Indeed, in the discussion of the HFEA already quoted, it is maintained that its work covers 'a field uniquely intimate *and religious* as well as scientific' (Deech 2003: 23, my emphasis). Of course, ethical behaviour is by no means the sole preserve of those who are adherents to particular religious traditions. But the word 'religious' should be considered to mean more than just 'adherent of a religious tradition'. The root meaning of the word 'religion' is disputed, but it is usually said to be derived from the Latin verb *religare*, meaning to bind. A religious perspective is one to which the adherent is bound: he or she cannot change that perspective without in some deep and significant way ceasing to be the person he or she is. And this, surely, is the nature of ethical behaviour. Any consistent ethical agent makes a commitment to behave in particular ways. These ways may or may not be derived from the teachings of a particular religious tradition, but the decision to live by them is a religious decision, involving commitment. It is a decision which binds, voluntarily, the will of the person who takes that decision.

A Secular Ethic?

Fukuyama recognizes the importance of ethics in addressing the issues with which modern biotechnology confronts societies today. As a way into ethical discussion he urges a re-examination of such concepts as 'human nature' and 'human dignity', which have fallen out of favour in recent decades through their historical use to support (often unsavoury) ideologies. However, his appeal is not (at least, in the first instance) to the traditional religions. Instead, he asks: 'Is there a secular ground for believing that human beings are entitled to a special moral status or dignity?' (Fukuyama 2002: 151). The answer to that question is, surely, 'no'. There are, however, many different *religious* grounds for believing precisely this, some of which have traditionally been labelled as such, and others of which have traditionally eschewed the label 'religious' on ideological grounds.

Conclusion

It is apparent that we may agree with Fukuyama's verdict that we have not, after all, reached the end of history. If his analysis is correct, and biotechnology does indeed hold out to us new potential for the future of our species, then we may further suggest that if we are wise in our applications of it that future need not be of the 'posthuman' kind which Fukuyama fears. That is because culture, and the wisdom it embodies, has also not reached an end. Herein lie grounds for hope: the wisdom embodied in culture, which has guided and inspired human beings down the centuries, can continue to do so – for as long as it is not itself allowed to come to an end.

Fukuyama is surely correct, too, in his assertions that issues like human nature and human dignity should continue to be of the greatest significance for us, and in his identification of biotechnology as an area of activity which throws such issues into sharp relief. However, the search for a new, 'secular' form of ethics with which to address these issues is both chimerical and redundant: chimerical, because any consistent ethical system can only be, at bottom, a religious system; and redundant, because in the culture which our history has transmitted to us we already have a rich variety of ethical resources on which to draw in approaching novel issues. The wise person, surely, is the one who draws most fully on these resources in addressing the dilemmas biotechnology sets before us. And, if we concede Moltmann's point about the divorce of science and wisdom, it is surely in such scientifically and ethically informed dialogue that we may see a potential locus for their reintegration.

References

Brazier, M.
  1990   'The Challenge for Parliament: A critique of the White Paper on *Human Fertilisation and Embryology*', in Anthony Dyson and John Harris (eds), *Experiments on Embryos* (London: Routledge): 127–41.
Chambers
  1983   *Chambers 20th Century Dictionary* (Edinburgh: W&R Chambers).
Deane-Drummond, C.
  2000   *Creation Through Wisdom* (Edinburgh: T&T Clark).
Deech, R.
  2003   'The HFEA – 10 Years On', in Jennifer Gunning and Helen Szoke (eds), *The Regulation of Assisted Reproductive Technology* (Aldershot: Ashgate): 21–38.
Fukuyama, F.
  1992   *The End of History and the Last Man* (London: Penguin).
  2002   *Our Posthuman Future* (London: Profile).
Gould, S. J.
  2001   *Rocks of Ages* (London: Jonathan Cape).
Hare, R. M.
  1987   'In Vitro Fertilisation and the Warnock Report', in Ruth F. Chadwick (ed.), *Ethics, Reproduction and Genetic Control* (London: Routledge): 71–90.
Moltmann, J.
  2003   *Science and Wisdom* (London: SCM Press).
Pattinson, S. D.
  2003   'Current Legislation in Europe', in Jennifer Gunning and Helen Szoke (eds), *The Regulation of Assisted Reproductive Technology* (Aldershot: Ashgate): 7–19.

Plato
    1982   *Apology* (Loeb Classical Library; London: William Heinemann).
Scherer, J. A.
    1990   'Why Mission Theology Cannot Do Without Eschatological
                Urgency', *Missiology* 18: 395–413.
Warnock, M.
    1985   *A Question of Life* (Oxford: Basil Blackwell).

Food Safety and Food Justice

Impacts of Scientific and
Religious Cultures

Antje Jackelén

The topic 'food' is well suited for a discourse on wisdom, sought through the cultural dynamics of science and theology, because it is characterized by an integration of all different kinds and aspects of knowledge. I will exemplify this by using the dimensions of knowledge suggested by Ralph Burhoe. Other models may be used and will probably lead to similar results. Burhoe (1967, 1981: 53–63) distinguishes between several kinds of knowledge: genotypic knowledge, perceived and intuited knowledge, culturally transmitted knowledge, rational knowledge, and scientific knowledge (see also Breed 1992: 37ff., 88).

Genotypic knowledge is genetically derived knowledge, also called the wisdom of the body or the knowledge of the vegetative system. In the case of food this can be said to be the knowledge from hunger and thirst. Perceived knowledge comes to us via sense perception, also called the revelation of the senses – here the sense perception of food. Intuited knowledge comes from intuition and imagination; it is revelation from beyond the senses. In the case of food it might mean the ideas of new kinds of food or new ways of preparing food, as well as an intuition of which nutrient is craved by the body at a certain time. Culturally transmitted knowledge, also called the revelation of the tradition, is what comes through the mores and myths of culture. Culture-type knowledge contains all cultural and religious traditions about what and when to eat and what and when to avoid eating. Rational knowledge, or the revelation of reason, is the result of deductive reasoning or logic. To this area, Burhoe allocates pre-modern science – geometry, philosophy and theology; but obviously, the modern sciences should be included, too. I suggest that what Burhoe calls scientific knowledge as the final stage, be renamed wisdom, because it implies revelation by a systematic involvement of all previously mentioned types of knowledge.

Burhoe interprets these 'knowledges' as steps in evolution. This interpretation easily evokes the impression that the different types of knowledge relate to each other as steps of a ladder, with scientific knowledge being the pinnacle. However, I prefer the view that these knowledges relate to each other in the manner of overlapping circles. This claim is supported by theories in both neurobiology and neuropsychology about how our brain works in memorizing and decision-making (e.g. Damasio 1994; Gärdenfors 2001). Also, recent concepts in philosophy and theology suggest that we are right to be suspicious of hierarchical classifications.[1] The turn from substance to relationality (Jackelén 2001) has taught us to question the often-precipitate choice of pyramid or stair metaphors. Their linear hierarchy tends to build in reductions at the very beginning of a research project, whereas the use of metaphors that lead us to envisage spherical, concentric and holistic structures of thought is likely to widen the horizon of research and knowledge.

The Interconnectedness of 'Knowledges' in the Current Food Discussion

The debate about genetically modified food displays a degree of inter-connectedness of knowledges that may surprise many. As Celia Deane-Drummond, Bronislaw Szerszynski and Robin Grove-White (2003) argue in their book *Re-Ordering Nature*, the richness of religious themes and dimensions underlying these debates has been underestimated and underexplored. By contrasting public policy statements with how ordinary people talk about and discuss these issues, the authors find that, while expert or government state-ments often display a clear-cut one-question approach, people's reasoning witnesses to a much broader approach, including thoughts about the essence of a human being and what it means to be a human being in nature. They argue that the public response they found is not only *ethically* significant, a fact generally acknowledged by public policy-makers as well as the writers of church statements, but it is also *theologically* significant, because it displays an engagement with the deeper, ontological significance of genetic science and technology. Behind the fear of poisoning and the sense of blasphemy against nature and agriculture expressed in debates about food, there loom theological questions about the place of humanity relative to other living species. In other words, there is more to public anxiety about genetic engineering of animals and plants than irrationality and emotionality. The public seems to have a profound sense both of mystery about the character of the universe, and of the essential openness of nature (Deane-Drummond *et al.* 2003: 35). This is contrasted by the sense of certainty often displayed by government regulators in their way of handling biotechnology. Also in respect of ethical deliberations much of public reasoning seems to be misunderstood by both official government policies and church statements. 'Both the consequentialist language and reductionist

---

[1] For philosophy, one might think of postmodern concepts; for theology, especially of feminist and postcolonial discourses. Already Paul Tillich (1976: 12–17) in the third volume, from 1963, of his *Systematic Theology* discards the concept of hierarchies, favouring dimensions, realms and degrees instead.

evaluation framework embodied in the regulatory processes, and the deonto-logical ethics that often comes more easily to the churches, look like inadequate responses in the context of these ambiguities' (Deane-Drummond *et al.* 2003: 35). For the public, neither cost–benefit analyses that fail to take into account the entire scope and context of an issue, nor the application of abstract ethical principles, can provide satisfactory answers to questions about the responsible use of science and technology with regard to food safety and food justice. Instead, space needs to be provided for questions like: What is natural order and the place of humanity in it? Where does consequential ethics leave us and how can we get beyond its deficits? How can fatalism and cynicism on the side of the public be avoided? What conflicting representations of the human are at stake (e.g. anthropocentrism, biocentrism)? What is humanity's place in the world?

The authors of *Re-Ordering Nature* argue that asking for the theological content of public response leads to at least two insights. First, these responses are far more reasonable and sensitive than perceived by the official bodies. Second, public statements that are shaped as one-issue-at-a-time scientific assessment, and that almost exclusively build on a consequential ethics approach, miss the point of public discourse. If these perspectives are omitted, official and lay pictures will continue to drift apart. Hence, neglecting the theological dimensions of problems related to science and technology poses a serious threat to democracy, for democracy cannot survive without successful public communication.

The hypothesis built on these observations is intriguing for scientists, theologians, opinion leaders and political oversight bodies alike: '[T]heological perspectives may now be indispensable in helping explain to largely secular institutions the sources and dynamics of conflicts now threatening to paralyse the development of what is being posited as a key technology for the twenty-first century' (Deane-Drummond *et al.* 2003: 22).

While the interpretation in terms of virtue ethics and wisdom propagated by Deane-Drummond and Szerszynski may be too benevolent toward religion, the basic thesis remains worth consideration. Significantly, the request for a more virtue-oriented ethics as a complement to '[t]he alliance of utilitarianism and scientific thinking in public debates about genetic engineering in the agri-foodsector' (Verhoog 2003) has been voiced even by scholars outside the realm of theological ethics. Much like Deane-Drummond and Szerzynski, Henk Verhoog argues and exemplifies how so-called 'intrinsic' issues are ruled out by 'extrinsic' reasoning. Intrinsic concerns refer to common-sense attitudes towards nature, as held by human beings in general. They are often misrepresented as feelings less of moral concern than of disgust and revulsion – a collective 'yuk-factor' effect, as it were. Extrinsic issues refer to the translation of the issues into the language of the knowability of consequences and the controlling of the risks, that is, into a utilitarian cost–benefit analysis. Focus on calculations of specific case studies eliminates from the very beginning a debate on underlying concepts.[2] The examples mentioned by Verhoog[3] confirm the hypothesis advocated by Deane-Drummond and Szerzynski: the one-issue-at-a-time approach and the confinement to consequential analyses miss where public debate actually is. Thus they are counterproductive in that they do not help to increase knowledge, to create a balanced discussion, and to pave the way for just regulation.

These examples also indicate that scientists cannot dismiss the discussion by referring to it as a matter of technology only. Issues like the public's sense of ecological integrity, that nature has rights and sacramental value, in matters where governmental analyses are perceived as superficial, pertain to the whole spectrum of science and technology. Both sensitive science and informed religion can register with these perceptions, and each can contribute to informing and refining the public position, and assisting its articulation.

This leads me to my *first conclusion*: the current debate about food must be understood within the framework of the dialogue between religion and science or else it is not understood at all.

Food and Culture

Food makes an ideal topic for a conversation that seeks to involve religion and science with a theme that is of practical relevance for everybody, because it is, and has always been, so central to human survival and culture. From societies of hunters and gatherers to highly technological societies that need special clinics to treat eating disorders, food is a defining trait of what constitutes existence and culture. Problems connected with food escape easy generalizations about traditionally rich and poor countries. The simplified image of people in the 'poor' countries chasing calories while everybody in the 'rich' countries is trying to run away from them is, of course, not true. Obesity is a problem not only in the USA; countries in the developing world also note high rates of people suffering from it (Food and Agriculture Organization of the United Nations (FAO) 2002). In a global perspective, obesity is quantitatively a bigger problem than underweight (World Health Organization (WHO)). On the other hand, malnutrition and hunger are not problems of the poor countries only. In the USA an estimated 11 million households – that is more than 10 per cent of all households – cannot help themselves to a sufficient amount of healthy food at

---

[2] Similar concerns have been raised by the Danish Centre for Bioethics and Risk Assessment (CeBRA) in their 21 October 2003 conference on the limits of biotechnology (Kan økologisk risikovurdering give tilstrækkeligt svar på, hvorvidt gensplejsede planter vil skabe problemer i naturen?; www.bioethics.kvl.dk, accessed 21/1/04).

[3] Verhoog (2003) mentions the following three examples: an analysis of a US Presidential Commission on biotechnology in Barbara Katz Rothman, *Genetic Maps and Human Imaginations: The Limits of Science in Understanding Who We Are* (New York: W.W. Norton, 1988); a public debate on 'Food and Genes' in the Netherlands at the end of 2001; and the report *Genetically Modified Crops* by the Nuffield Council on Bioethics, 1999.

all times.[4] Changed patterns of preparing and eating meals, in connection with a lifestyle that makes acceleration a value in itself, require highly industrialized countries to face socially caused malnutrition in young people. Fast food and convenience food pose a threat to time-honoured knowledge about the preparation of food and the specifics of ingredients. Year-round availability makes the knowledge of seasonal rhythms of growth and harvest fade away. The microwave makes common mealtimes superfluous. In the modern kitchen, time and space are suspended, and the connection with the production and distribution story of food is widely lost.

At the same time, functional foods, especially yogurt, margarine and bread – although neither legally defined (in Europe) nor scientifically proven in terms of health effects – represent a rapidly growing market. Often, self-aware consumers display split personalities: they are aware of ethical questions involved in the production and distribution of food and in principle favour alternative products declared as fair trade, ecologically sound, etc. Yet, in practice they go for the cheapest staple foods regardless of their ethical conviction, while at the same time being prepared to pay almost any price for functional food, regardless of the scientific documentation of its effects. There is a huge gap between thought and actions, especially if the latter have a price.[5] One may take this to confirm the image of the public as a bunch of irrational, unreliable, gullible and easily scared individuals. And this may well be accurate as long as people are regarded as consumers only. However, the picture changes as soon as they are understood and understand themselves as citizens who are able to turn technical consumer concerns into public concerns about shaping a good society (Brom 2000). The difference that this alteration of perspective makes is similar to the difference between attempts at understanding public opinion with or without its theological underpinnings.

Food and Society

In European countries citizenship is widely interpreted as a matter of freedom of choice, which is the motivation behind legislation regarding labelling of genetically modified food and the core of the discussion whether agriculture with genetically modified organisms (GMOs) can be permitted in the EU. Freedom of choice is dependent on the safe coexistence of different types of agriculture as a real option, as well as on adequate information and

[4] In 2000, 10.5 per cent (11 million) of US households were food insecure, i.e. without access by all their members at all times to enough food for an active healthy life (ERS Food Assistance and Nutrition Research Report (FANRR) No. 21, 2002, 3–8).

[5] 48 per cent of Nordic consumers claim to prefer organic commodities, even if they are often a little more expensive, according to The Nordic Council of Ministers, *Food Labelling: Nordic Consumers' Proposals for Improvements* (TemaNord 2001:573), 38. Yet, in Denmark only 5.6 per cent of the total food consumption is organic, according to the main organization representing organic food production in Denmark, Organic Denmark (figures for 2003). I thank Christian Coff for these references.

transparency. Concerns have been raised especially regarding the safe coexistence of different types of agriculture. The achievement of this goal will
require 'clean' production all the way from handling the seed through growing,
harvesting, transportation, processing and distribution. However, it seems
hardly likely that contamination-free processing can be guaranteed all the way
through. It should also be noted that so far there are no scientific data available
that can serve as a basis for discerning acceptable levels of 'contamination'. The
levels that are being used have been set arbitrarily for political reasons in order
to create a system that is manageable. This means that, if indeed gene-transfer
cannot be controlled sufficiently, as some agencies have cautioned, increasing
contamination will in the long run eliminate conventional and organic agriculture and thus undermine the freedom of choice for consumers as well as for
producers and distributors (Tappeser, Hermann and Brauner 2003). Again, the
arguments used are not only scientific; to a high degree they are based on ideas
of consumer-rights, which are derived from a conglomerate of philosophical,
religious, ethical and political concepts. In comparison with the idea of citizenship, the consumer perspective is impaired by some serious reductionist
flaws. Although freedom of choice *per se* is important, its effects are negative
when it is separated from intrinsic values.

Today, the structures of production, processing, distribution, preparation
and consumption of food are shaped by an intricate interplay of global and local
elements (Tansey and Worsley 1995). Agriculture shows two faces: the face of
culture and cultivating, but also the face of an activity that is ecologically
deeply destructive. Science and technology have profoundly changed agriculture
and led to the development of agribusiness in ways that affect everybody. The
trend from family farming toward large-scale operations continues to bring
fundamental agricultural and social changes to many regions in the world. Yet,
farmers often maintain a vocational understanding of their work and express
their relationship to the soil in religious terms. In analogy to seeing people in
general not only as consumers but as citizens, farmers often look at themselves
as more than producers. Modern technology is often experienced as a blessing,
while economic pressure toward large-scale production and monoculture tends
to be perceived as a threat.

Agricultural subsidies affect both local farming and global food trade. The
dynamics of abundance and scarcity in combination with first-world agricultural and food subsidies have deep impacts on developing countries. These
issues need to be addressed in discourses that take seriously religious and
spiritual understandings of food, of agricultural work, of the soil, of technological practices, as well as of local, regional, national, international and global
solidarity. They raise the question whether and how global science and local
wisdom can together provide 'glocal' solutions that contribute to the *food
democracy* much called for in both rich and poor parts of the world. It seems to
me that this call transcends religious and cultural differences as well as disagreements about the assessment of technology. Therefore, it has the potential
of playing a key role in facilitating conversation on food issues in a cross-

cultural perspective. Let me illustrate this with an example: Vandana Shiva, world-renowned environmental thinker and activist from India, writes about the need of a global movement for food democracy (2000: 122–3). She is highly critical of how research is used by the food industry and claims that the success stories about genetically modified crops are greatly overstated. Dennis Gengenbach, a Nebraskan farmer serving on the Rural Desk Advisory Committee of the Evangelical Lutheran Church in America, speaks about the power of the seed companies that exceeds the power of any government. In his opinion, only a grassroots movement can make a difference. Both agree on the need of food democracy, but they strongly disagree about the use of genetically modified corn. While he is strongly in favour, she is equally strongly opposed to it. Agreement in some respects overcomes differences between religions and cultures, while at the same time in other respects the lack of facts and experience as well as the interpretation of accessible facts create differences that cut across lines of consent. Many of these issues are deeply controversial, and loaded with significant amounts of individual and communal passion as well as massive economical and socio-political interests (Pence 2002). But a great number of the issues are also common to such an extent that a discussion of them can be projected to disclose consent where it is not expected and to help forming alliances that otherwise are difficult to achieve. In my view, the request for food democracy is one of the most important if not the foremost among these issues.

The significance of food is social and political and may again become increasingly so. It is at the core of questions about economy, peace and justice. There are indications that conflicts about oil will be succeeded by conflicts about water, which also means conflict about food. If current trends prevail, such political tensions or conflicts will have religious undertones. Even if theologians and sociologists agree that the use of religion in conflicts often is a pseudo-use that transforms religion into an ethnic or economic marker, the religious dimension carries considerable weight and its neglect will retard progress, and in some instances prevent it altogether.

Food and Religious Values

Food is at the heart of many religious and spiritual traditions (e.g. Schmidt-Leukel 2000). It forms a vital symbol in liturgy and rite. Basically every religious and spiritual tradition deals with food: sacred meals, rituals around meals and their preparation, restrictions in eating certain things or at certain times. Rituals around the fertility of the ground count among the oldest religious practices. The spiritual values of fasting (Ware 1984: 13–68) seem pertinent to issues of food justice as well; learning the art of expectant preparation conveys meaning in regard to both physical and spiritual nourishment. By fostering appreciation of the balance between the outward and the inward worlds, these values protect against spiritualization and affirm the value of the material world. In that sense they are likely to include a positive interest in the progress of science and technology. The spiritual values of fasting also counteract a false sense of autonomy and self-sufficiency, thus strengthening the awareness of dependence and interdependence. In this, they are in consonance with what currently are the best scientific descriptions of our natural world. Rules such as abstaining from animal products on certain days may have a concrete balancing impact on ecological systems. The goal of making 'all our eating spiritual, sacramental and eucharistic' (Ware 1984: 25) translates into secular language as: fostering discernment about the structures and implications of production, processing, distribution, preparation and consumption of food individually and in community with others, looking both behind and beyond what is or is not on the plates of children, women and men on this planet. Also sacramental meals can and need to be theologically interpreted in the context of everyday nourishment.

The centrality of food to religious symbols and experience is in glaring contrast to the reality of how religious people respond to actual questions of food safety and food justice. Among many other interesting features the Eurobarometer on *The Europeans and Biotechnology* (2000) reveals some embarrassing facts for religious communities.[6] The percentage of negative responses to the question whether one has ever discussed modern biotechnology falls in line with the degree of religious inclination. As many as 66 per cent of those people who described themselves as 'extremely religious' had never discussed modern biotechnology with anyone, whereas only 26 per cent of 'agnostics' had never discussed these issues. With 53 and 41 per cent respectively, the gap is less between 'quite religious' and 'atheists', but it is still remarkable in size. Sociodemographic analysis of the data shows that in a number of respects religious people are less informed about and less engaged in central issues pertaining to citizenship in democratic states than their anti-religious, agnostic and atheistic fellows. While religious and spiritual values are pertinent to the dialogue and while religious traditions are in charge of powerful concepts that could contribute to lifting a conversation, often limited by emotions and rigid opinions, to a higher level, religious communities do not seem to be good stewards in making these resources available for a fruitful and successful public dialogue.

This obvious disharmony between the possibilities and the reality compels me to give my *second conclusion* in the shape of a challenge directed especially to leaders of religious and spiritual communities: given the provocative presence of the food topic in science, in societies all over the world and in religions, religious leaders must find more effective ways of promoting education and involving their communities in informed dialogue over the whole breadth of the issues involved, or else they will deprive the global community of resources essential in addressing some of the most urgent issues of our time.

---

[6] The analysis is based on data from 1999.

References

Breed, D. R.
 1992   *Yoking Science and Religion: The Life of Ralph Wendell Burhoe* (Chicago: Zygon Books).
Brom, F. W. A.
 2000   'Food, Consumer Concerns and Trust: Food Ethics for a Globalizing Market', *Journal of Agricultural and Environmental Ethics* 12.2: 127–39.
Burhoe, R. W.
 1967   'Five Steps in the Evolution of Man's Knowledge of Good and Evil', *Zygon, Journal of Religion and Science* 2: 77–95.
 1981   *Toward a Scientific Theology* (Belfast: Christian Journals Limited).
Damasio, A.
 1994   *Descartes' Error: Evolution, Reason, and the Human Brain* (New York: Putnam).
Deane-Drummond, C. and B. Szerszynski with R. Grove-White (eds)
 2003   *Re-Ordering Nature* (London: T&T Clark).
ERS Food Assistance and Nutrition Research Report (FANRR) No. 21
 2002   *Household Food Security in the United States, 2000* (www.ers.usda.gov/publications/fanrr21/, accessed 16/1/04).
Eurobarometer
 2000   *The Europeans and Biotechnology* (http://europa.eu.int/comm/public_opinion/archives/eb/ebs_134_en.pdf).
Food and Agriculture Organization of the United Nations (FAO)
 2002   *The Developing World's New Burden: Obesity* (www.fao.org/FOCUS/E/obesity/obes1.htm, accessed 16/1/04).
Gärdenfors, P.
 2001   *Blotta tanken* (Nora: Nya Doxa, 3rd edn).
Jackelén, A.
 2001   'From Drama to Disco: On the Significance of Relationality in Science and Religion', *Currents in Theology and Mission* 28.3–4: 229–37.
Pence, G. E. (ed.)
 2002   *The Ethics of Food: A Reader for the 21st Century* (Lanham: Rowman & Littlefield).
Schmidt-Leukel, P. (ed.)
 2000   *Die Religionen und das Essen* (Kreuzlingen: Hugendubel).
Shiva, V.
 2000   *Stolen Harvest* (Cambridge, MA: South End Press).
Tansey, G. and T. Worsley
 1995   *The Food System: A Guide* (London: Earthscan).
Tappeser, B., A. Hermann and R. Brauner
 2003   'Gutachterliche Stellungnahme zu den Vorstellungen der EU-Kommission zu Fragen der Koexistenz gentechnisch veränderter,

konventioneller und ökologischer Kulturen' (www.oeko.de/ oekodoc/91/2003–004-de.pdf?PHPSESSID=73ca7e3dd07651fdb 69e1dcef25afe63, accessed 6/9/05).

Tillich, P.
1976   *Systematic Theology*, vol. 3 (Chicago: University of Chicago Press).

Verhoog, H.
2003   'The Alliance of Utilitarianism and Scientific Thinking in Public Debates about Genetic Engineering in the Agrifoodsector', in *Proceedings from the 4th Congress of the European Society for Agricultural and Food Ethics* (EurSafe; Toulouse, France, 20–22 March 2003): 37–9 (www.eursafe.org, accessed 18/1/04).

Ware, K.
1984 [1978]
            'The Meaning of the Great Fast', in *The Lenten Triodion* (trans. Mother Mary and Archimandrite Kallistos Ware; London and Boston: Faber & Faber): 13–68.

World Health Organization (WHO)
            Controlling the Global Obesity Epidemic (www.who.int/nut/obs.htm, accessed 16/1/04).

To Know is to Make

Knowledge, Ignorance and Belief in a Technological Society

Walther Ch. Zimmerli

The Arguments

What I would like to do first is to summarize my arguments in three sentences in order to afterwards elaborate on them.

The first sentence is:

Knowledge, especially scientific knowledge, seems to be different from wisdom.

The second sentence is:

If we understand correctly what technology is with regard to scientific knowledge, we then know that technology actually is the making of what science has only thought so far.

But then again if you do, if you make, if you literally produce what you have so far only thought, then you suddenly find out that things are different, or that what you thought would happen is not going to happen, or that something is going to happen which you have not really in your wildest dreams imagined would happen.

Therefore what I'm claiming in my third sentence is:

Technology leads to wisdom via reflection on ignorance.

'To know is to make' – under this title I would like to comment briefly on knowledge, ignorance and belief in a technological society. I will not discuss sociological or societal issues in detail. Rather I will try to focus on what a philosopher's focus should be: the contents, the concepts and the ideas. In order to do that I would like to point out the following four topics.

First, I would like to discuss a tiny little question humankind has dealt with for millennia: What is truth?

After having discussed without having answered that question I will focus on a specification of the first question: What is scientific truth?

After having discussed without having answered that question either, I would like to reflect on what I will have answered so far: ignorance as the driving force of knowledge.

Finally, in my fourth and concluding remarks I would like to focus on something that seems to be different from truth and ignorance: magic and technology – not magic and theology, but magic and technology.

Truth

Let us start with something most of you probably know. Neither things nor facts are 'true', neither words nor exclamations; only statements can correctly be called 'true'. That is what we call the 'statement view' of truth and this is of course corroborated by one of our leading authorities of philosophy, by the great Aristotle himself. He does so in numerous places, and I am not just focusing on the locus classicus in 'Perihermeneias' and in his *Metaphysics*: to say of what is that it is not, and of what is not that it is, is false, while to say of what is that it is, and of what is not that it is not, is true. That is true, obviously. This now is truth. But as you know there are some doubting Thomases around – even in philosophy . . .

For example, let us focus on the Aristotle of the twentieth century, the German Aristotle, I should say, on Martin Heidegger. He is asking the question: 'Can something more fundamental be added beyond the boundary of the essence of truth as the character of a statement?' What he is asking is: What forms the basis of the fact that we call statements true? Is there something which we intend to say when we are saying a statement is true which is not just this: that the statement is true. Again it is a question, it is not an answer.

Let me quote another question which you all know of course (John 18): 'Pilate therefore said unto him, Art thou a king then? Jesus answered, Thou sayest that I am a king. To this end was I born, and for this cause came I into the world, that I should bear witness unto the truth. Every one that is of the truth heareth my voice.' Now hear the philosopher speaking: 'Pilate saith, *What is truth?*'

What I tried to show by means of these three quotations is that, within religion, within philosophy, within philosophy of science, always the same question is asked: 'What is truth?'

And the answer of course is that we have to distinguish between descriptive truth, the truth we are focusing on when we are talking about for example the statement view of truth, and the truth we are focusing on – remember Heidegger – when we talk about the non-statement view, about what lies behind the truth of statements.

If I am for instance saying: 'I am not saying anything now', this could be literally true because I could be talking rubbish, and it could be false because the statement itself in its pragmatic utterance is falsifying its content. So you have to distinguish between what you are doing while uttering a statement and the content of the statement. Every philosopher and every linguist knows this difference. But still, if we talk about scientific, non-scientific, technological, religious truth, we have to focus on this difference between the statement view and the non-statement view; the pragmatic view, between the non-statement view and the content-oriented view.

But then there is still another truth. If I were asking you to behave like human beings should behave, or to put it differently: to behave morally (because 'to behave morally' doesn't mean anything else but to behave like human beings are supposed to behave), then you would say: Well that's true we should do that. But this is a different kind of truth; it is not the descriptive, it is the prescriptive truth we would be talking about. And therefore one might suppose that there is something behind descriptive and prescriptive truth which is more than just the one or the other.

Again, if you look at the prescriptive truth from an ethical point of view we then know that there is a deontological view, a view which focuses on conscience and on what people ought to do and what people ought to be. And then there is the teleological point of view which judges the actions of people not by what they ought to do or ought to be, but by the outcomes of their actions. And of course we know that even in Scripture again we find both types of prescriptive truth.

Now let us briefly look at religious truth. Religious truth seems to be both a prescriptive and a descriptive kind of truth – descriptive because all the fundamentalists – and not only the fundamentalists – believe in what is written, in Scripture, in the written word which is both descriptive and of course prescriptive. On the one hand it is a narrative; we know what happened three days after Jesus Christ was crucified because we know the narrative. But still it is not the same kind of narrative truth we are intending as the one we are intending when we are talking about history, although it is historical truth. On the other hand in religious truth there is the pragmatic or non-statement view behind the narrative descriptive truth, the eschatological view – if we take into account what is going to happen at the end of history, at the end of humankind, what is going to be the end and goal of everything. So this is some teleological type of prescriptive truth, but nevertheless it is not just teleological and prescriptive because it is again more than that, having also an element of narrative in it. So if you don't believe in narrative it is also hard to believe in the prescriptive, the eschatological view in the same way as somebody who believes in both the narrative and the eschatological view. Therefore it looks as if the difference between the descriptive truth, the prescriptive truth and the religious truth is that religious truth seems to be some kind of underlying bridge or merger between descriptive and prescriptive truth. – So much for philosophy.

Scientific Truth

Now let us look at epistemology, let us look at scientific truth. – We still don't know what truth is but we seem to have a hunch what the difference between descriptive truth, prescriptive truth and religious truth is. Epistemology consists, like most artificial theories, of myths. Myths are important, of course, they are narratives, but again they are still myths. So we have to 'demythologize' the myths. Look for instance at the myth of correspondence. The radical concept of truth of course relies heavily on correspondence. Correspondence between – remember the quotation from Aristotle – what we say and what is; the only problem is that we as human beings can see only what we can see; we can't see what we can't see. Therefore how should we see what is, except with our own eyes? Except within our own view? Thus the only correspondence we actually have is the correspondence between what we see and say and what we see and don't say. Truth in this respect suddenly becomes property not to human beings, not to finite beings, not to beings who are within their own worldview but to some infinite absolute being which obviously is not a human being. Therefore truth as correspondence is not for human beings, although it is the kernel of what human beings understand when they talk about descriptive truth. Truth as correspondence is a myth because human beings are not able to compare what they say about what is with what actually is; they can compare only what they say about what is with what they say about what is.

Second, human beings ask for logical coherence. But if you go for example to a psychiatric clinic, you see that there are many human beings who are very coherent and at the same time mentally very ill. Thus, coherence could be a definition of mental illness.

How do we distinguish between somebody who is quite coherent although schizophrenic and somebody who is quite coherent although knowledgeable – if there is a difference at all (which might not always be the case). The answer again is: as human beings we don't have the possibility to really distinguish between these two cases, because coherence in itself is not coherent. Coherence in itself is just one element of a more aesthetic kind of a definition of truth.

Now let us turn to a third aspect: if we as human beings are really incapable of distinguishing between what we say and the state of affairs within things, and if we are not really capable of judging whether our coherence is something pathological or is knowledge: then at least we rely on progress. Regardless of whether we know if something were true or not, regardless of whether we know if the coherence were pathological or were knowledge, we still can judge whether it makes some progress, whether it contributes to progress. But then again we know there are different directions and different notions of progress. And how should we know whether what we are doing here – PowerPointing each other to death – is better than what my unfortunately deceased colleague Plato was doing when he was teaching his students without any kind of PowerPoint presentation?

Is it progress that we are PowerPointing these days? How should I know?

The only thing I know is that we obviously are doing more PowerPointing without knowing than we did before. So this then is the pragmatic turn. If we look at that part of the linguistic field which is dealing with the pragmatic aspect of our utterances then we of course come across the famous title of Austin's book *How To Do Things With Words*.

There is not really a difference between talking and doing because talking is one way of doing, the speech act, and by acting by speaking, we do something very similar to what we would do if we were acting without speaking because we are responsible for speech acts too. We change things with speech acts. Speech acts are the human way of implementing our knowledge in the world. And the philosophical pragmatists – like in this case William James – have of course dealt with that. If we now look at our non-pragmatist history of philosophy we suddenly see that all of the philosophers, including the giants of philosophy like Aristotle whom I have just mentioned but also Thomas Aquinas and even Hegel or Kant in this respect, are pragmatists. They are not explicit pragmatists but they are talking about truth in notions which are relying on the utility of truth. Even if Kant is trying to criticize the utilitarians, he is focusing on the utility aspect of truth, of what is going to happen if we stick to truth. If we lie, for example, if we say something which is not true to somebody else, if we intentionally do so, then of course we are changing something: we are changing the behaviour of others and we are trying to protect what we ourselves think, what our intentions are. And therefore the whole argumentation concerning the categorical imperative within Kant is a pragmatist argumentation. So transcendental truth, that is, what is behind truth, what is behind the difference between theoretical and prescriptive practical truth, is what we practise, if we talk about ourselves, if we talk about the fundamental instance which unites the theoretical and practical truth. We try to talk about the ego, about the idea of the ego which necessarily has to accompany every other idea, as Kant in his famous §16 of the transcendental deduction in the *Critique of Pure Reason* has pointed out. If we focus on what we are doing when we are addressing ourselves then we are trying to reach the foundation, the pragmatic foundation underlying the different kinds of truth.

In our quest for scientific truth let us now focus on something which has been neglected within philosophy of science and within philosophy at large. Let us briefly discuss the very fact that it is not technology which is the application of science but that it is science which is the abstraction of technology. Because as human beings – long before we ever started to be scientists, long before we ever started to apply philosophy, long before we ever thought of developing logic – we were already acting technically. We were tool-using animals. The definition of human beings as tool-using animals is the fundamental definition. But over the course of the last 400 years of progress in science and of scientific results we seem to have forgotten that we as human beings are technical beings, are beings who are changing the world by means of applying tools. And that all of our science is related to the application of tools, all of our science including the most abstract mathematics, even if it might not be applicable – yet. But we never know: suddenly, the most abstract theories become evidently applicable. The successful application on the other hand is just some kind of internal corroboration of what we are actually doing.

Remember one slight little fact: thermodynamics, the most fundamental theory of physics since the middle of the nineteenth century, is the theory of steam engines – we tend to forget that. And you have to suppose that our universe is a steam engine in order to believe in the laws of thermodynamics.

Our universe, however, is of course not just a steam engine, therefore we have to add a non-equilibrian thermodynamics to the thermodynamics which we used to apply in the nineteenth century: in order to understand that our universe is not just a steam engine but a living being and is thus developing like living beings. And we will add and add and add to that. But what is true behind all this is that technology is the truth of science, and it was again Martin Heidegger who spelled that out quite clearly by focusing on the 'unveiling', the, if I may say so, revealing character of technology.

Technology reveals the truth of both human beings and science. And if we again have a look at the history of ideas we then see quite clearly that philosophers have always known that. Francis Bacon, the famous or infamous British Lord Chancellor, is supposed to have said 'Knowledge is power.' However, he never said that, but 'ipsa scientia potestas est' – science itself is power. Not because science is science, but because science is technology. And from a different angle also our classical authority with respect to humanities and social sciences, Giambattista Vico, has formulated his famous Vico-axiom: 'verum ipsum factum'. To translate: True is only what we ourselves have made or are making or are capable of making. Since he wasn't that much interested in technology he was focusing on history and society and therefore he was of the opinion that the humanities, especially historical humanities, are the real sciences, the kernel of science, because they deal with objects we human beings ourselves have made whereas natural sciences are not real sciences because there human beings try to understand (and to deal with) objects God has made, not we ourselves.

If we apply this to our world of today we can easily see that our whole universe has become the laboratory of what we ourselves are capable of doing. So 'verum ipsum factum' implies that we now do have a criterion for truth. The criterion is: does it work in real life technology? From old to new technology there is but a short step, although an important one. And there is a step to understanding that new technology is the merger of what we so far have called both science and technology. By using information technology, by using all the tools which we are capable of using, we are capable not just of demonstrating things but of proving hypotheses by simulation in the virtual world. So the virtual experiment becomes the most important part of knowledge, and of course the largest virtual experiment has become real in the world wide web and in what we are doing on the world wide web. It is science, it is technology, but nevertheless it is still ignorance. Let me briefly reflect on that before I come to my concluding remarks.

Ignorance

What we have demonstrated so far is that we are ignorant with respect to the definition of truth, and that we are equally ignorant with respect to the definition of practical or ethical truth. We have demonstrated so far that we are even ignorant with respect to the very kernel of knowledge which is science. We have demonstrated so far that we have become less ignorant insofar as we are capable of applying science, but then we have demonstrated that applying science is not really applying science but removing the blind spot which we had when we didn't realize that science was the abstraction of technology. Now, dealing with technology, we suddenly see that we are dealing with ignorance again. Because ignorance has a lot of different meanings.

Let me comment on three of them. The first type of ignorance is knowing what we are unable to know, even to be capable of proving that there are certain things which in principle we can never know, which we are incapable of knowing. We know for example that Goedel has put forward a powerful proof for this type of ignorance.

The second type of ignorance: we do know something but we don't know and we have no possible means to ever know what the consequences are of what we are doing. Everybody has heard about the so-called 'butterfly effect' in a non-linear universe. Of course, we know that whatever we are doing, that even what we are saying now might have consequences which might change the world. Unfortunately it only very rarely is the case that philosophers are changing the world with their ideas. And unfortunately it is not always the best philosophers who are changing the world with their ideas. But it is nevertheless amazing how to do things with words, how we irritate the universe by doing something very unimportant, such as uttering something.

The third type of ignorance: there is knowledge around, but we don't know about it. I was introduced as the person who is responsible for setting up the Volkswagen AutoUni, the postgraduate university of the Volkswagen group. The underlying idea is that Volkswagen would know much more if Volkswagen only knew what Volkswagen knows. And that applies to everything and everybody: knowledge actually consists in trying to get to know what one knows. Or to try to set up an inventory of what one knows. We wouldn't have dealt with the risk perception regarding nuclear power plants the way we did if we had known what psychologists knew the risk perception regarding the fear of flying. If I were a good scientist, I would never use a plane because there are many physical aspects not yet explained of why planes are capable of flying. Speaking from a physicist's point of view they are not capable of flying. But technologically they are capable of flying. And I prefer flying in a technological tool to flying in a scientific theory.

Magic and Technology

To conclude let me therefore focus on something which has also been forgotten: on magic. Say you hate somebody and stick needles into a little puppet, representing the person you hate, and then suddenly the person you hate is dying. Well, that is voodoo, I know. But it is also technology, a different kind of technology. You can kill somebody by shooting him, you can also kill somebody by hating him and applying magic on him. So the idea behind all this is that we have more at our command than just our physical technology, that we are technologically changing the world from the basic feelings we have up to our scientifically co-ordinated actions within technology. I am not advocating table-tipping here; we all know that one can tip tables in different ways, we can even do it technologically by physically moving them. On the other hand there are many people who believe in another kind of tipping tables. Nevertheless, both are technologies: they are applications of belief systems onto something else. But whenever you apply technology, you run the risk of becoming the sorcerer's apprentice. And that is what I have in mind here.

As I said before, I am not advocating table-tipping, I am not advocating voodoo or any kind of sorcery. I am talking about the sorcerer's apprentice, I am talking about the fact that whenever you apply what you seem to know you will run the risk which is explained here by Goethe's famous lines: 'Sir, my need is sore. Spirits that I've cited my commands ignore.' That is what we today call technology assessment: technology assessment is management of ignorance. We try to somehow deal with the unintended, unforeseen, unforeseeable con-sequences of our technology. So at the very end of the day any sufficiently advanced technology – that is what Arthur C. Clarke says – is indistinguishable from magic because it has the same structure, it is confronted with the same problems, with unforeseeable consequences, and it always ends with ignorance. Let us therefore end with the adaptation of another famous quotation from an even better known source: 'For now – scientifically, technologically – we see through a glass, darkly; but then face to face.'

Index

absence (paradoxical, presence in absence) 75, 82, 85–8
Akhmatova, A. 130
Annas, J. 57
anthropology 4, 33, 84
apologetics, theological 49
Aquinas, Thomas – *see* Thomas Aquinas
Aristotle 23, 51, 54–60, 62, 146
art 95
Athanasius 114
Artigas, M. 25, 29, 32f., 128
Augustine 14, 53, 54, 79f., 114
Austin 149
authority 39, 48
awe 104

Bacon, F. 60, 61, 150
Balthasar, H.U. von 7, 81, 108f., 116–19, 122
Barberini, M. 26
Barbour, I. 25, 29, 56
Barrett, P. 109
Barth, K. 116
Basil 53
beauty 7, 116–19
Beck, L. J. 62
Bellarmine, R. 26
Benn, A.W. 65
Beyer, P. 64
Bible 1, 43
biography 6
biotechnology 127, 136–42
Boethius 55

Brauner, R. 140
Brazier, M. 131
Breed, D. R. 135
Brom, F. W. A. 139
Brooke, J. 65
Bulgakov, S. 7, 108f., 111–19, 122f.
Burhoe, R. W. 135

Calvin, J. 58, 59, 61
Cassian, John 53
certitude 27–9
Chambers 129
Chargaff, E. 3
Christ 76–8, 81f.
Christianity 42
Christologus, P. 53
Chrysostom, John 76
Church 74–8, 80f.
Clarke, A. C. 152
Clement of Alexandria, 78
climate change 7, 109–11
co-creator 35
Coff, Chr. 139
Cohen, I. B. 60, 61
coherence 148
communion 73, 75f., 77–82, 85–9, 101
Comte, A. 15
conceptions of science and theology, popular 39
consciousness 81–3, 85–7
consilience 29f.
Copernicus 11, 26

153

corroboration 13
creativity 8, 33–35
Creator 33, 79f. 82
Cross, R. 56
culture/cultures 5, 39, 44, 138
Curie, M. 40, 44

Damasio, A. 136
Darwin, C. 15, 44, 119
Davies, O. 117f.
Dawkins, R. 3, 65
Deane-Drummond, C. 111, 113, 114,
    121, 128, 129, 136–8
Dear, P. 62
Deech, R. 131f.
democracy 127
Descartes, R. 62, 93
Desmond, A. 65
Despland, M. 63
determinism 85
Dionysius 120
divine action 34
divine omnipotence argument 26
Dondeyne, A. 84
Donne, J. 67
Draper, J. W. 32
Duns Scotus, J. 55, 56
Durbin, W. 65
Dürr, H.-P. 3

Ebeling, G. 59
Eccles, J. C. 3
Einstein, A. 40, 44, 47, 65
embodiment 85
eminence 39, 40, 42, 43
empiricism 12
enlightenment 15, 16
environment 42, 43
epistemology 36, 148–51
eternity 14
ethics 30, 35f., 73, 131f.
Eucharist 75–7, 80–2, 89
Europe, medieval 43
evolution 33f.
evolutionism 34
existence (being) 76–87
experience 12, 95, 95–6
explanation 10
exploitation, environmental 12

faith, propositional 20
Fall 117
fallibilism 27, 28
falsifiability 13
FAO 138
Feil, E. 63
Feyerabend, P. 13
Ficino, M. 63
Finocchiaro, M. A. 25f.
Florovsky, G. V. 74
food (justice, safety) 8, 138–42
Foscarini, P. A. 26
Franciscan tradition 119
Fredoso, A. 54
freedom 11
Fukuyama, F. 7, 127f., 130–3

Gadamer, H. G. 94
Galahar, A. 112
Galileo Galilei 25–7, 62
Gärdenfors, P. 136
Gasset, Ortega y 94
Gaukroger, S. 61, 62
Gengenbach, D. 141
God 4, 26, 43, 79, 81, 87f.
Gödel, K. 14
Goethe 152
Gould, S. J. 30–2, 132
Gregory of Nyssa 116
Gregory the Theologian (Nazianzus)
    114
Grove-White, R. 136
Gurwitsch, A. 85f.

Habermas, J. 25
Hapgood, I. F. 76
Hare, R. M. 131
Harris, C. 56
Harrison, P. 58, 60, 63, 128
Hawking, S. 3, 65
Hegel, G.W.F. 149
Heidegger, M. 146, 150
Hermann, A. 140
hermeneutical task 17
Hildegard of Bingen 40, 44
history 14, 16, 91
Hodgson, P. 28
Horizon 93
    human 45

Houghton, J. 109–11
human subjectivity 74, 82–7
humanities 30f.
humanity 16, 44
Hume, D. 12
Husserl, E. 83, 85, 93
Huxley, T. H. 65
hypothesis 44

identity, cultural 20
ignorance 8, 18, 145, 151, 152
Inciare, F. 56
information 33f., *see also* worldview
Ingham, M. 57
interplay, reciprocal 4
Irenaeus of Lyons 76f.

Jackelén, A. 136
James, W. 149
Jardine, N. 62
Jenkins, G. 111
Jerome 53
Jesus Christ 147
John of Damascus 114
John Paul II, Pope 35
Jones, M. 62
journey 92

kairos 18
Kant, I. 15, 93, 149
Karol, M. 35
Kent, J. 111
Kepler, J. 11, 27
Keselopoulos, A.G. 116, 121, 123
Knox, J. 40, 44
Kraye, J. 59
Kuhn, T. 13, 28f.
Kusakawa, S. 60

Laguna, G. 84
Lash, N. 63, 112, 117
Laudan, L. 27
Leary, J. 61
Lebenswelt 19, 21
leitmotif 16
Leroy, D. 34
liberalism, Western 20
life (meaning, mystery) 39, 44
Livingstone, D. 65

Logos 81–7
Lohr, Ch. 60
Lossky, V. 113f.
Louth, A. 81
Luhmann, N. 64
Luther, M. 58, 59, 60, 61

magic 151–2
Marcel, G. 84
Maximus the Confessor 77, 80f., 86–8, 114
McMullin, E. 62
Melanchton, Ph. 60
Merleau-Ponty, M. 83
methodology of science 44
modernity 11, 66
Moltmann, J. 113, 129, 131, 133
Mother Teresa of Calcutta 47
Myers, N. 111
myth 148

natural dynamics 33
natural laws 34, 83
naturalism 84–6
nature 15f.
Nature, Book of 44
Nesteruk, A. V. 73, 79, 81, 87
Newton, I. 11, 27f.
Nichols, A. 116
NOMA (Non Overlapping Magisteria) 31

objectivity 63
Ockham, William of 54, 56
ontology 36
Origen 53, 79
Orthodoxy [Eastern] 74, 111–16

Palmer, G. E. H. 80, 87
paradox 75, 82–9, *see also* absence; human subjectivity
Pasternak, B. 130
patterns 31, 33, *see also* information; worldview
Paul 52–4, 59
Pence, G. E. 141
perception of science and technology 38, 40, 42, 46
Pérez-Ramos, A. 61
personhood 73, 75f., 82–88

personality 45–6
phenomenology 83
philosophy 52, 95–6
    natural 56, 60, 61
    non-pragmatist history of 149
Picolomini, F. 59
Pieper, J. 121
pilgrim 7, 91
Plato 52, 53, 55, 58, 129, 148
Pltonsky, A. 62
Polkinghorne, J. 32
Popper, K. R. 12, 25, 27f., 35
post-modern 20
presuppositions of science 31–5
Prigogine, I. 3
problem-solving 13
process, evolutionary 93
professionalization 64
progress 148
    pilgrim's 12
    qualitative 15
    scientific 27, 31–5

Rahner, K. 101
rationalism
    critical 13
    naturalistic 84, 86
rationality 16
reason, sapiential 18
reductionism 2, 29, 30, 85
Reed, D. 62
Reformation 44, 57, 58
reliability 25–33
Renaissance 44
retro-justification 31, 33–5
revelation 11, 16
rightness 41
Roberts, J.H. 64
Rorty, R. 62
Royal Society of London 61
Rubidge, B. 62
Russell, C. A. 32

sagacity, reputation for 40
sages 3, 38–9, 41, 43, 49
scepticism 45f., 48
Scherer, J.A. 128
Schmemann, A. 77
Schmidt-Leukel, P. 141

science, *see also* philosophy, natural
    and religion 25, 31–6, 74, 82–9
    environmental 7, 109–111
reliability of 6, 25–33
self-determination 11
self-knowledge 35
self-organization 33f., *see also* worldview
Sherrard, P. 80, 85, 87, 112
Sherry, P. 119, 120
Shiva, V. 141
Sitz im Leben 21
Smith, W.C. 63
society, modern pluralist 19
Socrates 52, 53, 129
Söling, C. 4
Sophia 112–16
soteriology 100
soul 2
speech act 149
Spencer, H. 15, 65
Sprat, Th. 61
standstill 16
Stohrer, W. 62
Symeon the New Theologian 116,
    123
Szerszynski, B. 136–8

Tansey, G. 140
Tappeser, B. 140
technology 8, 145, 149–50, 152
Tertullian 53
theology 16–17, 20–2, 33f., 42, 62f.,
    74f., 78, 81f., 84, 86–8, 97
theory of everything 14
thermodynamics 150
Thomas Aquinas 6, 15, 34, 51, 54–7, 59,
    63, 108f., 120–2, 149
Thomson, A. 62
Thunberg, L. 81
Tillich, P. 136
traditions, religious and cultural 21
Trinity 98–9, 100–3, 111–16
truth 18, 40, 146–51
Turner, F. 65
Turner, J. 64

underdetermination of theories 27
understanding 10
Urban VIII, Pope 26f.

validity, criteria of 28f.
Valliere, P. 112, 116
values 11
  scientific 28, 32f., 35
Vendler, Z. 62
Verhoog, H. 137f.
verisimilitude 13
Vicco, G. 150
view, eschatological 147
virtue 57f., 120–2

Ware, K. 80, 87, 141f.
Warnock, M. 131
way 91
Weber, M. 65
Weil, S. 120
Weizsäcker, C. F. von 3

what- and why-questions 73, 75, 79, 87
Whewell, W. 29f., 64
White, A. D. 32
Wilson, D. B. 32
Wilson, E. O. 3, 30
wisdom 19, 51, 111–23, 128–32
Wissenschaft 10 n.1, 16
worldview 11, 33f.
Worsley, T. 140

Yeo, R. 65

Zahm, J. 34
Zigliara, T. 34
Zimmerli, W. 128
Zizioulas, J. D. 77